PENGUIN
LIFE AND FOOD

Chitrita Banerji grew up in Calcutta,
Harvard University, and now lives in Cambridge, Massachusetts. She spent many years as a journalist, editor and translator. Her other books include *Bengali Cooking: Seasons and Festivals* and *The Hour of the Goddess: Memories of Women, Food, and Ritual in Bengal*.

Her articles, columns and short fiction have appeared in *Granta*, *Gourmet*, *Gastronomica*, *Boston Globe*, *American Prospect*, *Calyx*, *Petits Propos Culinaires*, *Phoenix*, and *Boston Magazine*, and she has received awards for her papers at the Oxford Symposium of Food and Cookery.

Praise for *Life and Food in Bengal*

'A loving tribute to her homeland and more particularly to its kitchen'

—Frances Bissell, *The Times*

'Banerji's skills and interests extend far beyond the kitchen. She blends anthropology, history, geography, gastronomy and fiction, forming a lasting record of lifestyles that are already disappearing, at the same time completely beguiling the reader with her eloquent enthusiasm'

—Sue Earle, *The Far Eastern Economic Review*

'At one level this is the complete Bengali cookbook with a cascade of recipes that beg to be tried. But it is not for the recipes alone that the book needs to be read. Banerji's writing is so fine and her enthusiasm for Bengal so infectious that she is capable of directing even the most cynical towards going to Bengal and trying out its food'

—Ravi Vyas, *The Telegraph*

LIFE AND FOOD IN BENGAL

CHITRITA BANERJI

PENGUIN BOOKS

PENGUIN BOOKS
Published by the Penguin Group
Penguin Books India Pvt. Ltd, 11 Community Centre, Panchsheel Park,
New Delhi 110 017, India
Penguin Group (USA) Inc., 375 Hudson Street, New York, New York
10014, USA
Penguin Group (Canada), 10 Alcorn Avenue, Toronto, Ontario, Canada
M4V 3B2 (a division of Pearson Penguin Canada Inc.)
Penguin Books Ltd, 80 Strand, London WC2R 0RL, England
Penguin Ireland, 25 St Stephen's Green, Dublin 2, Ireland (a division of
Penguin Books Ltd)
Penguin Group (Australia), 250 Camberwell Road, Camberwell, Victoria
3124, Australia (a division of Pearson Australia Group Pty Ltd)
Penguin Group (NZ), cnr Airborne and Rosedale Roads, Albany, Auckland
1310, New Zealand (a division of Pearson New Zealand Ltd)
Penguin Group (South Africa) (Pty) Ltd, 24 Sturdee Avenue, Rosebank,
Johannesburg 2196, South Africa

Penguin Books Ltd, Registered Offices: 80 Strand, London WC2R 0RL,
England

First published by George Weidenfeld & Nicolson Ltd London 1991
This revised edition first published by Penguin Books India 2005

For sale in the Indian Subcontinent and Singapore only

Typeset in Perpetua by Mantra Virtual Services, New Delhi
Printed at Chaman Offset Printers, New Delhi

For my mother, the inspired provider,
and in memory of my father, the discerning gourmet,
a daughter's gift

CONTENTS

PREFACE TO THE NEW EDITION

Fourteen years after its first publication, *Life and Food in Bengal* is being given a new life by Penguin Books. During this time, the interest in food and books related to food has seen explosive growth. The expectation of readers is both varied and enormous. Keeping that in mind, I would like to point out that the objective of this book was to create, as accurately as possible, a representation of the Bengali tradition as reflected in food, cuisine, ritual and lifestyle. It is not meant to be a compendium of convenient, easy-to-make dishes for the modern cook who has little time to spend in the kitchen. Nor does it purport to be a guide to any kind of 'health food'. Although I believe that the basic Bengali meal is both nutritious and tasty, this book is not meant to provide any kind of solution to the twenty-first-century urban angst about cholesterol, obesity, or hypertension. What I have tried to portray is a distinctive cuisine, which embraces the simple and the complex with equal ease, and whose dimensions have touched every facet of life in Bengal. Despite some minor changes and revisions, the book essentially remains its original self.

Cambridge, Massachusetts
January 2005

CHITRITA BANERJI

PREFACE TO THE FIRST EDITION

When Vicky Hayward first approached me about writing a book on Bengali food and life, my first reaction was, 'impossible'. It has been a while since then. The book is a reality, though how far it will match any reader's expectation is hard to predict. No one should expect a comprehensive representation of Bengali cuisine from this one book. What I have tried to do, through fiction and personal narrative, is to capture a little bit of the elusive taste of Bengal as it exists in my mind and my senses. Necessarily, the scope is limited. However, I can never do justice to Vicky's patience and understanding nor can I sufficiently acknowledge my debt to the frequent illumination of perspective she provided. My publisher, Michael Dover, made this book possible in another, though no less significant, fashion. I shall always remain indebted to him for his understanding and flexibility.

What I owe to my parents is immeasurable. Not only were they a wonderful living connection between the present and the past where memory took me travelling, they were also a constant source of information, elucidation, support, encouragement and affection during the one year I spent in Calcutta researching the book and writing the first drafts.

Unexpected help and generosity were shown to me by Mr Shakti Roy, librarian, *Anandabazar Patrika*, Calcutta. Giving freely of his time, he helped me find obscure bits of reference material and also loaned me his personal books. My friend Sunil

Gangopadhyay also helped me in numerous ways—a measure of his spontaneous generosity of soul. Tapan Das, also of *Anandabazar Patrika*, provided me with valuable photographs at the shortest possible notice and without any expectation of return. My gratitude to him is immense.

To Bangladesh, where I spent seven fraught but rewarding years, I owe half of this book. The experience of living there enlarged my vision about Bengali life and reality and brought me dimensions of appreciation I could never have imagined before. I hope all my friends there, particularly Abu Abdullah, know how I feel, without my inadequate words. It was a reality which is no less present within myself even when it is part of my past.

As for my husband, Jai Chakrabarti, I will always be in his debt for his forbearance with an irritable and impatient wife struggling to meet her deadlines, as well as for all the painstaking proofreading he did for me. To all my other friends in India and the United States I owe much, not the less significant because it is unquantifiable. If I succeed in guiding the reader into unexplored pathways and a few memorable tastes, and arouse a greater desire to know about life in Bengal, it will all have been worthwhile.

Cambridge, Massachusetts   CHITRITA BANERJI
February 1991

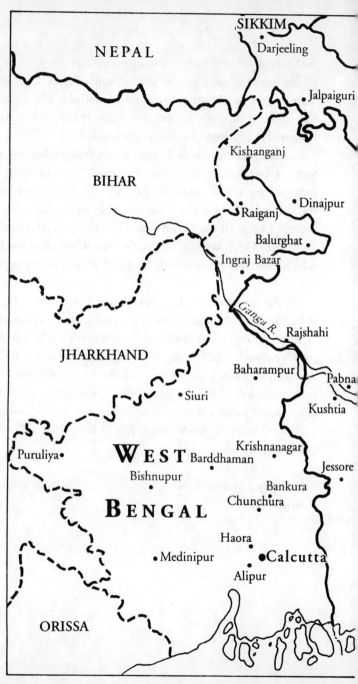

MAP OF WEST BENGAL

BHUTAN

ASSAM

Brahmaputra R.

Koch Bihar

Rangpur

MEGHALAYA

Bogra

Sylhet •

• Mymensingh

BANGLADESH

Kishorganj

• Tangail

TRIPURA

MIZORAM

• **Dhaka**

• Narayanganj

Faridpur

Comilla

• Maijdi

Khulna

Barisal

Rangamati

Patuakhali

Chittagong

MOUTHS OF THE GANGA

Cox's Bazar

AND BANGLADESH

INTRODUCTION

If you ask a Bengali for the shortest description of Bengali food, the answer is likely to be fish and rice; unless he is a vegetarian, in which case he may say greens and rice. If he invites you to his house for an elaborate, well-cooked meal that includes varieties of fish, vegetables and meat, not to speak of sweet dishes, he will probably say, 'Do please grace my poor hovel with your presence and share our simple meal of pulses and rice.' In this fertile tropical delta that serves as a basin for innumerable rivers, rivulets and tributaries, it is rice that has been the common sustaining staple from pre-Aryan times until today. Thus, the commonest way of enquiring if a person has had a meal, especially lunch, is to ask if he has taken rice. Most people, if asked, will agree that a basic Bengali meal will consist of rice, pulses, vegetables and fish.

But the minute you get into the details of cooking, a startling polarization of ideas and approach begins to emerge. If you happen to talk to someone from West Bengal, a Ghoti, he is likely to tell you that the uncivilized Bangals from East Bengal know nothing about cooking, that they ruin food by drowning it in oil and spices, that they eat half-cooked fish, that even the best of fish can be ruined by their peculiar habit of adding bitter vegetables to it. For his part, the East Bengali will declare that the Ghotis are the greatest philistines on earth, who can cook nothing without making it cloyingly sweet, that the freshest and most succulent of fish will be reduced to leather by the way they fry it, that their miserliness with spices renders all their dishes bland and colourless, that they are hardly true Bengalis for they prefer to eat wheat-flour chapatis instead of rice at dinner.

If, by chance, the warring factions belong to the Hindu and the Muslim camps, then you will also hear about the shortcomings of the Muslim, who cannot cook without onion and garlic and stinks of them himself, and of the Hindu whose meat sauces are no better than cumin-flavoured water. These jocular rivalries between Bengal on this or that side of the border—or this or that side of the River Padma in the days before a border—are likely to leave the newcomer utterly bewildered, for initially the whole range of Bengali food will seem broadly similar wherever you are.

But if you have the mind, the heart, the taste to explore, you will find an enormous variety in a cuisine where richness and subtlety are closely interwoven. With an array of ingredients ranging from water lilies to potatoes and gourd peel, to fish, meat, crab, tortoise and prawn, the Bengali has also devised a combination of spices that is both ingenious and delicate. From the simplest mashed potato enlivened with mustard oil, green chillies or fried, crushed red chillies, raw onions and salt, to the exquisite prawn coated with spices and baked inside a green coconut, to the hilsa fish in mustard sauce, to the tantalizing meat *rezala* made by Muslims—the Bengali takes an equal delight in whatever he happens to have. By medieval times we already find an extensive list of spices in works of literature that includes turmeric, chillies, mustard, cloves, bay leaves, cardamoms, cinnamon, cumin, fennel, ginger, fenugreek, asafoetida and nutmeg. The variety of items is matched by a variety of cooking techniques despite the limitation of cooking being done on a stove. Vegetables are fried, boiled, roasted on a fire, combined with others and seasoned richly or lightly, or stir-fried with a pinch of whole spices which add their aroma to that of the vegetables. Fish can float in a most delicately suggestive thin stew—the *jhol*—be made into a rich and spicy *kalia*, be fried crisply, or be made into a self-contained *jhal*, red with ground chillies or yellow with ground mustard. Even the humblest of pulses gains an unforgettable identity because of the *phoron* or flavouring added at the end. Every one of these items is eaten separately with a little bit of plain boiled rice.

But even that plain rice has variety, depending on the size of the grains, the natural flavour of each species and whether it is parboiled or not.

The importance of such gourmet considerations to the Bengali can be measured by a political history written around 1788 by Sayyid Ghulam Husain Khan Tabatabai. In it he wrote that the Bengalis considered the people of Maharashtra uncivilized, not because the latter were continuously carrying out raids in Bengal and pillaging and torturing, but for the unpardonable sin of not adding phoron to their dal! Similarly, a popular story goes that when the British shifted capital from Calcutta to Delhi, those Bengali families who necessarily followed because of their work, could easily be identified because smoke from their cooking fires started coming out at four in the morning and did not stop till midnight.

But the real food of Bengal, whether Hindu or Muslim, East or West, is not easy to reproduce on a mass scale, nor does it maintain its nuanced flavours after repeated heating or long hours in storage. Perhaps this explains the absence of a successful restaurant serving typical Bengali food in either West or East Bengal, despite the increasing urban trend of eating out. Most places tend to serve an imitation of northern Indian food as do restaurants run by Bengali people settled in the US or the UK. Even in Dhaka, where Muslim meat dishes appear on the menu in many restaurants, the eating experience is seldom as satisfying as at somebody's house. I remember a restaurant called Pithaghar that bravely opened in Dhaka purporting to serve real Bengali delights like *pithas* and *khichuri* with *bhuna* duck. It did not survive. The kabab joints with their nan bread and varieties of kababs are flourishing, but there is hardly any difference between those and similar places in Delhi, Lucknow or Allahabad.

As a result, many outsiders, Indian and foreign, tend to

conclude that there is no such thing as a Bengali cuisine, or that it is an extremely limited one. Partly it is the fault of the Bengali himself, for he cannot bring himself to serve, much less flaunt, some of the simplest things which are also the best he has devised over time. No honoured guest nowadays is likely to be served plain potato *bharta*, or *begun pora*, or fried *matar shak* (leaves of the green pea), or the thinnest of fish jhols, redolent of panch phoron and with pieces of brinjal, potato and *bori* floating in it. These are the common daily items, and therefore not good enough for guests unless specifically requested. But they are also some of the best the region has to offer because they have been developed over centuries and are based on a meticulous selection of local ingredients. Even at very traditional Hindu weddings, say thirty years ago, the food was typically Bengali, but consisted only of the richer, spicier dishes.

The land of these food-loving characters, Bengal, is made up of the Indian state of West Bengal and the sovereign country of Bangladesh (formerly East Bengal or East Pakistan), altogether an area of over 228,000 sq. km (88,000 sq. miles). Bangladesh has a population of 141 million and West Bengal of 81 million. So the Bengali nation is larger than most sovereign states. Most of the terrain is flat, delta land, crisscrossed with rivers, with a few hills and forests dotted here and there. Parts of the north are bordered by the Himalayas and the western part of West Bengal is an extension of the rocky plateau of Chhotanagpur in the neighbouring state of Jharkhand. Overwhelmingly, though, this is a flat green land, most of it cultivated and divided into fields, primarily growing rice, the staple food crop. In the northern districts of Bangladesh and West Bengal, the land is drier, a red laterite soil replacing the alluvial richness of the central areas. To the south where Bengal slopes down to meet the Bay of Bengal, are the famous mangrove swamps, the Sundarbans, home of the Royal Bengal tiger and the huge *gharial* or Bengali crocodile. Like the rain forests of the Amazon delta, or the Everglades in Florida (which they resemble in appearance), the Sundarbans are one of the few places where the mystery, beauty and terror of nature are still to be felt. Yet man can coexist with nature, for these mangrove swamps are the home of a whole community of boat people who live by the catch they haul in from the Bay of Bengal.

The rivers of Bengal have served many purposes in sustaining life and prosperity. The great rivers—Ganga, Padma, Meghna, Jamuna or Brahmaputra, Damodar, Ajoy, Tista, Karnaphuli and others—have always been conduits for goods moving from one place to another, while the Bay of Bengal has provided a natural entry for the incoming sea trade. Their fascination has been perennial, whether in the imagination of the poet or the mind of the ordinary peasant. Through the seasons their mood and appearance change dramatically. Attenuated in summer, they swell with life and energy with the monsoon rains and often become forces of destructive fury, only to be reduced to a tranquil fullness under an autumn sky. In winter the waters start shrinking, yielding the best possible catch of many kinds of fish for the food lovers of Bengal.

Though the raging fury of a great river in flood during the height of the monsoon strikes terror in the hearts of the people, these same floods leave rich deposits of silt when they withdraw, replenishing the earth which has been over-cultivated. Sometimes shoals of land appear in the middle of the river and traditionally people have fought and killed to acquire control over these extraordinarily fertile pieces of land. All of this has been conducive to a primarily agricultural way of life and to Bengal acquiring the reputation of a golden granary in later years. The rivers have also ensured the livelihood of the peasant, the boatman, the fisherman and the merchant who are the most notable images of the Bengali people. In almost every folktale

or fairy tale, there are three young protagonists: the prince
and his friends, the son of the townkeeper and the son of the
rich merchant. The merchant or trader, owner of a large fleet
of trading ships travelling over the rivers and high seas, has
also made his place in the medieval narrative poems of Bengal.
The *Manasamangalkabya*, for instance, is centred around the figure
of Chand Saudagar (merchant) who was a rigid follower of Lord
Shiva and refused to pay his homage to Shiva's daughter Manasa,
the snake goddess. She, in turn, plagued him with one disaster
after another, including the death of his only beloved son
Lakhindar, until peace was made by Chand's remarkable
daughter-in-law Behula.

All the rivers, ponds, canals and lakes have contained a wealth
of life. As the evidence of literature shows, fish has been part
of life from ancient days to now. True, written evidence is scarce
before the eleventh century, but as the historian Dr Nihar
Ranjan Ray points out in his definitive text, *Bangalir Itihash*, the
terracotta sculptures on the walls of Buddhist viharas in Paharpur
and Moinamoti (now in Bangladesh) which go back to the days
of the Pala and the Sena dynasties that ruled Bengal from the
eighth to the eleventh centuries, do provide reliable indications
of lifestyle. Realistic portrayals show fish being cut, cleaned
and transported in woven baskets. Nothing can be greater
testimonial to the continuity of food preference than to see the
subsequent depiction of fish in folk art down the years. The
nineteenth-century Kalighat *pat* paintings show an abundance
of fishy themes, of fisherwomen selling their goods in the market
and of babus carrying their fishy purchases. Throughout the
intervening years, fish has figured as a theme in the quilts
embroidered by Bengali women, in the *alpana* or decorative
patterns drawn on floors or walls or seats, as a shape for home-
made sweets and in innumerable proverbs and phrases. The
eighteenth-century narrative poem *Annadamangalkabya,* by

Bharatchandra, gives us a list of fifty-one varieties of fish that Bengalis ate in those days. And a food-loving poet in the nineteenth century, Iswarchandra Gupta, said that since Bengalis lived on fish and rice, nature had given them a land full of rice fields and rivers full of fish.

The greater part of this alluvial delta is eminently suitable for the cultivation of rice and the planting, transplanting and harvesting of rice is the main activity of the Bengali peasant even today. There are three plantings every year, the major one, Aman, being planted during the monsoon and harvested in the late autumn. The Boro planting, a relatively modern practice made possible by improved irrigation techniques, takes place in winter, the crop being harvested in early summer. Immediately after that, around May-June, the least important Aush rice is planted to he harvested by late monsoon, around August-September. For main meals the Bengali tradition, in common with that of China, Southeast Asia and the Pacific islands, is to eat plain boiled rice with vegetables and fish. It was not until the establishment of Islamic rule in India that pilaf, or *polao* as Bengalis call it, became a common item at feasts and banquets, the Muslim rulers, in keeping with the practice of the entire Middle Eastern region, finding it unpalatable to eat rice without first frying and then cooking it. In ancient and medieval times, the Bengali did, however, moisten his rice sometimes by pouring clarified butter, ghee, over it after it was served. A succinct description of an average person's meal can be found in the *Prakritapaingala*, written around AD 1400, in which there is a quotation from a hundred years earlier: 'Fortunate is the man whose wife serves him on a banana leaf some hot rice with ghee, Mourala fish, fried leaves of the jute plant, and some hot milk on the side.'

The Bengali calendar year is a solar one based on the six seasons—two months for each—of Grishma, summer; Barsha, monsoon; Sharat and Hemanta, early and late autumn; Sheet, winter and Basanta, spring. The year begins with the month of Baisakh in mid-April, when the heat of the summer is on full blast. The whole landscape looks parched, the leaves on the trees start drooping, and any cultivated plot that is not irrigated seems forlorn. Of course in terms of felt temperatures and other natural manifestations, spring and summer overlap considerably. The heat of the summer is palpable even in March. The most important season in Bengal is Barsha which lasts well into what is supposed to be early autumn. Torrential rains infuse the parched earth with new life and wash away the dust and grime of the previous months. Everything glows with green vibrancy and the life-sustaining rice crop is planted, transplanted and lovingly nurtured throughout the season. Nothing can be more beautiful than stretches of emerald-green rice fields under the slate-grey monsoon sky. The rivers assume their full majesty at this time, and rush along at full spate towards the sea. The autumn is a quiet time when the excessive moisture of the late monsoon starts to evaporate and the golden harvest stands ready in the fields. This is followed by the slow aridity of winter when balmy temperatures make the tropical delta a desirable resort.

The gentle rotation of the seasons, the garnering of the earth's resources and an active folk imagination have generated a large number of local rituals, some secular, which are indicated in the Bengali proverb of thirteen festivals in twelve months. Many of these are closely rooted to the ground and reflect a purely rural reality even though some of them have survived into modern urban times. Others are the Muslim festivals based on a lunar calendar, which became part of Bengali life after the conversion of large numbers of people to Islam. In a parallel rotation to the seasons, the two Ids, the fasting month of Ramzan, the 'Night of Destiny' and other occasions touch the various calendar months in turn.

The memoirs of Hiuen Tsang, a seventh-century Chinese traveller who came to India to study at the centres of Buddhist learning, provide some indications of the food habits of those times. Onion and garlic were taboo items; the common items of food were rice, wheat, milk, sugar, mustard, fish and meat. Onion and garlic did not become a part of ordinary diet in Bengal until Muslim rule had become well-entrenched after the fourteenth century and then, too, it was the local converts to Islam who accepted them. The Hindus resisted until well into the nineteenth century. Not only did these two ingredients have heathen associations, they were also supposed to have a libidinous effect on the character!

Of Bengal Hiuen Tsang mentioned only the elaborate feasts he attended. Had he spent time in the hinterland he would undoubtedly have listed fish and rice as the two foremost items in the local diet. The Bengalis continued to subsist on them through the centuries despite the advent of new influences, religious and political. Neither the disapprobation of non-violent Buddhism, nor the frowns of the vegetarian Brahmins of north or south India made any significant changes in the fish-loving Bengali's food habits. Brahmins all over India tended to be strict vegetarians until recently and Bengali Brahmins came to be considered no better than heathens because of their weakness for fish. In desperation, some of our own ancient scholars like Bhavadeva Bhatta have had to invent all kinds of specious justifications for including fish in the Brahmin's diet. Some scholars in medieval times even used to quote chapter and verse from the Sanskrit Puranas to demonstrate that fish was permissible except on certain religious occasions. Brahmins were let off with the half-stricture debarring them from eating several kinds of fish, especially those of the eel variety.

The abundance of fish in the land also led to techniques for

preserving excess supplies. Not content with sun-dried fish,
Bengalis in some areas have also developed a taste for fermented
fish. In Sylhet, where the huge lakes, *haors* and *baors*, are full of
large, plump punti fish, people put them in earthen pots filled
with mustard oil, seal the mouths and bury the pots
underground. When they are taken out after a specific period,
the fish has become an oily paste which is stored like a pickle.
Little bits of it fried with chillies can be served as a relish with
rice, or it can be put into a fresh fish stew to add its cheesy
flavour to it.

But fresh or preserved, fish by itself would have no meaning
for the Bengali. For the pleasure of savouring the taste of fish,
he needed to have his portion of rice. The spectre of an empty
larder with no rice is so dreadful to the Bengali mind that he
cannot even bring himself to articulate it. To indicate that the
stock of rice is dwindling, the Bengali housewife says that the
rice is 'increasing'—as if hoping to avert bad luck by the use of
the opposite word. To the rural Hindu Bengali, rice is almost
synonymous with Lakshmi, goddess of wealth and prosperity.
Even today, many sophisticated urban Bengalis, who do not
directly participate in the cultivation or processing of rice, find
it irrationally difficult to waste a single grain of rice. Even
when the portion on the plate is too much, they will try to
finish it because wasting rice is almost tantamount to insulting
the goddess.

By medieval times, Bengali literature began to contain
elaborate descriptions of available and cooked food, thus
unfolding a picture of a leisurely lifestyle among a certain class
who loved good food and devised many elaborate and subtle
ways of cooking it. Some of these texts list numerous kinds of
fish most casually; I doubt if you can walk into any fish market
in cities like Dhaka, Calcutta or Chittagong and find half that
many on any given day. The noticeable thing was that most of

them were sweet-water or brackish-water fish, not any marine varieties. The preference still remains.

The dual entity of rice–fish which is at the heart of Bengali cuisine is reflected in a thousand and one ways in the rituals and ceremonies of the Bengali Hindus. Unhusked rice, called *dhan*, is an inevitable part of any ceremonial offering to the gods. In parts of West Bengal there is a custom that when a new bride arrives with her husband to his house, she is welcomed with a platter of offerings containing dhan. For her part, she would have to hold a live fish in her left hand. This fish would later be released into the family fishpond to breed and multiply. During the ceremony of eating the *shadh* or desired foods, which takes place towards the end of pregnancy probably based on the assumption that if the mother has no unsatisfied cravings left she will produce a healthy child, rice and fish are the compulsory items. From the preferences of the living it is not such a big transition to the preferences of the dead. The spirits of ancestors are appeased at funerals by a final offering called the *pinda*, cooked rice and fish mixed together in a lump.

Apart from rice and fish, Bengalis have always taken advantage of the greens, vegetables and tubers that grow all over the land. Historians, basing their conclusions on a study of linguistics, think that modern vegetables like brinjals, several types of gourds and colocasia, as well as the bitterish leaves of the jute plant, figured in the pre-Aryan Bengali diet. The same goes for the indigenous fruits like *taal*, bananas, mangoes jackfruits, coconuts and sugarcane. Bananas were probably cultivated by the people who originally inhabited the land. Both the fruit and the tree are abundantly represented in inscriptions and stone reliefs that date back to Bengal's antiquity (which precedes the Muslim conquests beginning from the eleventh century). Like the rice plant, the banana tree also has a strong mythical significance in Bengali life. A young specimen is always placed outside the front door, together with a green coconut sitting atop an earthen pitcher, when a wedding or any other auspicious ceremony takes place. The same tree is pictured as the wife of Ganesha, elephant-headed god of success, son of the goddess Durga, Bengal's greatest deity. If a person dies on a Tuesday or a Saturday, the banana blossom has to be given as an offering.

Medieval poetry also gave its due to this tree. In the *Manasamangalkabya*, when the young and beautiful Behula finds herself widowed on her wedding night because of the malignancy of Manasa the snake goddess, she decides to win her husband back to life. Setting out all alone with her husband's corpse, she makes her momentous journey down the rivers to the underworld, in a raft made from the trunks of banana trees. Ever since, the phrase 'crossing the ocean on a banana raft' has come to signify incredible or impossible feats based on faith and courage and little else.

One of the most striking differences of staple between ancient and contemporary times is the absence of any kind of pulses in the food of ancient Bengal. The *Charyapadas*, the earliest examples of Bengali literature dating back approximately to the eleventh century, depict fishing and hunting for game, and mention rice, sugarcane and many other crops. But there is no reference to any kind of dal. It is only in post-fifteenth-century literature that several kinds of dal, as well as ways of cooking them, begin to be mentioned. It seems that in this respect ancient Bengal had more in common with Southeast Asia and China, where pulses except soyabeans (the source of tofu) are virtually unknown, than the Bengal of today. Even now, most of the dals consumed in West Bengal come from the other states in India. Apart from the natural cropping factor, the superabundant supply of fish made dal as a source of protein unnecessary. The shift in balance in medieval times can probably be attributed to the spread of the Vaishnav Bhakti cult whose followers were vegetarian. As a result, a substitute for fish or meat had to be found and the non-vegetarians also became familiar with this new element.

The relative scarcity of mustard, which has never been a major crop in Bengal because it is not that well suited to the soil or climate, meant that the cooking medium was often ghee—clarified butter—instead of oil. Though it seems infinitely strange to modern Bengali cooks for whom the main cooking medium is the pungent mustard oil, greens and vegetables were often fried in ghee in medieval times. As for rice, it was unthinkable to eat plain boiled rice without pouring ghee over it liberally, no matter how many other items there were. From the fourteenth century onwards, we find many descriptions of hot, steaming rice, each grain unbroken, drenched in ghee which has given it a yellowish tinge. No wonder the prosperous ease-loving Bengalis found a little pot belly the most natural of developments and aesthetically not unpleasing. Though we no longer fry green vegetables in ghee, it is still used in special preparations of vegetables like the *dalna* or the *ghanto*, as well as in rice preparations like polao, khichuri and biryani and the Muslim meat dishes. On occasion, even today, ghee will be poured over plain boiled rice if the first course consists of boiled or deep-fried vegetables.

In feudal Bengal, ghee also acquired an elevated status as the preferred cooking medium for the wealthy. In nineteenth-century Calcutta, many of the great feudal families would die rather than serve food cooked in mustard oil, which was considered only fit for the poor. There is an apocryphal story about an old lady from one of these families who was sick on hearing that her nephew had taken to eating mashed potatoes flavoured with mustard oil—something that most Bengalis today would gobble up with relish.

A stable agricultural way of life also meant the presence of cattle. Milk and milk products became an important part of Bengali food from very early times. Apart from being drunk by itself, milk was often served at the end of a simple meal, when it was mixed with a little cooked rice and white sugar or date-palm sugar. In rural households nothing could be a more welcome symbol of plenty than the brown and white cows standing in their sheds and the pitchers of foaming milk they produced. Even today, this symbolism remains in some houses. For when the new bride arrives at her husband's house, her first step over the threshold is timed to coincide with the boiling over of a pot of milk in the kitchen.

Yoghurt, too, has been an important part of daily food, especially in the summer when it is thought to aid digestion. Aryan culture attributed auspiciousness to it and Bengali Hindus continue to believe in that. A *tika* or dot is made on the forehead with yoghurt by well-wishing mothers or sisters whenever a child or sibling sets out on an important undertaking. Unsweetened yoghurt was used in cooking from fairly early times. The *Naishadhacharita*, probably written around the tenth century before the Sena dynasty took over in Bengal, mentions a dish spiced with mustard and yoghurt served at a royal wedding. Apparently this was so hot that the guests had to shake and slap their heads from the ferocity of it. The Muslims later used yoghurt as a substitute for wine. They developed a drink called *borhani*, which is yoghurt mixed with water and whipped together with salt and ground black pepper. This continues to be served even today at Muslim feasts where a lot of rich meats and polaos are supposed to be digested with the aid of the borhani. Many of their meat dishes require a little marinading in yoghurt and the korma and the rezala in Bangladesh are both based on a yoghurt sauce. As for the Bengali Hindus, some of their classic fish and vegetable dishes are cooked in a yoghurt sauce.

The most sophisticated transmutation of milk in Bengal has been in the form of an infinite variety of sweets, some made at home and some professionally. Certainly, no other region in India has shown such passionate absorption in sweets and appreciation of subtlety or variety in their preparation. The plump Bengali with his sweet tooth takes seriously the ancient Sanskrit recommendation, *madhurena samapayet*, a meal should be finished with something sweet, to the heights of finicky epicureanism. The Aryan tradition of central India gave us rice pudding and kheer or evaporated milk. To this the Bengali added his repertoire of sweet pithas, made with rice or wheat flour, coconut, milk, even pasted dal, and sweetened with sugar or gur from the date-palm tree; he was content with this for many centuries.

Despite warring kings in pre-medieval times and successive Muslim conquests by Turks, Arabs and Afghans from the thirteenth to the mid-sixteenth centuries, when the emperor Akbar made Bengal a part of his Mughal empire, the prosperity of Bengal remained unchanged, as did her social and economic inequalities. So great was her income from a flourishing export trade, that even at the tail-end of Mughal rule the entire imperial army was sustained exclusively by the revenue sent by this province to the Delhi treasury. It was during the fourteenth century, when Bengal was under the Turkish Sultan, Ilyas Shah, that the entire region—East, West, North and South—came to be commonly referred to as Bangla, Bengal.

Literary evidence from before the tenth century reflects the wide disparity between the diets of the rich and the poor. While ordinary people ate plain rice with a little fish and vegetables and some milk, it was common for the affluent to serve elaborate meals, especially at weddings and other festive occasions. The feast served at the wedding of the princess Damayanti, as described in the *Naishadhacharita*, included so many dishes that guests could not keep track of what they ate; nor, even, could they sample every dish. Venison, goat meat and gamebirds were served, as were fish and vegetable preparations, some of which were cleverly made to resemble meat. For sweet dishes there were many kinds of pithas and the inevitable sweet yoghurt. But the only drink served was water. Finally, the guests were served paan, betel leaves wrapped around sweet spices. These basics of a festive menu did not change for many centuries.

Much later, during the medieval period of Bengali history, when the *mangalkabyas*, narrative poems, as well as a lot of Vaishnav poetry and biography were written, we begin to find Bengalis sitting down to fairly elaborate meals at home even when there is no festivity. A Bengali phrase refers to the sixty-six dishes which made up a proper banquet. This figure is probably based on several centuries of an elaborate eating tradition, where the male was the god, the woman his cook and servitor and the rice on the centre of a huge platter was surrounded by individual bowls containing a variety of items. There was no tradition of men and women eating together. The males of every household had the right to sit down first and eat the best and the most. This practice can be seen all the way down the caste and class scales. Even in a very poor peasant family in Bangladesh where the menu is minimal, the male is served by the female. The wife, mother or daughter-in-law sits in front, her face half-covered with her sari, and attentively offers extra helpings whenever needed. In the hot weather flies would be a bother, and it was the woman's job to ply a palm-leaf fan to keep them away and increase male comfort. A turn-of-the-century novelist, Sharatchandra Chattopadhyay, made a cliché out of the image of this patient, submissive, fan-wielding Bengali woman, but like all exploited groups, women utilized this situation to their advantage sometimes. In a story written around 1916–17, the noted Bengali writer and poet, Rabindranath Tagore, describes a woman planning to win over her husband to her own choice of a daughter-in-law by cooking his favourite dishes, serving them to him at lunch and gently broaching the subject at a well-judged moment. As it happened, her plan did not work out, but it could have.

Hindu widows in Bengal were forced to go on a vegetarian diet for as long as they lived, a cruel stricture rigidly enforced by their families. One explanation for this could be the equally cruel supposition that these poor creatures, often in their youth, were considered potentially troublesome charges. They were not allowed to remarry and one false step into temptation would bring shame to the entire family. So a deficient diet and other hardships were indirect ways of despatching them to the next world, sometimes to the pecuniary advantage of their in-laws. But not all widows were obliging enough to drop dead fast. They lived and did their share of the drudgery, particularly in the kitchen. Tradition ascribes to these women who made the best of a bad bargain the excellence, range and subtlety of Hindu vegetarian cooking in Bengal. A noted food writer of the nineteenth century is supposed to have quipped that it was impossible to taste the full glory of vegetarian cooking unless your own wife became a widow.

The long period of Muslim rule from the eleventh century to the demise of the Mughal empire and the takeover by the British in the mid-eighteenth century, firmly established Islam as the second most important religion of Bengal. Mass conversions took place from the lower castes of Hindu society whose members had been oppressed and exploited by the higher castes under the well-entrenched forces of orthodox Brahminism. The remnants of the Buddhists who had survived the tyranny of aggressive Hinduism under the Sena dynasty were also tempted to accept the faith of the Muslim rulers.

This process continued until, by the latter half of the nineteenth century, Muslims constituted almost half the population of Bengal. In northern and eastern Bengal they were the majority, but they had little besides their strength of number. Land, power, good education and professional opportunities were all mostly for the Hindu elite. This inequality and geographical concentration sowed the seeds of discontent which eventually led to East Bengal becoming East Pakistan when the Indian subcontinent gained independence in 1947. But with inequality and disaffection continuing to be the lot of Bengali Muslims within Pakistan, they decided to break away in the hope of a better future. The sanguinary birth of Bangladesh in 1971 has created yet another South Asian country, but substantially belied the sanguine expectations on which it was based.

Culinarily, the impact of Muslim cooking was at first mostly to be seen among the leisured and affluent classes, especially the Nawabs who represented the Mughal empire in Bengal. But, however restricted initially, it led to the development of a Bengali Muslim cuisine which is distinctly different from the Mughal cuisine of northern India and the Nizami cuisine of Hyderabad. It is less rich and more subtle than both of them, tending to substitute yoghurt and lemon juice for the cream and solid kheer of other Muslim cooking. Beef and chicken were also introduced into the diet; the former a bitter bone of contention even today, the latter becoming a part of Hindu households. Onion and garlic too became commonly used ingredients in Muslim households, even the poorest ones. By the nineteenth century, the prejudiced Hindu image of the Muslim was a character reeking of those two spices. One of the best-known specialities developed by the Bengali Muslims is the rezala made with *khashi* or castrated goat, in which lemon, yoghurt, milk and spices are combined with the almost heretical addition of lots of hot green chillies. Fragrant and sharp, the chillies produce an uplifting sensation for a palate cloyed with an excess of ghee or other ground spices.

Bengal also owes the taste of many kinds of polaos, biryanis, kababs and the *parota* bread to the Muslims. The last, made with a flour dough and fried in ghee, can mean many things to many people. The average Bengali household, Hindu and Muslim, will serve a flat three-cornered piece of fried bread and call it a parota. In others, where the cook or the hostess takes pride in her art, a circular parota of five or six layers will be served. But if you are dealing with a first-class Muslim cook or *baburchi*, he can present you with a deluxe circle the size of a small dinner plate, with fifty or sixty flaky layers underneath a golden-brown surface. Rich and heavy though it is, this Dhakai parota, as it came to be known all over Bengal, eaten with judiciously chosen meat dishes, definitely justifies a trip to Bangladesh.

It must he remembered, though, that these sophisticated meat, rice and wheat dishes did not develop immediately after the Muslims came to Bengal. The Sultans who preceded Mughal rule were no patrons of local culture. They were far more interested in battles against local rivals, profit and self-aggrandizement than in creating a stable environment for the development of the fine arts. Though they and their followers made meat a major part of their diet, the methods of cooking probably remained confined to the simple techniques of grilling and roasting over open fires. The sophistication so evident in fish and vegetable recipes did not come to meat cooking for a long time. Even under the emperor Akbar, who ensured peace and stability in Bengal, the food-loving poets of the mangalkabyas make no mention of the rezala, korma, bhuna or biryani that is trotted out at weddings in Bangladesh today.

The last Nawab of Bengal lost his throne and his life after the Battle of Plassey in June 1757. But the two centuries of British presence in Bengal did not really make much difference to the way urban or rural Bengal continued to eat. In common with the rest of India, the colonial presence here resulted in an Anglo-Indian cuisine which remained confined by and large to the ruling race and the mixed race of Anglo-Indians. The one noticeable contribution this has made to everyday Bengali food is the inclusion of two extraordinary misnomers, chop and cutlet. These English words which have now become Bengali were probably adopted by the cooks who worked in British households to denote their crossbreed concoctions. The chop today means a round or oval potato cake with a fish or meat stuffing, which is dipped in egg and breadcrumbs, then fried crisply. The cutlet, which can be meat, chicken or prawn, usually means one of those elements seasoned lightly and pounded to form a long, flat oval, which is then coated and fried the same way, the prawn tail or a piece of bone sticking out at one end like a trademark device. From the baburchi's kitchen it did not take long for these two items to end up in urban eating joints, and there are many shops in Bengali towns that specialize in 'chop-cutlet' as a genre. Vegetarian versions of both have also developed, but the mustard that is inevitably served with these is not the Colman's mustard favoured by the British; it is Bengali *kasundi*, a mind-blowing (even if I say so myself) mixture of pungent mustard paste, mustard oil, lemon juice or sour green mango, traditionally served with greens or bitter gourds and rice.

The only overwhelming British tradition we have developed, in common with many other races, is that for tea. However, the first time on record when a Bengali drank tea was probably when the renowned Buddhist scholar Atish Dipankar Srignan went to Tibet in the eleventh century at the invitation of the king to propagate Buddhist teachings in Tibet; and that was certainly Chinese green tea.

The innovative genius of the Bengali cook, both Hindu and Muslim, has found expression in modern times in an amazing array of sweets, most of them based on milk. The concept of pithas being synonymous with sweets is now an archaic one. Instead there are the *sandesh*, the *rosogolla*, *the pantua*, the *chamcham*, or the *rosomalai* to be enjoyed. All of these are made, fully or partly, with *chhana*, the solid part of curdled milk. These chhana sweets are Bengal's contribution to the world of Indian sweets. In other parts of India, sweets are either of the halva category or based on kheer thick enough to be solidified. This is probably because for a long time people there believed that 'cutting' the milk with acid to make chhana is a sin. Krishna, whose idyllic pastoral childhood among the cowherds of Brindaban has been the subject of such a large body of poetry in central and northern India, is depicted as a mischievous boy stealing butter and cream, but never chhana.

This passion for chhana and its offspring is something very recent in the history of Bengali eating. Even into the mid-nineteenth century there is no mention of sandesh or rosogolla, the twin pillars of Bengali sweet repute. The eminent Bangladeshi historian, Professor Abdul Razzaque, was convinced that there was no domestic midwifery in the birth of these sweets. They were probably devised by the professional sweet-makers in the markets during the latter half of the nineteenth century. This is probably the reason for the sweets still continuing to be mostly made in shops rather than at home. Over the last fifty years, famous sweet shops have risen and fallen in the cities of Dhaka and Calcutta, and each in its heyday has been famous for one or two particular products. The sandesh from Bhim Chandra Nag, the rosogolla from K.C. Das (whose father Nabin Chandra Das is supposed to be its creator), the *mishti doi* from Jalajog, are all indications of the importance of the *moira*, professional sweet-maker, in Bengali society.

Tradition pictures the moira as a huge, immobile mountain of flesh, sitting in front of his stove or in front of a huge platter of white chhana which he manipulates with the ease of long practice. He is utterly oblivious to all else in the world and so satiated with his own products that he never touches them himself. Of course not all moiras are embalmed in stupor. The great Bhim Chandra Nag was once challenged by Lady Canning, the then Vicereine of India, to create a new sweet for her birthday. In response, the master craftsman invented something which is neither the pantua (akin to the *gulabjamun* served in Indian restaurants everywhere), nor the *langcha*, a similar, bolster-shaped creation. This new product, large, spherical, succulent and fragrant, became known as the *ladikanee* after its patron, Lady Canning. While many shops make them today, the Bhim Nag ladikanee is still considered special.

What a Bengali eats today is determined as much by his means as by his personal preference. For the very poor, it has always been a struggle to get even an adequate supply of the basic rice. The image of empty cooking pots keeps recurring in Bengali literature from the eleventh century *Charyapadas* to medieval lamentations by Phullara, wife of the hunter Kalketu, down to modern Bengali fiction. Many poor peasants in Bangladesh remain content daily with just rice, an onion or two, some chillies and the handful of *shak* or boiled potato. Urban workers living in slums often feel lucky if they can manage a regular supply of rice and dal. Ironically, if such people do happen upon a bit of fish, they cannot even enjoy that for want of fuel or the oil to cook it. During the famines—1943 in all of Bengal, 1974 in Bangladesh—the skies have echoed with tormented voices begging only for some *phan*, the starchy gruel drained out from rice.

Even without such stark conditions, there is bound to be a marked contrast between the food of the very rich and the very poor, as everywhere in the world. But throughout history there has always been an intermediate group—landed gentry, fairly prosperous peasant, merchant, businessman, middle-class professional—that has managed to eat well, with variety of taste and material, and without having to spend huge sums on food. The nineteenth-century figure of fun and comedy, the plump, sleek, indolent, pleasure-loving Bengali babu, is a product of many centuries of such gustatory gratification. And over the course of a lifetime, his eating experiences have been like the beautifully soft quilts the womenfolk have made out of torn old saris during their leisure hours. Some of these were very plain, only a crisscross grid of stitches holding them together, but aesthetically pleasing because of the woven borders or motifs on the original saris. Then there were the others, the *nokshikanthas*, patterned quilts, which were works of art. Some of them took a lifetime to complete and displayed the most exquisite and complex designs in subtly graded colours—but always using the same simple stitch and always based on everyday life and reality. The hand of the artist plied the needle in and out of the quilted cloth and the stitches fell so fine that they were hard to make out individually.

In the kitchen the same artist's hand would throw together the simplest of spices and use the most humble everyday ingredients in cooking meals for the whole family. But despite the simplicity, this taste of Bengal remains hard to define, quantify, memorize and reproduce, though easy to recall with nostalgic longing. It delights with nuances and suggestions. But like the fabled golden deer, it will elude the outsider until he decides to take the risk of bridging all distance, to enter, observe, feel and absorb Bengal. The pursuit may lead to encounter and involvement with Bengali characters. If he chooses, he can watch some of them, their life, food, interactions, family events through the Bengali year. Once the first excursion is completed, it could well be impossible to cease from exploration.

EATING AND SERVING
BENGALI FOOD

The Bengali people are perhaps the greatest food lovers in the Indian subcontinent. A leisurely meal of many items which requires long hours of labour and ingenuity in the kitchen to be produced, has been as much a part of Bengali culture as ceremonious eating in France. The traditional way of serving food is on the floor where individual pieces of carpet, called *asans*, would be spread for each person to sit on. In front of this seat would be placed a large platter, made of bell metal or silver depending on the family's economic status. Around this platter would be arrayed a number of small metal or silver bowls in which portions of dal, vegetables, fish, meat, chutney and dessert would be served. In the centre of the platter there would be a small mound of piping hot rice flanked by vegetable fritters, wedges of lime, whole green chillies and perhaps a bit of pickle. Finally, in the centre of the mound a little hole would be made to pour in a spoonful of ghee or clarified butter to flavour the initial mouthfuls of rice.

The star of the eating scene was inevitably the male: husband, father, son, son-in-law, and others. The women would hover around, anxiously serving extra helpings or directing the servants to bring them. Some of the women would sit and ply palm-leaf fans to cool the heated male brow as the pleasures of intake intensified! But in traditional homes, there would always be the secondary eating scene where the women could finally sit down and enjoy their meal. True, the best portions of fish and meat would be gone, devoured by the superior sex, but that did not detract significantly from their enjoyment. The long-established female tradition of savouring the ultimate pleasure from concoctions of vegetables and fishbones or succulent stalks cooked with tiny shrimps or various kinds of pickles and chutneys, is rooted in this practice of making the best of secondary resources.

The approach to food is essentially tactile. As in all of India,

Bengalis eat everything with their fingers. Neither table silver nor chopsticks are used as aids to convey food to the mouth. What, after all, could be better than one's own sensitive fingers to pick out the treacherous bones of fish like hilsa or koi? Quite apart from this functional aspect, the fingers also provide an awareness of texture which becomes as important as that felt by the tongue. The various mashed vegetables or the different kinds of rice or varieties of fish we eat are all appreciated by the fingers before they enter the mouth.

Each individual has a particular style of dealing with his food. Some people pick up their rice and accompaniments very daintily, their fingers barely touching the food. This is supposed to be the style of the elite. Others prefer to mash their rice in their fingers before mixing it with the other items. Yet others will form balls of rice and other items in their palms before popping it in their mouths. Children are inevitably fed this way by their mothers. And then there are those hearty, somewhat coarse eaters who can be seen licking their palms all the way to their wrists. 'Up to one's wrist in food' has become a Bengali phrase to denote gluttonous indulgence. The other peculiarity about the Bengali eating scene is the unashamed accumulation of remnants. Since succulent vegetable stalks, fish bones and fish heads, meat and chicken bones are all meticulously chewed until not a drop of juice is left inside, heaps of chewed remnants beside each plate are an inevitable part of a meal. The custom of immediately and scrupulously wiping clean the part of the floor—now the table—where food has been eaten is probably related to the presence of such remnants.

Whether you have five dishes or sixty, the most important part of eating in Bengal is eating each dish separately with a little bit of rice in order to savour its individual bouquet. Not for the Bengali an indiscriminate mixing of fish, meat, dal or vegetables together with the rice in one graceless huddle, as outsiders tend to do in Indian restaurants at home or abroad. Any cook who takes pride in his or her art, feels outraged at this kind of tasteless tasting of food. The more delicate tastes always come first and it is only by graduating from these to the stronger ones that you can accommodate the whole range of taste. Vegetables, especially the bitter ones, are the first items followed by dal, perhaps accompanied by fries or fritters of fish and vegetables. After this comes any of the complex vegetable dishes like a ghanto or *chachchari*, followed by the important fish jhol as well as other fish preparations. Meat will always follow fish and chutneys, and *ambals* will provide the refreshing touch of tartness to make the tongue anticipate the sweet dishes. Of course, modern everyday food is limited to only one vegetable, one dal and either fish or meat—but the order remains the same.

colour, spice and smell

The simplest and most graphic way of visualizing and understanding the world of Bengali food and its place in Bengali culture would be to take you into the intimate domestic life of an ordinary middle-class Bengali family. Through the interactions between the characters I hope the patterns of daily life, the manifold symbolism of food in human relationships, the importance of food and festival and the place of food in memory will come to life in such a way as to bridge distance, unfamiliarity and degrees of incomprehensibility.

Chhobi woke with the first pale light of a February dawn. Looking over the half-curtains covering her window, she could see the vivid scarlet flowers of the *shimul* tree outside, the fleshy petals forming a bell that did not hang down but looked up to the sky. She decided to get up and go downstairs. No one stirred in the huge old house as she crept out of bed, sneaked past her parents' room and padded softly down the stairs to the first-floor landing from where she could see the *dalan*, a huge central hexagonal space. Though there was a formal living room for guests on the ground floor, this first-floor dalan served as the informal gathering place for the family and old friends. Now, however, all the furniture had been moved and the eastern light coming in through rows of glass windows softly highlighted the alpana on the gleaming red floor.

All major social and religious occasions were honoured in their home by the meticulous drawing of these decorative patterns on the floor, in rooms and passages, even on the steps. Her mother was particularly gifted in the art and Chhobi loved to squat on the floor, watching her mix rice flour with water to achieve the right consistency and then dip a bundled piece of rag, somewhat like a fat tapering wick, into the thick white liquid and start to paint on the silky smooth, deep-red floor with its black borders. The incredibly varied flowers, fruits, leaves, vines and conch shells that emerged as the white liquid dried on the floor, however fantastic, were always perfect in their execution and had a strange tenacity, surviving the mopping cloth of the maid and the endless feet that walked over it. Well after every event was over, they lingered as a memento of festivity.

This morning's alpana was a special thrill, for Chhobi's mother had told her the night before that she was going to experiment and mix some other colours with the white. She had shown her the red and yellow powders that had been bought. But though Chhobi had begged to be allowed to stay up and watch, her mother had firmly sent her upstairs to her room.

'No dear, I won't be able to start until the furniture has been moved to the dining room and your uncles have gone to bed. By the time I finish, it will be well past midnight. Besides, it will be there for several days, you know.'

So Chhobi had sighed and turned her face into her pillow. But the image of her mother sitting on the floor, the shoulder end of her sari, the *anchal*, wrapped tightly round her waist and tucked in, her hair drawn back in a bun, and painting with slow absorption, had lingered before her eyes. As she stared this morning at the fantastic design that was spread out before her in white and red and yellow, the daylight deepened and gave a jewel-like quality to each colour. She looked and looked, entranced by the magic of colour and form, until suddenly her grandmother's, Dida's, door opened and the old lady came out to the dalan. As the old and the young eyes met, they smiled silently, content in the knowledge that they were bridged by the person who had created this beauty. Curiously, neither of them had the same gift.

'So, Didi, you had no problem getting out of bed this morning, eh?' said Dida, gently laughing at Chhobi's usual aversion to early rising. She always called Chhobi didi, or older sister. 'I have so much to do I don't know where to begin. You'd better go back to bed or you'll fall asleep just when the ceremony starts.'

'No Dida,' pleaded Chhobi, 'I want to watch you do your puja.'

Every morning Dida went to the little room where the images of gods and goddesses were kept, together with special sets of brass and copperware, beautiful brass lamps, bells, carved conch shells, vases, incense holders and a large copper jar full of the holy water of the Ganga. As soon as you entered, you were overwhelmed by a sense of other-worldliness, for the pervasive aroma of sandalwood paste and incense, coupled with the lingering presence of yesterday's flowers, created a tenuous but definite distance from the rest of the house. And each time, she went through an intricate set of rituals that never failed to mesmerize Chhobi. When all the divinities had been worshipped, she would turn to Chhobi and give her some of the sanctified offerings: leaves of the *tulsi* or wild basil, two or three *batashas*, meringue-like sweets of white or brown sugar, and some fruit.

'No Didi, it's too early for you to start the day. And I have to bathe and change before I can do my puja, you know that. Besides, you'll have enough excitement later. Go on, get back to bed before your Ma knows you've been prowling around.'

Though disappointed, Chhobi did not argue. Dida never raised her voice, but she left no doubts that she meant what she said. And she was right. This was the day of the *annaprasan*, or first rice ceremony of Chhobi's little cousin Bilu, the only boy and male heir in the family. Only after the annaprasan could Bilu move from mother's milk to rice and other solid foods. After the ceremony guests were coming for a special lunch, and two professional cooks had been hired for the day to do justice to the occasion.

Back in bed, snuggling under the saffron and brown cotton quilt (made from one of her mother's old saris) that kept out the slight chill of a spring morning, Chhobi stared out of her window and tried to count the shimul flowers. In a few days, it would be almost impossible to see the branches, much less count the flowers: the whole tree would be a scarlet flame. That and the *kadam* tree in the southeast corner of their garden were the two landmarks that signalled their house from a distance. Chhobi counted both as her friends, though the kadam, which blossomed during the monsoon was a more intimate friend. It was part of their garden, unlike the shimul, and it was considered holy because of its association with Lord Krishna and his beloved Radha around whom the medieval poets of Bengal have woven many romantic stories of assignations, passion, separation and loss. Chhobi's devout grandparents had built an altar around the huge kadam and on certain religious days friends and family assembled in the garden for an evening of *kirtan*, devotional songs performed in front of the altar. Since grandfather's death, however, there had been very few sessions. Somehow, none of Chhobi's uncles had inherited either the devoutness or the musical passion of their father.

But the kadam flourished in spite of death and neglect, and Chhobi loved to see it from afar as she came home from school. Beyond the high branches was the house with its long entwining verandas and the wide open central courtyard around which rose the three floors. Here lived her family, her grandparents, their four sons—one of whom was married—and their only daughter, Chhobi's mother, with her husband and child. Chhobi did not quite understand how she and her parents had come to live in this house instead of with her paternal grandfather, whom she had visited every Sunday until his death when she was eight. But she knew, instinctively, that it was better not to ask any questions about this. She and her parents occupied two rooms on the second floor.

For Chhobi, the only child in the house for a long time, the nicest part of the house was the first floor where Dida lived. The southern veranda there had a huge array of potted plants that throve under Dida's care. Many of them were tulsi or wild basil plants, sacred to Krishna. Her family belonged to the Vaishnav sect, followers of Krishna, an incarnation of Vishnu, the lord of preservation. Everyone in the house had to chew and swallow several of the leaves culled daily by Dida and offered to Krishna during her daily puja. There were varieties of lilies, white and coloured, as well as two kinds of jasmine and a plant called *kamini*, whose tiny white flowers studded in the mass of small, dull green leaves made the evening air heavily redolent with fragrance in summer. Many years later, when Chhobi was a woman, she would remember her grandfather laughing and telling her that the word kamini meant woman, and that women were as intoxicating as the fragrance of this flower. The other plant that grew on Dida's veranda, the *hasnahana*, was also fragrant, but it bore associations of mystery and danger. The flowers, greenish white and hard to make out from a distance, bloomed during the monsoon, opening only at night. So sweet was their perfume, that snakes were supposed to be drawn irresistibly to its source, which was why Dida had demurred when Chhobi's eldest uncle brought the plant home. But he had dismissed it as superstitious nonsense, and Dida had been wise enough to give in on a small matter. So the hasnahana had been there for years, although Chhobi had never had the thrill of seeing a snake.

Meanwhile, on weekends it was a quieter kind of pleasure to wake up before her parents, run downstairs and catch Dida just as she finished her bath and went to the veranda to pluck her daily quota of tulsi leaves and some flowers. Dida's long grey-black hair would hang down her back in wet strands and the keys tied to her anchal would jingle quietly with her movements. Unlike Chhobi's mother who loved to dress in warm-toned saris, Dida would always wear white cotton saris with wide coloured borders displaying a variety of woven motifs. With the onset of middle age, most traditional Bengali women changed from colours to white, the absence of colour signifying a withdrawal from the passions and desires of youth. Later, when Chhobi's grandfather died and Dida became a widow, the Hindu strictures imposed asceticism on her, and all she was allowed to wear were white saris without borders or the least touch of colour.

As Chhobi followed her up and down the length of the veranda, Dida would smile from time to time, but there would be no conversation. She would be humming a devotional chant set to the morning raga, Bhairabi: *'Bhajo Gouranga, kaho Gouranga, laho Gouranger naam re . . .'* Gouranga was another name for Sri Chaitanya, the medieval founder of the intense Bhakti movement to which the Vaishnavs of Bengal were heirs. Perhaps it was this quiet, pensive beginning to the day that gave Dida the calm poise to deal with the problems of daily life, especially in the final year of her married life. For Dadu, grandfather, had suffered from a protracted illness before he died and his irritability had been hard to bear. Chhobi, with a child's selfish instinct for self-protection, tended to avoid going into his room, despite her mother's urgings to cheer up the old man. But no amount of irritability on his part robbed Dida of her smile, or hampered the grace of her movements or the authority with which she ran the household.

Saturday was Chhobi's favourite day. There was no school and yet all the grown-ups, including her mother, would go to work, which meant she could monopolize Dida, pottering around after her as she went through the daily chores. When Dida became too preoccupied with other things, or talked to Dadu, Chhobi would run out to the veranda and stare down at the *dumur* tree, whose round berry-like fruits, a species of fig full of tiny, gritty seeds, were made into a spicy dish to be eaten with rice. Chhobi hated dumur, but she was fascinated by the tree, for her eldest uncle had told her that no one had ever seen its flowers. In Bengali the term was synonymous with something invisible, much as a 'snake with five legs' was with something impossible. Chhobi would sit on the floor of the veranda for minutes at a time trying to find even a single flower on the dumur tree, but she had never had any success.

At the end of these vigils, she would go skipping back to the dalan to find Dida ensconced in her usual spot, chopping vegetables. This was the vantage point from which Dida could see the passage in front of the kitchen: the passage where the spices were ground and where Keshto the cook would squat and tell Dida about the market prices, or some incident at the government ration shop, or some garbled political news he had culled from his morning forays. Not that Dida paid much attention to his rumbling voice and doomsday forecasts. This was one of Chhobi's favourite times. Traditionally, the midday meal had always been the most important meal of the day in Bengal, and since two of Chhobi's uncles, who were practising doctors, always came home for lunch, and Dadu, having retired, was always at home, a proper lunch had to be cooked every day of the week. A routine of daily shopping for fish and vegetables, grinding of spices, cutting of vegetables and the cooking of rice, dal, several vegetable dishes and the all-important fish stew, occupied Dida and Keshto till midday. For Chhobi, Saturday meant being in the centre of it all, her nostrils assailed with the pungency of raw spices as they were ground on the stone to be followed by the mingled flavours of fish or vegetables or dal being cooked, while around her were the purples, greens, yellows and whites of all the vegetables brought from the market.

The child watched her grandmother with grave absorption as she chopped the vegetables for the day. She would sit in the classic posture for cutting, her right leg folded and tucked under her body, the left folded and raised so that the knee reached the chest and the foot rested firmly on the narrow slab of wood from which rose a shining arc-like blade. This was the Bengali *bonti* in front of which countless generations of Bengali women had sat and dismembered their vegetables. It came in several sizes, the large ones generally used for cutting fish and meat. Every traditional household had at least two, one for the vegetables and the other, called the *ansh-bonti*, for fish, flesh and fowl as well as for onion and garlic, those two accompaniments for meat and poultry. And God help the poor fool who chopped vegetables on the latter. Chhobi was to see all hell break loose once when a maid had done that. Of course, by then Dida had become a widow and therefore condemned to purely vegetarian food. She could not stomach the contamination of her vegetables by the ansh-bonti; an entirely different lot had to be prepared. Chhobi had dared to protest against what seemed a pointless bit of orthodoxy, but retreated under the double glare of maternal and grandmotherly eyes.

The dietary strictures of widowhood, however, were no hardship for Dida. As far back as Chhobi could remember, her grandmother had seemed to prefer vegetables and fruit over fish or meat. The morning ritual of cutting the vegetables gave her much pleasure, and she rarely entrusted the job to Keshto or the maid. Around Dida, as she sat on the square piece of carpet called an asan, the vegetables would be stacked in woven baskets. The little girl would watch as she started with the potatoes, the compulsory daily ingredient aside from rice and dal. Scrape, scrape, scrape: Dida would turn the potatoes skilfully against the bonti and they would be neatly peeled. Then came a few moments of silent calculation. How many potatoes for the fish jhol? How many for the mixed vegetable dish? How many for the *bhaji* to be eaten at night with hot chapatis or luchis, those round fried breads so loved by Chhobi?

If the vegetables were not the right shape, the dish would never taste good, such was the long-held belief among Bengali women. Long flat slices for the fish jhol; tiny cubes for the dry bhaji spiced with salt, dry red chillies and a pinch of *panch phoron*, the combination of five whole spices (fennel, cumin, mustard, onion seed and fenugreek) so dear to the Bengali nose and palate; slanting but small pieces for the mixed vegetable concoctions; halves for the meat or chicken curry; quarters or whole new potatoes for the mouth-watering *dam*, potatoes cooked slowly in a thick, spicy sauce.

'Are we going to have *begun* bhaja?' Chhobi would ask, as her grandmother turned to brinjals, her eyes gleaming at the thought of the brinjal quarters fried and served with hot rice and ghee.

'Yes. That's why I have to be so careful and watch out for any bugs hiding inside. Of course, if we made round thin slices of the begun, instead of cutting them into quarters, it would be very easy to see the worms. But I don't like doing that as the slices absorb too much oil.'

'They have round slices in aunt Tota's house,' said Chhobi, remembering the lunch at the house of her mother's closest friend.

'Well, you see Didi, Tota is a Bangal,' said Dida, dismissing the entire race of Bengalis who came from East Bengal as lovers of rich, oily food. 'We Ghotis don't like our food so oily or so hot.'

'Why don't we buy begun without any bugs at all? And why do you call me didi? I am not your elder sister, am I?'

'Because you are the wise old woman of all time. And most of these beguns don't have worms. Now I'll do the *patols* and then we can move to the kitchen.'

'I hate patol,' declared Chhobi looking with aversion at the pile of pale green gourd-like vegetables, something like the length of a small courgette or zucchini, but tapered at both ends and plump in the middle. Once the thickish skin, alternately striated in pale and dark green, was peeled and the vegetable cut open, a mature patol would display a double row of white seeds in the creamy flesh. During the summer and monsoon Bengalis used it in a hundred and one ways without getting tired of it: the halves could simply be fried and served with rice and dal, or they would be dipped in batter and fried to be served as an occasional snack with hot tea, or they would figure prominently with the potatoes in the fish stew. At other times the vegetable would be made into *dolmas,* stuffed inside with cooked, flaked fish or even ground meat. And when there was no more scope for eating, the patol-mad Bengalis would go into ecstasies over its shape, comparing the eyes of beautiful women with halved patols. Traditional wisdom decreed that nothing was a better cure for dysentery than overcooked, pulpy rice with a stew made out of a species of catfish called shingi in which floated very small, very soft and immature patols. The very thought of these dishes brought tears of nausea to Chhobi's eyes and she inevitably had to be cheered up by her youngest uncle, who read her stories about a droll boy called Palaram who lived in a place called Patoldanga and who lived on a diet of patol and shingi stew because he was continually suffering from dysentery.

'If you hate patol, you are not wise at all. Just a silly little girl,' said Dida. 'Why, your father would pay a fortune to buy patols out of season. And you say you hate them!'

'The seeds are terrible. And the rest of it is mushy.'

'You know you like them fried. Besides, they are really good for you. My father, who was a famous doctor, used to say that the patol goes straight to the mouth of the liver and keeps it healthy.'

Chhobi had no idea where the liver was or how the patol travelled there from the mouth. But she knew better than to question anything proclaimed by Dida's father. The patols being halved and quartered, Dida called Keshto the cook to come and pick up the bowls containing all the vegetables as well as the bonti. Slowly, she got up, stretched, flung the anchal of her sari firmly backwards so that the bunch of keys jangled, and walked into the kitchen.

The absence of much morning light did not make the kitchen a particularly cheery place. But Chhobi was always a prey to the gloomy fascination of watching Keshto hover over the two coal stoves in the far corner, stirring something and humming tunelessly. There was some mesmerism in the cavernous, sooty darkness of the kitchen, the imprisoned smells, the sight of the earthen stoves glowing with red hot coals, that dominated Chhobi's imagination more than any of the other rooms, even Dida's puja room. The food that was produced in that kitchen was the basic coin of human exchange: love, anger, exuberance, jealousy, contrition, devotion. All seemed to be expressed in the house through the cooking and serving of food. There was that time when Chhobi's father had had the most unexpected row with Dida. Everyone was shocked at the violence of the exchange, for the relationship between the two was one of extraordinary affection. Somehow, Dida fancied a slight in a comment that was probably quite innocent. But when tempers had cooled, she must have realized her mistake. Instead of apologizing, she sent her eldest son to the market for the choicest fish and vegetables, slaved in the kitchen all day and produced a lunch that was nothing short of a miracle. Was it only her family that was particularly wordless, or was it a common pattern of Bengali behaviour, Chhobi was to wonder sometimes in later years. On the whole, she would decide, the latter.

Although Dida and Chhobi's mother and aunt often cooked for the family, Chhobi always perceived Keshto, the cook from Midnapore, as the lord of the kitchen. He was always surly, always hungry, looked half-starved, consumed mountains of rice and had a genius for transforming all vegetables, fish and meat into tasteless watery mush. Yet nobody ever thought of firing him. He was the faithful old servant, the known devil who aggravated you in a hundred ways but would never rob you or let out family secrets. But since good food was a must, the women of the family had to share the burden of cooking. On holidays, or when guests were invited, it was always Chhobi's mother who made the special dishes. Once two other uncles were married, the new aunts would also do their bit, but not often enough. On a day-to-day basis, however, it was Dida who made the important fish stew and at least one vegetable dish.

The refrigerator was an unknown, though Chhobi's eldest uncle sometimes talked about getting one. On these occasions, both grandparents would immediately make an outcry against such needless extravagance and the subject would be dropped. Most cooked food was finished daily. Fish and vegetables cooked in the morning were kept in wired meatsafes and reheated in the afternoon and evening. Milk, too, had to be boiled several times to keep from spoiling. If there was a large amount of unused milk for some reason, Keshto would sit in front of the stove in the evening, stirring the milk over a low flame until it became almost solid. This kheer or *ghano dudh*—literally thickened milk—was sweetened with sugar and served as dessert with dinner.

Spices, too, were ground fresh every day, though in some houses they preserved them for a few days by adding salt. Chhobi's family, however, were too finicky to do that and every morning you could hear the grinding sound of stone on stone as Patoler Ma, the part-time maid, worked on the spices. She was as much of an institution as Keshto, her emaciated body wrapped tightly in a striped sari, her mass of hair piled high in a round bun at the back of her head. She came early in the morning and left around noon. By then she had ground the spices, swept and mopped the whole house, washed the clothes and done the dishes and pots and pans from the night before. She would show up again around teatime, wash the dishes used at lunchtime, sweep the floors, fold the dried clothes and depart.

Chhobi found the sight of Patoler Ma grinding spices perennially absorbing. She would squat in the passage outside the kitchen, the spices ranged in little bowls on one side, a big bowl of water on the other and the grinding stones in front. The instruments were the *shil*, a flat, broad piece of stone with a carefully pitted surface, and the *nora*, an equally pitted stone pestle which was held horizontally in both hands and rubbed against the shil. A little water would first be sprinkled over the portion of spice to help form a paste, and then the rhythmic back and forth movement of the nora would start. The stones would throb and rattle on the cement floor and Chhobi would watch in utter amazement as the long, dry red chillies gave up their seeds, then their skin, and were transformed into a red paste. The portions of dried turmeric were hard as rock and Patoler Ma would first hammer away with her nora until they were pulverized, and then add water to make the yellow paste. Ginger, however, was soft, juicy and easy to transform, so were cumin, coriander and mustard. It seemed nothing short of magic to the little girl as Patoler Ma finished her daily grinding and ranged the spices in dabs of different colour on the special wooden plate, the whole effect being like that of an artist's palette. But whenever she crept up behind the maid and put out a finger to touch the red or yellow or brown pastes, the ever watchful Keshto would bellow at her.

The shil and the nora were also used for grinding other things. On Sundays or other holidays, Chhobi's mother and aunts would sometimes decide to have green mango relish with their lunch as an additional treat. By then of course Patoler Ma would have left and it was Keshto who peeled the small green mangoes, halved them, discarded the seeds and proceeded to crush them on the stone with one or two green chillies. This would then be mixed with ground mustard, salt and pungent mustard oil, and served as a hot-and-sour relish. At other times a chutney would be made with ground mint or coriander leaves, mixed with tamarind pulp, chillies, oil and salt. Though Chhobi had usually finished her lunch and gone upstairs by the time the chutney was being made for the grown-ups, she would invariably hear the grinding sound and creep downstairs. Then Keshto would give her his big wolfish grin, and never shout when she put out an eager little finger, dipped it into the dark or light green paste still on the shil and licked it with slow savouring pleasure. Popular belief ascribed to women a particular fondness for these chutneys as well as other sour things like lime and certain berries. But in Chhobi's family all the men seemed to enjoy the hot-and-sour chutneys as much as the women.

When Dida came into the kitchen after doing the vegetables, the two stoves in the corner would be occupied with two large pots, one bubbling with rice, the other frothing with the dal, both stoves fuelled with a judicious mixture of coal and *ghunte*, dried cow-dung patties. When Dida or Chhobi's mother or aunts made something for the family, they would use two smaller stoves in another corner. But none of them could stoke the stoves with coal and ghunte and get the fire going. That was one of Keshto's first and most important duties.

Though he cooked rice every day, he never seemed to have an accurate sense of the time it took. For daily meals the family preferred a firm, parboiled variety of rice that was always drained after cooking. Somehow, Keshto was never sure of how much water he had put in or how long the rice would take. Each day he went through the same process, testing the rice for softness several times before being sure it was ready. Then he put the lid on the huge pot before carefully carrying it over to the sink to drain the water. No one but Keshto could have lifted that enormous pot day after day without mishap. He would hold the pot and the cover tightly together and slowly tip them forward to drain the water.

Once the rice was taken care of, it was time to deal with the dal. Keshto would put a long-handled wooden *ghutni* or whisk into the pot and stir vigorously, holding the handle between both palms until the grains of dal blended smoothly with the liquid. After this came the spicing of the dal, yet another thrill for Chhobi. Each dal, whether the orange *masoor*, pale yellow *moong* or creamy white *kalai*, or any other variety, had several combinations of approved spices to be used as flavouring agents. Sometimes it was panch phoron. Or it could be only mustard and green chillies. Or cumin, bay leaves and dry red chillies. Or onion and garlic, or—one of Chhobi's favourites—ginger, cumin, green chillies and bay leaves. Whatever the combination of spices, they always had to be fried in oil or ghee. Keshto would put the iron *karai*, a wok-like utensil, on the stove. Oil would be heated in it and the combined spices fried for a few minutes. Then the hot dal would be poured into the karai. The sizzling noise of the liquid meeting the hot oil never failed to thrill Chhobi.

While the dal was being done, Dida would go over to her corner and start the mixed vegetable dish. Keshto's next job would be frying the salted brinjal quarters, followed by the pieces of carp or other fish that had been bought that morning. Most Ghoti families would fry their fish before putting them in the jhol. But the actual cooking of the jhol was something Dida never entrusted to Keshto unless she was unexpectedly busy. For the creation of this thin, watery stew which had the most delicate yet irresistible taste and flavour was an art. If Chhobi happened to be upstairs, she would always know when Dida was making the jhol, for the cumin–coriander–turmeric flavour enhanced by fresh green chillies and varying spices like asafoetida or black onion seeds or green coriander would inevitably rise up to the floor above. But if she was downstairs, Chhobi would sit on a little stool near the kitchen door and eagerly watch Dida as she removed the big karai containing the bubbling jhol. Then she would move forward and peer inside at the floating pieces of fish, potato, patol and the bori, little sun-dried mounds of spiced dal. Ah, the pleasure of surreptitiously dipping your fingers into the pot and popping a bori, succulent with jhol, into your mouth.

While Dida instructed Keshto about other things, Chhobi would go back to her stool, slowly chew her stolen titbit and stare at the rows of jars on the shelves containing all the spices: turmeric and red chillies, cumin and coriander, fennel and fenugreek, cinnamon and cardamom, cloves and peppercorns, *posto* (white poppy seeds) and bay leaves. On the bottom shelf stood two baskets containing potatoes and ginger. Onion and garlic, those two accompaniments for meat and chicken, were considered non-vegetarian, and therefore banished to a separate corner. In a locked wall-cupboard in the storeroom, Dida kept a few other ingredients like nutmeg, mace and saffron, together with camphor, rose-water, *keora* water (flavoured with a synthetic floral essence), all of which were rarely used.

Though Dida's natural self-restraint allowed her to put up with Keshto's minor vagaries, there would be the rare days when Chhobi would hear voices raised, one in anger, the other in self-righteous exculpation. Dida would berate him for his extravagant use of *garom mashla*, cinnamon–cardamom–clove, or of mustard oil, and Keshto would interpret that as an accusation of dishonesty and tell her to find a new cook. She would also tell him off for putting so much asafoetida in the kalai dal that it was completely inedible, and Keshto would again threaten to leave. But such exchanges never lasted long and everyone knew that Keshto would never be fired, nor would he leave. He was as much a part of the family as they were, and there was no real bitterness in Dida's exasperation with him.

On some days there would be no big fish, neither any of the carp family like rui, katla or mirgel, nor the great Bengali favourite the hilsa, nor the bhetki. Those were the days when neither Chhobi's father nor her uncles had been able to go shopping. Keshto would be sent to the market, and since big fish were expensive and his judgement of their freshness not always dependable, he would be instructed to buy inexpensive small fish like punti or mourala. These were usually cleaned but left whole, most of them being only 7-10 cm (3-4 in) in length, like small sardines. Mostly they were made into a very dry but very spicy concoction called chachchari. Or they would be fried to a crisp, to be eaten with rice and lots of dal. Those were the days when eating a meal was the most painful experience for Chhobi. Oh how she hated those bony little fish that others found so delectable. Her mother or grandmother would force-feed her, telling her how good it was for her eyes, her hair, even her brain. Patoler Ma, said Dida, had such a wealth of hair because she only ate small fish. But not even the dream of having a dark cloud of hair cascading to her knees, like that of all the princesses in fairy tales enabled Chhobi to acquire a taste for small fish. Argument, however, was never any use. In matters big and small, what Dida said was final. Chhobi's mother, too, had her moments of rebelliousness, but under Dida's calm reproving gaze, she would inevitably give way. Even Dadu, the male head of the household, the traditional figure of authority, surprised Chhobi by the way he deferred to Dida's judgement on most matters.

Though they were orthodox Hindus of the Vaishnav sect, which laid great emphasis on non-violence, Chhobi's family was not averse to eating meat. No beef or pork though, just goat meat. It was a much prized delicacy and was usually bought on Sundays so that everyone could enjoy it at lunchtime. Holidays, in fact, were synonymous with that particular pleasure: gorging oneself with a spicy meat dish at lunch and then having an afternoon nap. There was not much variety in the cooking of meat in comparison to fish and vegetables, but no one was ever heard to complain. For Chhobi the biggest pleasure was sucking the marrow out of the pipe-like bones of the front legs. And if sucking was not enough, then you banged it a few times on your plate until the recalcitrant marrow emerged with a plop.

Chicken was a rare item on the menu, being expensive, but whenever it did appear, it was Chhobi's mother who did the cooking. Neither Dida or Dadu would touch it. To them, as very orthodox Hindus, the bird was taboo because of its association with Muslims and Westerners. It had been introduced into their house by Chhobi's uncles, but even though they were grown men by then, they were in absurd awe of their father's anger. So the first attempt to cook and eat the bird had been surreptitious.

'I was waiting to get married at that time,' reminisced Chhobi's mother once, 'when your two eldest uncles smuggled a chicken into the garden one day. Your grandfather would skin them alive if he knew about it. So those two came to me for help. I sneaked out a cooking pot, spices and a new kerosene stove from the storeroom, then we dressed and cut the chicken and started cooking in the far corner of the garden. We were quite confident that we could not be seen from the house because of the bushes there. But somehow your grandfather got a whiff of what was cooking. He followed his nose into the garden and there we were, caught red-handed. I was sure he was going to kill us. But you know what he did? He stared at the pot of chicken in dead silence for a few minutes and said quietly, "If you wanted to eat this bird so badly, why not tell me?" And off he went. Ever since then, we have had chicken in the house.'

Game birds were acceptable though. Chhobi could never forget the first time she tasted pigeons brought over by Dilip, a grateful patient of her uncle's who became a friend and adoptive uncle of the family. The novelty of eating a bird that had been hunted instead of being raised, coupled with the firm texture and strong flavour of the flesh, lingered in her memory for years. Dilip's family had been big landowners in the old feudal days and even now there was enough property to keep them in comfort and supply them with game. In the winter there was another bird that appeared on the menu as a treat: tiny snipes that were carried live in woven baskets covered with rope nets and sold door-to-door by itinerant hawkers.

Meals were eaten, as they had been for generations, on the floor, in the dining room. Individual asans would be placed on the floor by Keshto at mealtimes and large bell-metal plates with raised edges, *thalas*, placed in front of the seats. No one thought of eating off china or ceramic plates. Each plate had several small bowls ranged alongside to receive the servings of dal, fish jhol or meat, milk or yoghurt. Rice would be served in a heap on the centre of the plate and around the edges would be placed fried vegetables like potatoes, brinjals or patols, wedges of lime, one or two fresh green chillies, a little bit of salt and a portion of the mixed vegetable dish. Sometimes ghee would be poured over a portion of the hot rice and mixed in quickly to lend its flavour. Since everything was eaten with the fingers, washing your hands before a meal was a compulsory ritual. Though neither Chhobi's father nor any other uncles were strong on the observances of orthodox Hinduism, she could always remember the little ritual Dadu used to enact at mealtimes as long as he was well enough to sit down with the family. Even though he had washed his hands before sitting down, he ceremoniously picked up his glass, poured a little water into his right palm and sprinkled it on the floor. Then he touched his Brahmin's sacred thread with this purified right hand and closed his eyes for a few seconds, silently saying a prayer. Next he took a few grains of rice and placed them on the floor, offering them to the gods and the ancestors. Only after this was he free to eat. The same meticulousness could be seen in his observation of the food on everyone's plate. Repeatedly he would call Keshto and ask him to serve seconds or thirds to each member of the family, though he himself ate little. Sometimes, Chhoto mama, Chhobi's youngest uncle, would tell her a funny story and she would choke as she laughed. Dadu, in his concern, would immediately insist on thumping her on the back so vigorously that tears of pain joined the tears of laughter streaming down her face.

Custom decreed that men, as superior creatures, had to eat first, the women waiting to anticipate their needs and serve them. For centuries the classic image of the Bengali woman had been that of a figure seated before her husband, her sari pulled modestly over her head, waving a palm-leaf hand-fan to keep away the flies and plying her lord and master with more and more food. Though no such scene was ever enacted in Chhobi's house, some discrimination did prevail between men and women. Whenever there were guests, it was Chhobi's mother, and later her two aunts, who did the serving. They themselves would eat only after the guests had finished. As for Dida, as the female head of the household, she inevitably ate after everyone else, every single day. And after her widowhood, it was not permissible for her to sit down with anyone who was eating non-vegetarian food.

Once the meal was over, Keshto would come in and take away the plates, bowls and serving dishes. The asans would be folded and piled in their usual corner. Then he would bring a wet rag, kept for this particular purpose, and wipe the floor clean. This act, called *enthho para*, was absolutely essential. Even if not a speck of food or droplet of water had fallen on the floor, it had to be wiped, simply because of contact with the food and the act of eating. If a lot of people had to be fed in separate batches, the floor would be cleaned between batches. No one would sit down at a place that was enthho.

In those days of innocence Saturday afternoons meant blissful storytelling sessions after lunch. In the big wide bed in Dida's room, Chhobi would lie next to her grandmother and stare up at the embossed floral patterns on the ceiling. Dadu, who never slept in the afternoon, would be reclining in his lounge chair with a book. Dida's voice would unfold the magical fantastic world of Bengali fairy tales where a princess lived in a faraway land and a prince had to cross seven seas and thirteen rivers to come to her, only to find her submerged in the depths of an enchanted sleep, the result of a witch's spell. A gold pin lay at her head and a silver one at her feet. The princess would awaken only if the prince touched her with the gold pin. But even after that, there were numerous dangers to be overcome and enormous distances to escape before the lovers could live happily ever after. Or there would be the story of the king and his two queens, the good one who was kind and virtuous and the wicked one who was beautiful to look at, but in reality a *rakkhashi* or female demon. True to a pattern of male folly, the king would be enslaved by the latter and banish the good queen and her son to the forest, where they lived a life of hardship until some catastrophe opened the king's eyes. Or there would be tales of adventure where the prince set out with his friends, the son of the minister and the son of the merchant, and sailed away to distant lands in search of fabulous wealth and beautiful ladies. There were ghost stories, stories of gods and goddesses, stories from the epics, the Ramayana and the Mahabharata, and above all, stories about Krishna and his childhood among the milkmaids of Brindaban.

No story, however, had had the impact of a particular tale of witchcraft which Dida had told Chhobi one winter afternoon. It was about a wicked witch who hated her stepdaughter. When a prince from a distant land happened to see this poor girl washing dishes by the village pond, he was so overcome by her beauty which shone through her rags, that he instantly wanted to marry her. Confronted by the prince and his entourage, the wicked stepmother could not openly refuse. She asked them to return a little later so that she could dress her stepdaughter in the clothes and jewellery befitting a bride. As soon as she was alone with the girl, she made her put on a beautiful brocade sari and decked her out in the most lavish jewellery from head to toe, tiara to anklet. And then, as the girl stared in a mirror, dumbstruck at this reversal in her fortunes, the stepmother muttered a charm that transformed every item of jewellery into live, writhing venomous cobras which twined and twined around her limbs injecting their fiery poison into the poor girl with a thousand hissing bites. In a terrifying transposition, Chhobi suddenly saw herself as the victim, remorselessly entwined in a slithery serpentine embrace, and she screamed over and over again. Nor could she be calmed until Dadu held her close and taught her a Sanskrit mantra which was supposed to frighten away all snakes.

The loss of innocence—of these long Saturdays—came with the marriages of her two uncles and Dida's battles with her two daughters-in-law. The first one, who was married to Shejo mama, Chhobi's third uncle, when Chhobi was six, provoked Dida by her loudness and her over-jovial manners, her bossiness and her arrogant presumption in inviting people to the house without bothering to consult her mother-in-law. It was she who introduced the meat of the *khashi*, castrated goat, into their house. Any objections about buying this rich, fatty meat from the Muslim butchers, who had a monopoly over it in Calcutta, were swept away in a strident voice. By the time she finished cooking, the kitchen would be in chaos and inordinate quantities of ghee and spices would have been used. Neither Dida nor Chhobi's mother appreciated this lavish preparation, nor did they feel happy about having hordes of guests, mainly relatives, descending on them every month. Many bitter exchanges took place. But these were pardonable faults in the long run. Chhobi found that her aunt also had a very generous side to her, was lavish in her gifts on festive occasions and never tried to set her husband against his family. Perhaps her childlessness made her need the family even more.

This aunt also brought the fine art of making patterned quilts into their house from her Bangal mother. Both Dida and Chhobi's mother made quilts out of their old torn saris. The borders would be cut off and several of the thin washed out cotton saris pressed together and stitched with minute quilting stitches. There were two large wooden chests in Chhobi's house, one on the first floor and the other on the second, where the family's quilt collection was kept along with extra sheets and pillowcases. Everyone had one or two light quilts that were used whenever there was a chill in the air, either during the spring or autumn, or during the damp but stormy days of the monsoon. These were not heavy like the cotton-filled winter quilts, but infinitely comfortable. The women of East Bengal, Dida used to say, were far more industrious than Ghoti women, their domestic crafts being legendary. And Shejo mama's wife could spend hours in total concentration over the most exquisite patterned quilts. They were too beautiful to be used by the family and were ceremoniously brought out when important guests or relatives came to stay. The many-hued flowers, fruits, animals and human figures that stood on those quilts reminded Chhobi of her mother's alpana. But these were permanent.

Another unexpected side of Shejo mamima, so strident and so lacking in feminine grace, was her skill in making paan or betel leaf. Chhobi loved to watch her aunt's nimble fingers. Each heart-shaped paan leaf would be split down the middle and the two halves placed together. Then Shejo mamima would dip her finger in the brass pot containing a thick lime-and-water solution and coat the top half-leaf with the white paste, the alkaline substance that protected the mouth from the sharp pungency of the paan juice. Next she would pick up the tiny pestle that sat in the pot of *khayer* solution. This brown liquid, obtained by grinding the resinous substance from the heartwood of a tree (*Areca catechu*) and mixing it with water, would go over the white paste and the green-brown-white tones of the paan then formed a perfect foil to the embroidery of spices to come. Finely chopped *supuri*, betel nuts, some dyed red and some naturally white-flecked brown, were followed by a few seeds of the smaller cardamom and a few of the larger cardamom coated with silver foil. Fennel seeds and a dash of keora water completed the spicing process and the paan was wrapped up to form a small cone, held together with a clove stuck through the edges.

Eating a paan after a meal was a tradition in their home, the cloves, fennel and cardamom inside the leaf acting as a chaser after the hot spices used in the food. But many people, like Chhobi's mother and her two older uncles as well as her aunt, were also addicted to chewing betel leaves with perfumed tobacco or *jarda* inside them. Children were always discouraged from eating paan and Chhobi had to plead hard before being allowed one on special occasions, though jarda was unthinkable. Once, overcome with curiosity, Chhobi had stolen a large pinch from her mother's supply and put it into her mouth. The experience of dizziness and vomiting, not to speak of the scolding she got from everyone, had killed all desire for the forbidden product. With or without jarda, however, everyone admitted that the best paan was always made by Shejo mama's wife.

It was the marriage of Chhoto mama, the youngest uncle, the apple of Dida's eye, that changed the dynamics of the entire set of family relationships. Dadu had died by then, and Dida arranged this marriage for her son on the recommendation of a family friend who knew the bride's father well. Within a few months, the whole family except Chhoto mama was conscious of a severe disappointment in the new bride. She came from a family that was very different in its cultural moorings. Her father, a wealthy barrister, had spent many years in England and he had no patience with the meaningless rituals of Hindu orthodoxy. How could his pampered daughter be expected to honour them? But Dida found it hard to accept that her favourite son's wife could neither perform puja rituals for the gods nor have a sufficient regard for the rules of *bichar-achar*.

'It's all my fault, of course,' Dida would say, 'I should have known better than to agree to this wedding even though she is from such a prestigious and well-connected family. In the home it is purity that matters, not prestige. I still remember that first time I went to see her at her father's house. I was appalled at the way she handled the plates and glasses. And I saw her, with my own eyes, eating the rice pudding with a spoon, putting the bowl down and not bothering to wash her hands afterwards! Then she went over to the bookcase and pulled down the book her father wanted, with the same enthho hands. The whole house was contaminated. If this is sophistication, God help us!'

For a long time Dida avoided open confrontation, not asking the spoilt daughter-in-law to do anything for fear of alienating her youngest son. But the resentment festered and one day it burst out and erupted like a volcano. The result was momentous for it led to the first break-up of the joint family. Chhoto mama, enslaved by his wife, decided to move out of the house with her and sever connections with the family.

Chhobi had a hard time accepting the apparent cause of this explosion as sufficient grounds for such a separation. At the time grandfather had been dead for several years and the loneliness as well as the strict observance of widowhood had robbed Dida of some of her placid equilibrium. The attenuation of her person caused by the many fasts she undertook was matched by a sharpening of the personality.

And she had developed a minor obsession with the hundred and one rituals to ensure the purity and cleanliness of food, of the kitchen and the *thakur ghar*, the room where the images of the gods were kept. Chhobi could never rationally accept the strictures of these rituals known collectively as bichar-achar. The ban on onion and garlic as non-vegetarian foods made some kind of sense since they were primarily used for cooking meat, itself a taboo item for widows. But why should the *pui shak*, a succulent leafy green, be banished from the community of vegetables, and why should the harmless lentil assume the same status as fish and meat? And why should it be better for a widow to eat non-parboiled rice?

For Chhobi the most irrational aspect of bichar-achar—and this had to be observed by everyone in the house—was the set of taboos centred around that basic item, the pot of rice. Anything that touched the pot or the grains of cooked rice, became *shokri* or enthho, and had to be washed to be reusable. Serving spoons, glasses, serving dishes of vegetables, even hands and mouth, all had to be rinsed after contact. Even a sick person was not permitted to eat rice, or anything that had touched cooked rice, while sitting on the bed, for that would mean washing the bed-clothes and sprinkling the holy water of the Ganga on the wooden frame! And in keeping with the fine irrationality of the whole system, uncooked rice as well as puffed and popped rice were not considered enthho. Bengali is probably one of the few languages that has two different words for raw and cooked rice: *chaal* and *bhaat*.

So ingrained was Dida's fear of enthho that she could not bring herself to drink water by putting her glass to her lips, but insisted on holding her large bell-metal glass a couple of inches from her mouth as she tilted her head back to drink the stream of water. Chhobi's mother and her uncles, too, had the same habit. But not Chhobi. I am the next generation, the first grandchild, she thought. I am allowed.

'Things are so easy for you these days,' said Dida to her one day, addressing the granddaughter but hoping to make a dent in the conscience of her youngest daughter-in-law. 'In the old days a woman would have to bathe first thing in the morning, summer or winter. And remember, there was no running water then, it had to be a dip in the pond. Then she would put on a red-bordered sari, less wide than normal saris so that her movements would not be hampered, and go to the kitchen and worship Agni, the god of fire, before she started the day's cooking. And remember, there was no one to help her build up the stoves with coal and ghunte. And you girls feel put upon because you have to keep the pots and pans separate or wash your hands a few times, or eat on a clean floor like all your ancestors have done instead of sitting at a table like the sahibs. That's what sophistication does for you.'

Chhobi sighed, thinking back to the days of earlier childhood, far less fraught with divided loyalties—for a part of her did sympathize with her youngest aunt's desire to modernize their lifestyle.

The rupture cast a pall of gloom over the whole house for a while. Between anger, sorrow and self-reproach, Dida became a silent shadow of her former gracious self. Even Chhobi's mother, normally so reserved, lost her cool one day and blamed Dida for being overly rigid about archaic rituals and letting her own pride break up the family. Dida retreated more and more into the room where the gods were and sometimes would not emerge for a whole day. Gone were the leisurely mornings of cutting vegetables in the dalan, listening to Keshto and smiling at Chhobi. Now it was Keshto who did the vegetables sitting in front of the kitchen, gossiping with Patoler Ma.

Bilu, Chhoto mama and his wife's only son, was born eighteen months after his parents moved out of Dida's house. Chhobi's three remaining uncles and her parents heard the news but were afraid to say anything to Dida for fear of increasing her misery. No one knew how best to reunite the family and yet everyone felt it was high time the youngest son came home with his wife and child.

Chhobi, too, was kept in the dark for fear she would blurt it out to Dida in unthinking excitement. The first she heard of it was when she saw her older aunt embroidering a beautiful quilt. What amazed Chhobi was that her aunt was quilting together several thin saris made of silk rather than cotton. They were old and frayed at the edges, but silk seemed too impractical for daily or even occasional use. How would they be washed? Chhobi had pestered her aunt about this until she was told under the seal of secrecy that this quilt was being made for a special cousin whom none of them had yet seen. The very next day, however, there was no need for secrecy. Her eldest uncle decided to take matters into his own hands and informed Dida about the birth of the first grandson. Pride and anger could never last in the face of such happy news. Dida, armed with special offerings made to the goddess Kali at the temple in Kalighat as well as the traditional symbolic gift of a gold coin, went with her eldest son and Chhobi's mother to visit the truants and look upon the face of the sole dynastic heir. The next thing that happened, of course, was the return of Chhobi's youngest uncle with his wife and son.

The presence of a child was worth a hundred good resolutions and brought so much spontaneous joy in the quiet house that the daughter-in-law's faults became secondary. She, for her part, decided to be gracious in her triumph and even made the occasional attempt to honour the rules of bichar-achar. To Chhobi, her little cousin Bilu brought only unalloyed joy. Fair, chubby and good-tempered, with his mother's wide black eyes and his father's curly black hair, he seemed to infuse a sense of well-being that made everything brighter. Patoler Ma, wiping the floor, would pause on her knees and admire the child's fair skin.

'Just like a sahib's child,' she would say in wonder.

Though Chhobi laughed at this evidence of colour-consciousness, she, too, would feel a sense of wonder at this new creature who had made such a momentous impact on her family. Playing with his toes that nestled in the palm of her hand like the tiny baby bananas inside the banana blossom, she wondered what life would be like in the future when she was not the only grandchild in the house, no longer Dida's undisputed favourite. So long used to the role of a child, she was surprised at the semi-maternal tenderness she felt towards this little human morsel.

Even surly Keshto went about whistling. Chhobi's three older uncles, all childless, were constantly in confabulation about the grand feast to be given on the occasion of Bilu's upcoming annaprasan. As for Dida, the presence of this grandchild and the preparations for the ceremony seemed to rejuvenate her into a second youth. Gone were the silence and languor of the past months. The images of the deities saw her only briefly, morning and evening. The old corner of the dalan saw her ensconced once more in front of her bonti with the vegetables piled around her. And her voice could be heard ever so often, instructing Patoler Ma, scolding Keshto for his wasteful habits or sniffing the odour of the phoron and the dal and telling Keshto he had ruined it with too much asafoetida. And of course there was her grandson to be cooed over whenever she had a chance. Chhobi would notice her own parents smile at each other as they looked at Dida holding up her chortling grandson who kicked her with his fat legs.

The date of the annaprasan was finally set. Bilu would be six months old, the right age for a boy's annaprasan. One day as Chhobi's father and uncles sat in the dalan planning the menu, deciding when to send out the invitations and estimating costs, Chhobi suddenly thought about her own infancy. She certainly had no memory of any such ceremony.

'What did you do for my annaprasan, Ma?' she asked her mother.

'Nothing like this dear. It's not the custom to have an elaborate ceremony for girls. Of course every child has to go through the ritual, otherwise nobody would be able to eat rice at all.' And Ma had laughed gently at the scowl of anger on Chhobi's face. With such an air of festivity enveloping the house, however, it didn't last for long.

Uncle Dilip, somewhat portly around the middle by now, arrived the day before the annaprasan. He had been informed of the happy event by Chhobi's eldest uncle and was determined to take part in it. This time he brought no pigeons with him but a whole sackful of the specially fine rice that grew on one of his estates. Throughout the day his voice could be heard from upstairs, berating the workmen who were covering the enormous roof with a canopy under which the guests would sit down to their meal. Under the red, white and blue cloth, tables and chairs were set out in rows. Once a beautiful teak dining table had been imported into the house by Chhoto mamima, the family had never gone back to the old days when meals were eaten on the floor. But in one respect Dida still had her way. For the beautiful polished surface of the table was kept permanently covered with an ugly piece of plastic which could be washed and scrubbed after each meal. Enthho para was not going to stop in Dida's house. Still, Chhobi was grateful that her grandmother's *shuchibai*, cleanliness mania, was not as bad as that of the old lady's next door where copious quantities of soapy water had to be poured over the dining table to make it really 'clean'. The wooden legs had already started rotting under such treatment.

By the time Chhobi woke for the second time on the day of the annaprasan, the whole house was astir with bustle. Many voices, raised disparately, told her that the preparations were well under way. Slipping out of bed, she saw her parents' room was empty. As she went downstairs, she could hear one particular voice from the ground floor that made her grin. Anath uncle had arrived. Like Dilip, he was no real uncle but a former patient of Chhobi's second uncle. Unlike the wealthy Dilip, however, he was way down the social and caste ladder, being a *jele* or fisherman who acted as a wholesale buyer of fish from individual fishermen and supplied the fish to the stall owners in the fish markets of north Calcutta. Ever since he had been cured of some painful intestinal problem by Mejo mama, he had often supplied the family with fresh carp or hilsa or bhetki at no charge. And on special occasions, he always undertook to supply all the fish needed. Not only that, he would turn up himself with a couple of helpers carrying the fish in huge baskets and spend the morning cutting, cleaning and portioning the fish in the way the cooks wanted.

This morning, too, Chhobi saw him as she peered through
the dalan windows into the courtyard below, sitting in front of
a huge ansh-bonti, wearing nothing but a thin red-and-white
checked *gamchha* or towel around his waist, holding a portion
of the carp he had just beheaded. His dark, wiry, muscular body
gleamed with the remnants of the mustard oil he regularly
massaged in before his bath, and the space around him was
awash in blood with piles of extracted gut and several fish heads
lying around. But from a distance and under the open sky it did
not seem so revolting to Chhobi. She called out to him and he
looked up, baring his teeth all stained with the red juice of
spiced paan. Anath's grin enveloped his face in such a way that
Chhobi was always reminded of the Bengali idiom which
translated literally as 'a cheekful of smile'.

In broad daylight the alpana on the floor looked no less
miraculous than in the pearly light of dawn. Soon, she knew, it
would be obscured, for the priest would come and all the rituals
would begin, including the lighting of a small fire where
oblations of ghee would be poured. Chhobi wandered over to
the kitchen and looked in, but neither Dida nor her mother
paid her any attention; even with the cooks hired for the day,
who were working on the roof, there were numerous small
things to be done in the kitchen and Keshto always needed
supervision. From there she moved to the dining room where
the table had been pushed against the wall and the chairs piled
on it to make room for the rattan furniture from the dalan. In
the middle of this chaos was a small empty space on the floor
where Chhobi found her elder aunt sitting with a big plate of
paan leaves and small containers of spices. Noticing the
supplicating little palm, Shejo mamima placed one on it. 'Off
with you now,' she said. 'You won't get another one. And if
your father sees you going around with that red-stained mouth

he'll have my head. So run along and brush your teeth and take a bath.'

With a sigh Chhobi got up to go. It was true. Her father, normally such a gentle, woolly-headed person, who never spoke a harsh word to his daughter, always became furious if he saw her chewing paan. He did not mind his wife's addiction to paan and jarda, seeing it as the influence of her family. But he himself would never touch it and was determined that Chhobi should not acquire the habit. That was why Chhobi so looked forward to the visits of Sadhubaba, a holy man whom her grandfather had encountered many years ago and made into an informal guru. Sadhubaba usually came to their house on the eve of some religious festival and inevitably, they would be deluged by visitors during his stay. Big bowls piled high with paan, with and without jarda, would be placed in Sadhubaba's room for he was not only an addict himself, but also loved to distribute paan to his admirers. And such was his power that even Chhobi's father did not dare protest when his daughter was given a sweet-spiced paan by the indulgent old man.

Chewing her mouthful of paan, Chhobi tried to look in on Bilu before going upstairs, but his parents' room was locked and Chhoto mamima called out from inside that she was giving him his bath. There was nothing to do then, but to go upstairs for her own bath. Once bathed, her teeth brushed to remove all traces of the paan, Chhobi happily put on the new blue dress Dida had given her for the occasion. As she got out of her room, she could feel the bustle of real action. The professional cooks were already at work. From the roof, where they were cooking, came the pattering sound of footsteps and the enticing smell of cauliflower and potatoes being made into a spicy dalna. And she could also detect the caramelly smell of hot ghee in which something was being fried. From downstairs came the mingled voices of Anath, Keshto, Patoler Ma and her uncles. The priest had probably arrived and was setting out all the items to be used for the ceremony. Chhobi wondered if Bilu was going to howl at the unprecedented sight of so many strange faces.

She decided to take a look at the roof before going down to the ceremony. One corner had been partitioned off for cooking. Several huge stoves had been brought in by the cooks, together with monstrous pots and pans for the rice, dal, vegetables, fish, meat, chutney and sweets that were going to be served. Close up, the mingled smells were still more wonderful. Anath's carp was already being made into a rich kalia, and one of the cooks was lifting fillets of bhetki fish from their lemon, ginger, onion and chilli marinade to coat them with egg and breadcrumbs before frying them. Those 'fries', as they were called, were a special favourite of her eldest uncle's and her father's. No important occasion in the family could be imagined without serving bhetki fries. But the most inviting smell came from the stove in the farthest corner where one of the cooks sat frying pantuas in ghee before dropping them into a pan of hot syrup. These dark brown balls were Chhobi's favourite sweets and her mouth watered at the sight of all the pantuas floating in syrup.

Not that she was a stranger to pantuas at other times. The family ate sweets, or *mishti* every day. Often her father or one of her uncles would bring back pantuas in an earthen pot from one of the famous sweet shops. Dida and Ma were always telling her not to drink water on an empty stomach. This was a wonderful excuse to pop a juicy pantua into your mouth! Guests were treated to the same conundrum and no visitor could leave the house without the ritual of mishtimukh, or sweetening the mouth.

Though her father and uncles were always complaining about the deterioration of all shop-made mishti and had endless discussions about the amount of rice flour, cream of wheat or plain flour which they claimed was used to adulterate these products, Chhobi never saw them eat any less of the sweets or buy them less often. In the fancy sweet shops of south Calcutta where Chhobi lived, you would find a variety of sweets—sandesh in many shapes and sizes, rosogolla, pantua, mihidana, kalojam, balushahi and gaja—all aseptically displayed in metal containers behind glass counters.

Mejo mama would sometimes tell Chhobi about the famous mishti shops of north Calcutta where he had been to college. He said that each of them had their own resident moira or sweet-maker, invariably a mountainous figure wearing only a dhoti tucked around his middle like a loincloth and a red-and-white checked gamchha flung over his shoulder. The gamchha, according to Mejo mama, was given to the moira by god to serve the purpose of a cow's tail, not only to wipe the sweat from his face but also to wave away the flies that constantly hovered around the sweets he was making. Chhobi would gurgle with laughter at the idea of a cow crossed with a moira and wondered how many of his own sweets the moira ate every day. She had a vision of this enormous pot-bellied man with bulging eyes and a face shining with perspiration constantly popping sweets into his mouth and chewing in bovine appreciation while a huge cauldron sat on a stove in front of him bubbling with syrup in which floated various sweets.

'Would you like a pantua, little girl?' Chhobi realized suddenly that she had come up close to the cook who was making the sweets. He was smiling kindly at her and Chhobi felt no embarrassment as she stretched out her palm for the hot sweet and put it into her mouth. Oh, how she loved the taste of those juicy brown balls made from a mixture of chhana—the solid part of curdled milk—and thick evaporated milk. A little piece of crystallized sugar was put inside each ball before it was fried in ghee: the sugar would melt in the heat and when the pantua was dropped into the hot syrup, the vacant space inside absorbed and retained the liquid, like a liqueur chocolate. Seeds from the larger variety of cardamom were also blended into the chhana mixture so that when you bit into one of them, a gentle explosion of flavour filled your mouth.

Savouring the taste, Chhobi smiled gratefully at the cook and went downstairs. From the first-floor landing she could smell the incense and sandalwood paste and hear the priest chanting in Sanskrit. The ceremony had begun. Despite the unprecedented melee of sight, sound and smell, Bilu behaved impeccably. Dressed in a miniature adult outfit made of cream satin, he sat in the lap of his maternal uncle for tradition decreed that only this relative could feed you your first grain of rice. Instead of screaming he calmly observed the fuss that went on around him with a satisfied air, as if he knew it was all for his benefit. His mother stood nearby, looking beautiful in the dazzling yellow silk sari with a green-and-gold border that Dida had given her for the occasion. Her long black hair, like that of the princesses in fairy tales, hung down in a cloudy profusion over her back. The great moment came and went and Bilu bared his toothless gums in the manner of a star expecting applause. Chhobi went over to take him in her arms and he happily nuzzled his face against hers.

Later, as the first batch of guests trooped upstairs for lunch, Ma urged Chhobi to go up and eat with them, but she felt too bashful to do so. So it was Dida who took her into the dining room and served her lunch on the floor, in the same place where her aunt had been making paan. Chhobi grinned happily as she looked at the bhetki fries and meat with luchis on her plate and deliberately regressed to earlier days of childhood.

'Tell me a story, Dida.'

'There you go again. Big girls like you are supposed to read stories, not to pester their grandmothers.' But she was smiling fondly at Chhobi.

'No Dida. Today you just have to tell me a story. Otherwise I won't eat.'

Dida laughed and reminded Chhobi about the time when, as a little girl, she had taken a plate of luchis up to the roof one winter morning so she could eat them in the sun, and a huge brown kite had come swooping down and flown off with her luchis. 'How you wailed that day—as if it was the end of the world! Your Ma made you some more luchis, but you just would not be consoled. I still remember you hiccuping through your tears and saying, "But why must the bird take my luchis?"'

Chhobi looked at the luchis that sat on her plate. They looked flaky and crumbled easily in her fingers. Somehow, she did not like the taste of them as much as she had hoped. When her mother or Dida made luchis, they had a trick of kneading the flour with water and ghee in such a way that the round, rolled-out luchis puffed up enormously as soon as they were dropped into the hot ghee in the karai. One of Chhobi's treats was to sit next to either of them and watch each luchi being fried and lifted out of the karai. Inevitably, she would be given one to taste before the meal and she loved to poke a hole in the puffed up outer skin of the luchi and feel the hot air rush out. Then, when you tore it apart, that luchi would always have a feel of elasticity quite unlike the crumbling flakiness of these.

'I don't think these cooks can make luchis as well as you or Ma.'

'Well, they have to make tons of them, and that's not so easy. Besides, those luchis are flaky because they kneaded the dough with a lot of ghee. Some people prefer that to the kind of luchis we make at home.'

Chhobi shook her head at the vagaries of such people and went back to her request for a story. Somehow it seemed important to recapture the essence of the lovely childhood bond with her grandmother on this day when she could sense so clearly that another child had come into their lives—another child who would be watched over by Dida, patted to sleep by Dida, lovingly fed by Dida and then lie next to her in the big bed and listen to her stories. Her grandmother must have felt some of the same things, for she suddenly started on one of Chhobi's favourite childhood stories about two princes, Nilkamal and Lalkamal. By the time the story had come to an end, Chhobi was savouring the last mouthful of the last pantua.

Once she had washed her hands, the loud orders and the buzz of conversation from upstairs told her that lunch for the guests was in full swing. Now that she did not have to eat in front of them, Chhobi felt bold enough to go up and take a look. Her father and uncles were doing the serving in the time-honoured custom of formal hospitality. Her mother and both her aunts stood around, urging the guests to have more. Chhobi regretted not having eaten on a banana leaf like the guests. Somehow, everything would acquire a new taste simply by being served on those wide, glossy green leaves. Before the guests sat down, the leaves would be embellished in the corners with a bit of salt, a wedge of lime, fried brinjals split lengthwise in the middle and with the stem still attached, a little dab of fried spinach and some fried patols. As the guests sat down, the serving would begin, each server carrying brass buckets in which the cooks had heaped the food. Hot rice, cauliflower and potato dalna, moong dal cooked with the heads of Anath's carps, followed by carp kalia and the fries. Finally came the meat curry served with those flaky luchis.

Chhobi loved to watch the little drama that inevitably resulted with some of the guests who really loved to eat but had to pretend, for the sake of good manners, that they did not. Whenever seconds or thirds were offered, they would extend both hands over the banana leaf, look panic-stricken and deny vehemently that they could eat another morsel. The server would of course refuse to accept this and threaten to pour the food over their hands until, good manners having been observed, the guests would remove their hands in mock dismay and allow the food to be served and consumed with relish. After the meat came the tomato chutney, a common winter favourite, and hot crisp salty *papors*. These were supposed to cleanse the mouth and prepare you for dessert. Once again, Chhobi chuckled from her vantage point as all the sweets—the white sandesh, the pink sweet yoghurt, the brown pantua and the yellow globules of mihidana—fell on the green leaves only to disappear in a flash despite all protests about overeating.

Once the meal was over, the guests trooped downstairs to wash their hands and both of Chhobi's aunts followed to serve them paan. But Chhobi lingered upstairs for she wanted to be around while her father, real and adoptive uncles and their helpers sat down in front of fresh banana leaves. Her mother supervised while Keshto and the cooks brought them food. Anath uncle always amazed Chhobi by the amount of food he could put away in his compact little body. His obvious relish for what he ate made him a favourite with both Dida and Ma. Chhobi pulled up a chair next to him and tried to act like a proper hostess, urging him to have more of everything. Anath was vastly amused and called out to her mother.

'Look, Didi, your daughter's growing up all right. It's time you married her off so she has her own home!'

Everyone, including Anath's two assistants, laughed and Chhobi turned scarlet. But soon she forgot her embarrassment and asked Anath to tell her a 'fish' story.

'Well, do you know what the koi fish is supposed to say? It has these terrible curving bones around the stomach, as you must have noticed. And any time you catch the koi, it says, "I'll remember the person who caught me and I'll also remember the person who cleaned me. As for the person who eats me, I'll make sure he never forgets me, for my bones will stick forever in his throat.'" And Anath roared with laughter at his own joke.

'Oh come on, Anath mama,' protested Chhobi. 'That's not a proper story. I've heard that one a hundred times.'

'You have? Well, you've got to give me time to think of another one.'

'Now, Chhobi,' said her mother, 'let him eat in peace. Why don't you go to your room and lie down for a while. Otherwise you'll be so tired you'll fall asleep in the evening.'

Somewhat reluctantly, Chhobi got up, for she knew her mother was right. It would be nice to get away from noise, bustle and loud conversation. The striped canopy overhead obscured the sky, but she could sense an oncoming darkness. As she moved towards the stairs, she could hear Dilip's voice.

'Looks like it is going to rain. Good thing we got everyone fed before it came pouring down.'

'Yes,' said Chhobi's father, 'it's time it did rain. This has been such a dry month. Of course it's too late for the proverbial rains of the end of Magh, but maybe this rain will also be good for the crops. I'm sure they need it.'

'Oh yes,' said Dilip. 'My fields could certainly do with a bit of water.'

Chhobi went into her room, flung herself down on her bed and pulled aside the curtains of the nearest window. Yes, there was no doubt it was going to rain, one of those unseasonable spring downpours. The sky was covered with slate-grey clouds and the shimul flowers blooming on the top branches were vividly scarlet against it. A cool wind came into the room and fluttered the pages of her book. Chhobi pulled out her saffron quilt, drew it over herself and snuggled her cheek into the pillow. It had been a beautiful day, she thought. One year ago, nobody would ever have dreamt of such a reconciliation, or of there being another child in the family. Who knows what the coming years would bring? But I will not be a child any longer, she thought, I will grow up and one day I'll leave them like the prince in the story and go out across the seven seas and thirteen rivers in search of adventures. Much later, having seen the world, I'll come back. I'll be the one to tell stories then and all of them will listen. And the house will be here, kadam on one side and shimul on the other, and inside will be the most wonderful alpana for I will describe all kinds of new flowers, fruits and leaves for Ma to paint. She will listen and paint and I'll sit by and watch, no matter how late it is and Dida will smile at us as she combs and braids her hair.

BASANTA

spring

GRISHMA

summer

Flagrantly scarlet on bare branches or covertly crimson amidst dark green foliage, the early flowers of spring arrive to signal an end to the mellow contentment of winter and to herald a brief unsettling season. Hardly perceived before it is over, spring in Bengal combines beauty and terror like the longer-lasting monsoon. The variety of colours ranged on the trees and the fragrance of mango trees in blossom carried by the balmiest of evening breezes create a lightness of being before the relentless weight of summer sets in. A little later in the season the heady scent of gardenia in the evenings heightens sensory awareness to a new pitch. But the changeable weather of spring is inevitably accompanied by outbreaks of chickenpox and measles. Not so long ago, a greater terror stalked the land at this time: smallpox, whose Bengali name, Basanta, is synonymous with the season itself.

According to the Bengali calendar, the two months of Falgun and Chaitra, mid-February to mid-April, are to be counted as the spring. But by the end of March, one can feel the cruelty of the summer sun and the long, dusty wait for the monsoon starts as moisture evaporates from leaf and land while a humid haze covers the sky.

Food in a Bengali household takes on the summer pattern fairly early in the spring. Daytime temperatures are hot enough for the traditional housewife to buy and serve 'cool' items to her family. This belief in the hot and cold quality of foods has been a fundamental part of local beliefs for a long time, probably dating back to theories of indigenous Ayurvedic medicine that developed under the Aryans. The *Charakasamhita*, an Ayurvedic text written by Charaka around the first century BC, contains detailed descriptions of the specific attributes of foods as well as detailed instructions on eating and keeping healthy. Having been a great drinker himself, Charaka extolled the virtues of alcohol, but this part of his teaching has not found root in Bengal.

Nor has his stricture, reminiscent of Jewish food practices, against the consumption of fish and milk together, on the grounds that they would burden the digestive system.

But the belief in the specific attribute of different foods has continued to flourish here because of a long tradition of Ayurvedic medicine practised by local physicians. Even now, women of my mother's generation will serve vegetables like *lau*, white gourd, or ladies' finger or patol, the small striped gourd known as parwal in other parts of India, during summer, with the conviction that these will keep the body cool. Meat, egg, onion and garlic, on the other hand, are studiously avoided. Ginger, though, is encouraged because it is believed to increase appetite and aid digestion if taken before meals with a little salt. As for biliousness, which seems to have been a universal affliction in the old days, Ayurvedic practitioners will recommend patol, cucumber and the two varieties of bitter gourd, *karola* and *uchchhe*.

The association of healthful properties with a bitter taste and the subsequent appreciation of that bitterness as a taste is a Bengali peculiarity that outsiders find incomprehensible. Even for the natives, it is an acquired taste. Most children, including myself in my pre-teen schooldays, recoil from these bitter vegetables. My mother, a determined woman, would force me to swallow bitter gourds, leaves of the neem or margosa tree, and a *shukto* made with mixed vegetables and the excruciatingly bitter leaves of the patol, even though tears rolled down my face. Years of force-feeding accomplished the intended miracle, for nothing tastes sweeter now than the bitter vegetables served with rice at the beginning of a meal.

My personal favourite is the simple *neem begun*, made with brinjals cubed small and fried with a handful of the bitter neem leaves. In spring, the coppery new leaves cover the branches and are ideal for making this dish, being slightly less bitter than the older leaves. The virtues of the neem are supposed to be many. Its oil is extracted to be made into beneficial soap, its twigs are broken off and chewed at the ends to make fibrous natural toothbrushes in rural areas. But the greatest of its medicinal properties is to be seen during the rampaging outbreaks of chickenpox. When the scabs dry and the whole body is one gigantic agonizing itch, neem leaves are boiled in water and used to sponge the patient to give exquisite relief. Sometimes, soft branches are tied together and used like an improvised brush to rub the patient's body. Though smallpox has now been eradicated, the memory of it still remains as a great fear in the Bengali mind and the deity that folk imagination devised as the patron saint for warding off this terrible disease, the goddess Shitala on her donkey, is still worshipped in small roadside temples.

The bitter gourds, karola and uchchhe, are not confined to the spring and the summer. In our house they are round-the-year favourites and can be eaten boiled and mashed, or sliced and fried crisp, or made into a soft chachchari with sliced potatoes, ground mustard and a little panch phoron. But their real glory emerges in shukto, the strange preparation over which Bengalis pride themselves so much. The term is derived from the medieval Bengali *shukuta*, meaning the dried leaves of a plant, usually the bitter jute plant. These leaves were stored throughout the year and used to make a bitter dish with seasonal vegetables. From mythical Shiva in the narrative poems to the historical figure of Chaitanya, the medieval Bengali loved his shukto, and all the more so because it was believed to be an antidote for excessive mucus in the gut, which was one sign of that common affliction, dysentery.

The shukto remains one of the best instances of a Hindu Bengali cook's ingenuity, with a combination of subtle half-tones rather than any dominant taste. The bitterness is rarely allowed to overpower the other flavours which include the sharpness of mustard, the grainy blandness of poppy seeds and the caramel-like flavour of ghee. In the old days no woman was considered a good cook unless she could produce a creditable shukto: a nursery rhyme in my childhood heaped ridicule on a poor girl called Rani because she knew so little that she had put hot chillies in her shukto and flavoured her sour ambal with ghee. Of course, there are the fifth columnists who declare that the shukto is a superb instance of the Bengali's low cunning, for anything you serve after a bitter item is bound to taste wonderful.

Whatever the motives for serving shukto, it is an integral part of the summer menu, regularly served to guests on formal occasions, even as late as twenty years back, and with infinite variations. The vegetables may vary according to season and availability, with the characteristic bitter taste produced either by the bitter gourds, or by the leaves of the patol or by some other leafy green.

SHUKTO

FOR FOUR PEOPLE

INGREDIENTS

500 gm (1 lb) of cubed or sliced mixed vegetables such as potatoes, brinjals, sweet potatoes, green papayas, local radishes, flat beans, green bananas, patols, ridged gourds or jhinge and bitter gourds

2 + 1 tablespoons of oil

½ + ½ teaspoon of panch phoron

1 tablespoon ground posto or poppy seeds

3 tablespoons of mustard (ground fine with a touch of salt)

1 tablespoon of ground ginger

2 bay leaves

2 teaspoons of flour

2 teaspoons of ghee

3 teaspoons of sugar
Salt to taste

METHOD

We often feel you cannot have too much of Shukto. For four people we usually take about 500 gm (1 lb) of cubed or sliced mixed vegetables. The thing to remember is that the bitter gourds should be sliced very fine and should not be more than one fifth of the total quantity of vegetables. Once all the vegetables have been washed, heat a little oil in a karai and sauté the bitter gourd slices for three to four minutes. Remove and keep apart. Add a little more oil to the pot (the total amount should be about 2 tablespoons) and throw in ½ teaspoon of panch phoron. A couple of minutes later, add the rest of the raw vegetables, stir for four to five minutes and add enough water to cook the vegetables. Keep covered until they are cooked, add the fried bitter gourds together with salt to taste and the sugar. Cook over high heat for another three to four minutes and remove from the stove.

To spice this dish we use ground posto, mustard and ground ginger. This is added in the second stage of the cooking, when 1 tablespoon of oil is heated in another pot, and another ½ teaspoon of panch phoron, together with the bay leaves and half the ground ginger thrown into it. Once this has been fried for a minute or so, the cooked vegetables with the gravy are poured in and brought to the boil. The posto and mustard are combined in a bowl with flour and a little water and the paste is added to the pot. After cooking these for three to four minutes, the ghee and the rest of the ginger are added. The salt and the sugar are checked, the whole thing stirred thoroughly to blend the flavours and the pot removed from the fire. The sweetness should balance the bitterness, so more sugar might be needed. It is up to the cook to decide how much sugar he or she wants to add; being Ghotis, we like our shukto to be sweetish, but others prefer it more bitter. The sauce should be thick, not watery, and whitish in colour. I find that the delicacy of flavour is heightened if the shukto is served warm rather than piping hot.

When shukto is not possible, the Bengali passion for bitterness finds expression in the addition of bitter vegetables to dal. There is both variety and a strict order in the cooking and serving of dals. Three or four different types can be served at the same meal, especially among the Hindus of East Bengal. You can start with a bitter dal with vegetables, then, after one or two vegetable items, you can have a roasted moong dal cooked with a fish head. Finally, after the fish and the meat but before the chutney and dessert, a sour dal, made either with green mangoes or tamarind or any other sour fruit like the star fruit, can be served. Such elaborate meals are rare now, but a surprising variety of dals is still part of the Bengali cook's daily repertoire. The proverbial phrase, 'poor man's rice and dal', can easily be made into a far-from-poor meal.

The most important thing about cooking dal is the phoron or spices used for flavouring it. Different dals will have different combinations for phorons and the same dal can have several different phorons, depending on the mood of the cook. The first step for all dals, though, is always the same: boiling in water until it is soft and soupy, the amount of water needed varying widely, depending on how thin or how thick you want your dal to be. My family thought of lentils as a rather thick potage with long slices of onion and green chillies and, of course, a sweetish undertaste. So when I first went to live in Bangladesh with my husband, I was very disconcerted at seeing the thin dal that appeared on my in-laws' dining table. The taste was different too, for the lentils had been flavoured with minutely chopped onions and garlic, together with bay leaves and dried red chillies, all fried in oil.

In summer the common dals in our home are moong and kalai rather than lentils, yellow split peas or pigeon peas. And while in winter the moong dal may be roasted in a frying pan before cooking, in summer it is preferred *kancha* or unroasted, because that is easier to digest and does not heat the system.

KANCHA MOONG DAL

FOR FOUR PEOPLE

INGREDIENTS

250 gm (½ lb) of moong dal
750 ml (1¼ pints) of water
1½ teaspoons of oil
2 dried red chillies
1 teaspoon of whole mustard seeds
2 teaspoons of finely chopped ginger
4 bay leaves
1 teaspoon ghee
1 tablespoon juice of freshly ground ginger
2-3 green chillies
1 teaspoon of panch phoron
1 teaspoon of turmeric powder
1 teaspoon of salt

METHOD

Take moong dal and rinse it in a colander under running water for three to four minutes. Somehow, this makes a difference even if the dal is clean. As you hold the dal under water, squeeze it in handfuls to make sure that the surface dust is thoroughly washed off. Heat water in a pot. When it comes to the boil, add the dal and salt. If you wish, you can also add turmeric powder. When the dal is cooked, remove from the stove. Heat oil in a karai or frying pan and throw in the dried red chillies. When they turn black, add the whole mustard seeds. As soon as these stop sputtering, add the ginger and the bay leaves. Stir for a minute, add ghee and pour the dal over it. Taste for salt, add a little sugar, keep on a high flame for three to four minutes and remove. The thickness of the dal can be suited to your taste. You can change the amount of water.

The same dal, once it has been boiled, can be treated a little differently. Before removing the cooked dal, add ginger juice and green chillies. Then heat some oil separately, fry 2 bay leaves, the ginger pulp from which the juice was pressed, and panch phoron in it. Pour the dal over this, cook for three to four minutes, taste and remove.

Though the kancha moong dal is a summer favourite, sometimes my mother would make an equally simple version of masoor dal. This dal, for some odd reason, is considered non-vegetarian by the Hindus and therefore forbidden to widows. Its usual recipe with onions is more suitable to the cooler temperatures of monsoon and winter, but this particular recipe, somehow, made it past all apprehensions of heat and appeared even in summer.

MASOOR DAL

FOR FOUR PEOPLE

INGREDIENTS

250 gm (½ lb) of masoor dal
750 ml (1¼ pints) of water
1 tablespoon of ghee
2 green chillies, finely chopped
Salt to taste

METHOD

The masoor dal is boiled in water with salt. Then, instead of any phoron being fried separately, ghee and green chillies are dropped into the dal. It is left covered for five minutes to let the flavours mingle and tastes so good that the absence of phoron is not noticed.

Once, in Dhaka, a good friend of mine, Salma Sobhan, was talking to me about Muslim Bengali cooking. She explained that among its intricacies were a few simple dishes, like lemon dal, that amazed one with their taste. What was that, I asked. And she was taken aback at such ignorance.

LEMON DAL

FOR FOUR PEOPLE

INGREDIENTS

250 gm (½ lb) of moong dal
750 ml (1¼ pints) of water
Thin slices of lemon or lime
Salt to taste

METHOD

For lemon dal it is the same kancha moong dal that is used. Once cooked with a little salt and water, it is sieved through a cheesecloth so that it comes out as a thick, creamy soup, without the fibres. Then a large porcelain or earthenware (never metal) serving bowl is taken and the bottom and sides lined with thin slices of lemon or lime. Bengalis prefer to use the fragrant *kagaji* or *gondhi* lemon, if they are available. Once the slices are in place, the sieved dal is put back on the stove, brought to the boil and kept there for two to three minutes, then poured into the lemon-lined basin and kept covered for about five minutes to absorb the taste and flavour of the lemon. This needs to be served with plain rice, preferably an *atap* (non-parboiled) rice like Basmati. The problem with this dal is that it can neither be reheated, nor kept overnight, for it tends to turn bitter. To serve it for guests, cook and sieve it earlier, then boil and pour it over the lemons just before serving.

Despite all considerations of health and cool foods in summer, the Bengali does, on special occasions, indulge his taste for rich and spicy concoctions. This is true of dal too. One of the great Bengali classics, *muror dal*, cooked with a fish head and strong spices, was often served at weddings and feasts even at the height of summer. In our family, my mother's third sister, whom I called Aunt from Shyambajar (in north Calcutta), was absolutely crazy about it and was quite prepared to give up all fish, meat, vegetable or dessert items for the pleasure of eating her fill of muror dal!

Bengal shares her great spring festival, Doljatra, held on the full moon of Falgun, the first month of spring, with all of central and northern India. In Hindi this event is called Holi, the festival of colours, commemorating the occasion on which the young Krishna, during his stay in Brindaban among the community of milkmen and milkmaids, played the tantalizing game of colours. The stories always centre around the passionate love affair between Krishna and his beloved, the beautiful Radha, with the 1600 attendant milkmaids providing added inspiration, strewing powdered colours over each other and generally having a rollicking good time. Food plays no part in this sensuous game of touch and go, of feigned escape, intent chase and breathless surrender. Though it is a very innocent game among children, young adults find many dimensions of romantic exploration as they pursue each other, mostly with coloured powders and sometimes with sprayers filled with coloured water. The normal social restrictions are lifted for a day and prim, post-Victorian Bengal suddenly goes back to an earthier past. In the evening the light of the full moon and a balmy spring breeze intensify the romantic mood and set the scene for the many weddings to come.

Though the days are filled with a dry heat, the aridity of summer is still far away. The fields look dry, but not parched and the new green leaves on the trees still retain some of their clean glow. In the gardens the smell of gardenias during the day is matched by the less powerful though no less heady fragrance of the first kamini flowers and of the bell-shaped golden champak. The mango blossoms are replaced by tiny budding mangoes and the long leaves of the litchi trees unsuccessfully hide the clusters of newborn litchis. One of the most beautiful trees is the tamarind, whose tiny feathery leaves in fan-like formations wave enticingly in the breeze. A Bengali proverb uses the smallness of an individual tamarind leaf as a metaphor for adjustability: if good men are together, even nine of them will manage to find space to sit on a single tamarind leaf. Among the strangest sights of this short spring is the huge *shojne* or *shajina* tree. These bear elongated pods in spring, but unlike the tamarind, the shojne pods are about 30 cm (1 ft) long and look like ribbed stems. The colonial British called them drumsticks and the appearance is the obvious reason behind its misnomer in Bengali, *shojne danta*, the word danta meaning a succulent stalk. Bunches of this firm, fleshy, chewy and short-lived vegetable are sold at high prices in the markets in springtime. They are cut into small pieces and combined with potatoes and brinjals to make a chachchari spiced with ground mustard. They are also added to machher jhol, fish stew, which is the centrepiece of the Bengali lunch all through the summer.

The jhol can be cooked in a hundred different ways, but its frequent appearance in the menu has made it the most well-known Bengali dish. It is a thin stew, usually of fish, though it can also be purely vegetarian. But the fish in a jhol is always combined with vegetables. Though several different ground spices are used in cooking jhol, the most important quality about a good one is its lightness. Too heavy a hand with the spices will ruin it. At the same time, bad cooks can also produce watery, tasteless, pallid jhols. Achieving the right balance only comes with much practice. But good or bad, the jhol is the mainstay of the Bengali lunch almost throughout the year. It is more of a Hindu institution, but there are many differences between the East and the West Bengali treatment of it. In our house, the fish, usually a carp, is always fried first before being put into the jhol. To the Bangals of East Bengal that is as good as throwing the fish into the dustbin. The individual cook who tries this recipe can suit his or her personal preference about frying fish.

MACHHER JHOL

FOR FOUR PEOPLE

INGREDIENTS

500 gm (1 lb) of fish
4 medium potatoes
1 medium brinjal
10-12 kalai dal boris
1 teaspoon of turmeric powder
2 teaspoons of ground ginger
1 teaspoon each of ground chilli, cumin and coriander
1 teaspoon of panch phoron
5-6 green chillies
2 tablespoons of chopped coriander leaves
3 tablespoons of heated oil
900 ml (1½ pints) of water
Salt to taste

METHOD

In Bengal the favourites are the rui, the katla, or the mirgel, though any big fish can be made into a jhol. Once the head and the tail together with the last 10-12 cm (4-5 in) of the body are removed and set aside, the cook decides which portion of the body will be used for the jhol. The body of the fish is cut lengthwise, the front or stomach portion being called the peti and the back being called the daga. The peti is preferred for almost any dish since it is oilier and tastier. But the bony daga is ideal for the medium of the jhol. Whatever the portion chosen, it is then cut horizontally into pieces 2-2.5 cm (¾-1 in) in thickness. Since most families are unable to buy a whole fish, it is common in Bengali markets for the fishmonger to portion his fish and cut it to the specifications of the client. The fish is rinsed carefully to get rid of all traces of blood and slime, dusted with salt and turmeric and slowly fried in hot oil, two or three pieces at a time. The oil should be heated well before the fish is put in. The salt and turmeric are used, not only to reduce the fishy odour, but also because they prevent the fish from crumbling or disintegrating (this makes them almost inevitable ingredients for frying fish, prawn or crabs). Since the skin is left on the fish and tends to sputter in the oil, it is wise to keep your pan covered. Once the fish pieces have been lightly browned, they are lifted out and set aside to drain off all excess oil. If the frying oil has turned too dark, it has to be discarded.

Since two of the several vegetables we commonly use in jhols—patols and green bananas—may not be available everywhere, I'll stick to the certainties of potatoes and brinjals.

Take the potatoes, peel and cut them into long, flat, 1.25 cm (½ in) thick slices. The brinjal should also be cut into matching slices. If boris made of dried dal paste are available, 10-12 kalai dal boris, white in colour like the dal they are made with, are a must for this jhol. The boris have to be fried first in 3 tablespoons of heated oil. When they turn brown, lift them out by drawing them up along the sides of the karai so that all the oil drains back. The potato slices should also be lightly browned in the same oil and set aside. Then fry the panch phoron, add the ground spices, and stir for a couple of minutes. Add the brinjals and potatoes and pour the water into the karai. When it comes to the boil, add the pieces of fried fish, the boris, the green chillies and a little salt. The salt has to be added carefully because there is already salt in the fried fish. As the jhol keeps cooking, you can taste and adjust the salt. The whole thing should be kept on the stove until the fish and potatoes are tender—about five to six minutes. Finally, the coriander leaves should be stirred in and the jhol removed from the heat. The gravy should be thin and fragrant, but as I said, how thin or how spicy it is depends a lot on personal preference.

A typical Bengali lunch menu on the long hot days of the summer could have a bitter shukto or neem begun to start with, then a vegetable dish containing at least one of the specially cooling vegetables, followed by the machher jhol and perhaps a chutney or sour ambal to finish with. The dal will figure either after the shukto or before the chutney, depending again on individual eating habits.

The three cooling vegetables, patol, jhinge and lau, all belong to the gourd family and are indigenous to Bengal, having a pre-Aryan history. Its versatility is most apparent in its combination with evaporated milk, ghee and sugar to make a dessert, a specialty of East Bengal. But my own favourites are *lau-chingri*, with shrimp, and *lau-ghanto*, with coconut, green peas (or brown chickpeas) and crushed boris. The former is a Bengali classic. In one of many stories about Gopal Bhar, court jester to Maharaja Krishnachandra of Nabadwip, he slips some shrimp into his tight-fisted widowed aunt's dish of lau and, threatening to tell the neighbours that she has been breaking the widows' code of vegetarianism, manages to extract some money from her.

LAU-CHINGRI

FOR FOUR PEOPLE

INGREDIENTS

750 gm (1½ lb) of young, tender lau
2 2.5cm (1 in) pieces of cinnamon
3 cloves
4 cardamoms
2 teaspoons of freshly ground cumin
2 teaspoons of freshly ground coriander
1 teaspoon of chilli powder
1 teaspoon of turmeric powder
3-4 green chillies
2-3 teaspoons of ghee
2½ tablespoons of oil
2 bay leaves
A pinch of flour
Salt and sugar to taste

METHOD

In lau-chingri the thick green peel of the gourd is not used, but is preserved to be chopped and fried later as a side dish. Chop the lau into fine narrow pieces about 2.5 cm (1 in) long, throwing out all the seeds. Steam it lightly with a touch of salt and 2 tablespoons of water. If you keep it covered over a low flame, the vegetable will release its own moisture and become very soft. (If it is a very young lau, then it does not even need to be steamed.) Set aside the steamed lau after draining off any excess moisture. The chingri, peeled and deveined, is dusted with salt and turmeric and fried lightly in oil. Grind the pieces of cinnamon, the cloves and cardamoms for garom mashla.

The lau, being watery, requires very little oil. So I heat the oil in a large karai, throw in the bay leaves and add the steamed lau. After stirring this around for a couple of minutes, I add the shrimp and all the ground spices except the garom mashla. The whole thing is then stirred and stirred until all the spices are blended and release their fragrance. Sometimes I sprinkle a little water over the lau as I go along, if I notice any tendency for it to stick to the pot. Then I add salt, sugar and green chillies and keep it covered over low heat for three to four minutes. The sugar should be perceptible, so it is best to start with 3 teaspoons and then to add more if needed. Finally, I uncover the karai, stir in the ghee mixed with a pinch of flour and the garom mashla, and remove the lau from the stove.

For those who are vegetarians and are forbidden to eat shrimps, the lau-ghanto is a delightful alternative. Not that non-vegetarians abstain from eating it—it is a perennial favourite in our house during the heat of the summer, and it has the advantage of being easier to cook.

LAU-GHANTO

FOR FOUR PEOPLE

INGREDIENTS

750 gm (1½ lb) of lau
4 tablespoons of ground coconut
120 gm (4 oz) of green peas

8-10 boris made of matar dal
2 teaspoons of ground cumin
2 bay leaves
2-3 dry red chillies
2½ tablespoons of oil
2 teaspoons of flour
2 teaspoons of ghee
Salt and sugar to taste

METHOD

For lau-ghanto, again, you need the lau (or any gourd substitute), peeled, chopped fine and steamed. All excess water should be pressed out. Fry the boris in hot oil. They should be set aside and a phoron of red chillies, bay leaves and whole cumin should be added to the same oil. When they darken and the cumin seeds stop sputtering, add the steamed lau, the peas, the ground coconut and ground cumin. All this is stirred thoroughly for four to five minutes. Then salt and sugar to taste are added and the boris crumbled and mixed into the vegetables. Once the lau is quite dry and the peas are tender, add the flour and ghee, mix them well into the vegetables, taste for salt and sugar and remove from the stove. Of course, orthodox Bengali cooks will raise their eyebrows at peas and boris figuring together, but I quite like breaking conventions if it means variation and improvement in taste.

The second great summer vegetable, patol, tends to drive most Bengalis into ecstasy. A small oval gourd, patol has a creamy firm flesh inside and is much firmer and less watery than the lau. The riper the patol, the harder its seeds, something the true aficionado like my father loves. Excellent fried unpeeled as an accompaniment to rice and dal or peeled and cut into pieces in jhols and chachcharis or even rich dalnas, or left whole with the seeds and part of the flesh taken out through a hole at one end and a stuffing of fish or meat put inside to make a dolma, the patol is essential summer eating. And in this the Bengali has the unequivocal support of Ayurvedic theory, which finds the patol to be light, digestive, a curative for worms, fevers, coughs, wind and bile, as well as pleasing to the mind.

DOI-PATOL

FOR FOUR PEOPLE

INGREDIENTS

500 gm (1 lb) of tender young patol

120 gm (4 oz) of yoghurt

3 teaspoons of ground ginger

½ teaspoon each of chilli and turmeric powders

2 bay leaves

1 teaspoon of whole cumin seeds

A tiny pinch of asafoetida

4 tablespoons of oil

1 tablespoon of ghee

For garom mashla, grind 4 cardamoms and 4 pieces of cinnamon,
      2.5 cm (1 in) long. No cloves.

Salt and sugar to taste

METHOD

These patols, being young, need to be peeled lightly, but they can be left whole with 1.25 cm (½ in) slits being made at both ends. Rinse them in running water and drain. Heat 2½ teaspoons of oil in a karai and lightly brown the patols. Remove and set aside. The oil will have turned black, so it will have to be discarded. Heat another 1½ tablespoons of oil in the karai, add 1 tablespoon of ghee to it and throw in a phoron of bay leaves, whole cumin seeds and asafoetida.

After a minute or so, add the ground ginger and the chilli and turmeric powders and a little salt. Fry the spices well, whip the yoghurt and pour it in. Add the patols, some sugar and sprinkle a little water over the whole thing. Cook uncovered for five to six minutes and taste. You can add more salt and sugar if needed. Finally, combine the ghee and garom mashla, add to the patols, stir once or twice and remove from the stove. Keep covered until serving time.

As spring moves on and the month of Falgun transits into Chaitra (in mid-March), the midday temperatures become quite taxing. In the villages the small ponds and canals start drying up, but the water shortage is not acute yet and village children enjoy catching all kinds of small fish from these dried-up water sources. On one such hot, dry, cloudless afternoon in late Chaitra, my grandmother told me the fable about the *chatak* bird, a strange swallow-like creature doomed only to drink rainwater. As the hot, dry weeks progress towards the height of summer, these poor creatures desperately circle the sky looking for the slightest trace of cloud that will bring them life-saving water; in years of excessive heat, their sufferings are unbearable. Popular belief goes that if you refuse to give water to a thirsty person, you will become a chatak bird in your next incarnation. Mythical though the story was, it made a great impression on my mind as I pictured the bird's waterless vigil of the skies.

In rural Bengal and even in certain urban areas, the last day of Chaitra sees the festival of Charak. The religious part of it is mostly observed by wandering sadhus, holy men who belong to the Shaiva (devotees of the god Shiva) sect. Having spent part of the month observing fasts and special rituals, they choose this day for masochistic performances in the hopes of pleasing Shiva the destroyer, the third of the Hindu trinity. In the old days they would pierce their cheeks and tongues with large iron hooks, claiming to feel no pain. Iron rods piercing the skin of their backs would be attached to a tall wooden contraption that would whirl them round and round until they fell to the ground unconscious and bleeding. Many of them died of tetanus and other infections. Thankfully, the government banned the use of iron hooks and rods in 1863, but lesser acts of self-torture are still performed in front of gawking audiences at the Charak fairs.

With the month of Baisakh the dry heat of summer is at its highest, to be followed by the oppressive humidity which will be relieved by the monsoon. A folk rhyme listing all the rituals that Bengali Hindus should perform through the months of the year describes the watering of tulsi (sacred to Krishna) plants as the appropriate one for Baisakh. In spite of this parching heat, Baisakh is a great time for Hindu weddings. The Hindu almanacs, based on ancient scriptural calculations, have designated several months of the year as *malomash*, inauspicious for weddings. So all weddings are scheduled during the other permissible months on the specific auspicious days marked in the almanac. The final month of the year, Chaitra, is a malomash and with the beginning of the new year, the mood is all set for the festivity of weddings. For some reason, the first month of the year has extra auspicious connotations.

When my mother and father got married in the early forties, wedding feasts still followed tradition. Banana leaves were spread in front of each guest; once the meal was eaten, the leaves would be thrown away and a new set of leaves placed before the next batch of guests, thus saving on washing up and forestalling the dangers of inadequate cleaning. First there would be luchis, thin golden discs of rolled out dough fried in ghee, to be eaten with fried greens and some other fried vegetable like patol or brinjal. Next would come the famous Bengali chhanchra, mixed vegetables cooked with the entrails and oil of fish, followed by a rich dal. Once all of this had been mopped up with innumerable luchis, a lovely rui fish made into a rich kalia redolent of garom mashla, would be served with polao.

This polao was no approximation or base imitation as is so common today. Only the best quality of rice, Basmati or some other fragrant variety, would be used. The huge quantities of ghee required to make polao for 300 or 400 people would also be absolutely pure, unadulterated with vegetable shortening. The water in which the rice would be cooked was called the *akhni* water, that is water in which whole garom mashla as well as other expensive spices like mace, nutmeg, saffron, *sajira* (a kind of cumin) and a handful of yellow split peas had been boiled for a long time—the usual duration was the time needed to reduce the original water to one-third of its volume. This incredibly fragrant water—once the spice bundle, like a bouquet garni, was discarded—would then be added to the rice fried in ghee, and the polao that was produced was a delight all by itself. Sadly, the fabulous prices of good ghee, fine rice and the ingredients for akhni water have made that polao a dream from the past. The 'fried rice' or 'vegetable polao' served at most weddings today is made with ordinary rice and cooked in peanut oil with a few chopped vegetables thrown in.

In very wealthy houses in those days, the rui kalia was often accompanied by another fish preparation, either of king prawn or of hilsa. But meat was usually not part of a Hindu wedding feast. For the vegetarians there would be an extra item of curried chhana or *dhonkas* made of ground dal. After the fish came a chutney (tomatoes, green mangoes, green papayas, dried plums, according to season and taste) served with crisp papor (papadam in other parts of India). Last, but not least, came the sweet yoghurt, mishti doi, with a variety of sweets and, as a final chaser, the sweet-spiced paan.

The average wedding menu today, especially in a city like

Calcutta, hardly bears any resemblance to this menu of the forties. As meat became more and more acceptable even in the most orthodox houses, it became the fashion to serve a meat kalia after the fish and, by the sixties, when I was old enough to go to weddings or observe the food at weddings in my own family, all the initial items of fried greens, chhanchra and dal were being dropped because they were troublesome. After the sixties, even the kalia made with rui fish disappeared: in its place the non-vegetarian guests were given fillets of bhetki, coated with egg and breadcrumbs and deep-fried in oil, or a fish 'chop' followed by a meat kalia.

Today's weddings have slipped even further. They often take place at houses hired for the occasion, the food is supplied by catering companies who bring the pre-cooked food, heat whatever needs heating and serve the guests on china plates. No longer for us the pleasure of touching the shining green of banana leaves, nor the excitement of the preparations. Each wedding in our house during my childhood carries memories of hectic activities in one corner of the huge roof, where the professional cooks would set up their wood and coal stoves and be busy cooking all day.

Even a couple of days before the wedding the house was full of relatives working away. Then would come the arrival of Anath uncle, the wholesale fishmonger whom my uncle had befriended, sitting in the courtyard in front of a huge ansh-bonti, dismembering one huge rui after another, the blood and entrails of the fish spilling all around him. And apart from the mishti doi, ordered from one of the famous Calcutta sweet shops, the other sweets were all made at home by those hired cooks. They never minded it when I slipped upstairs and stood watching their activities, and inevitably grinned when I reached out a greedy little paw for a surreptitious handful. I will never forget the fresh taste and fragrance of those sweets, still hot from the huge karai. Nothing tasted half as good when bought from the shops. Munching the sweets, I would wander over to the other cooks who were boiling the akhni water for the polao and take a few heady breaths before trotting demurely downstairs, my mouth and hands wiped clean of all sticky traces.

The wedding feast in Bangladesh is quite another matter. The Muslim elite's fondness for meat has set the standards for the middle class too, and the wedding menu probably has remained constant for the last half-century. The very first wedding I attended in Dhaka was that of a friend of my husband's. At the wedding feast the menu was simple, and I was to see it repeated, with minor variations, at all subsequent weddings during my six years in Dhaka. Instead of plain polao, there was a biryani, rice cooked with meat. There were round brown shami kababs and there was a jhal gosht made with beef. A yoghurt and cucumber *raita* and a dessert of *firni* completed the meal. All of these items are to be seen all over northern India and in Indian restaurants abroad.

The sameness of the Bangladeshi wedding menu tends to pall—'Yet another wedding invitation!' is a genuine expression of gustatory boredom—but, in the hands of the gifted cook, each of these items takes on the attributes of a classic. Of the many possible combinations of rice and meat, probably the tastiest is the kachchi biryani made with rice and khashi meat. Bangladeshi Muslims seem to have an exclusive preference for khashi or castrated goat meat over ordinary goat meat. Over the years the Hindus too have learnt to eat the rich, fatty khashi meat (in Calcutta mostly Muslim butchers sell it), but they also enjoy the special taste of the tender flesh of the kid goat. In Bangladesh this is almost unknown. Even chicken is made into capons by the Muslims, especially in Dhaka, Noakhali and Chittagong.

Unlike other rice preparations made with meat and rice, in

kachchi biryani the meat is uncooked when added to the rice. As a result the dish requires slow cooking over low heat and makes for very tender textured meat. Some people find it too rich to stomach. Others, like my friend Farhad Ghuznavi, whose feudal background is well reflected in his tastes, feel it is the only kind of biryani worth having. Just before leaving Dhaka for good, I was fortunate enough to be shown one way of making the kachchi biryani by Nilufar, a woman who worked with me. It is never a success if you try to make it in small quantities, nor is it too much effort to make a lot of it, since you can make a complete meal out of it with a salad on the side. The predominant flavour is that of the rich fatty meat transmuted into an unoppressive spiciness by the technique of sealed cooking. Though the process is painstaking, the results are well worth it.

KACHCHI BIRYANI

FOR EIGHT PEOPLE

INGREDIENTS

1 kg (2 lb) of fine Basmati rice

2 kg (4 lb) of khashi or lamb

2 large onions, finely sliced

A little ghee to fry the onions

2 tablespoons of ground ginger

1 tablespoon of garlic

6 cardamoms, 6 cloves and 2 pieces of cinnamon, 2.5 cm (1 in) long

1 whole nutmeg

1 tablespoon of cumin powder

A large pinch of mace

3 tablespoons of roasted red chilli powder

300 gm (10 oz) of yoghurt

4 tablespoons of keora water

500 gm (1 lb) of medium potatoes, peeled and quartered

360 ml (12 fl oz) of ghee
3 l (6 pints) of water
4 tablespoons of salt

METHOD

Bony pieces like lamb chops will be better than solid meat like the leg. When I went into the kitchen, Nilufar had already cut the meat into medium-sized pieces, washed it and left it mixed with 2 tablespoons of salt to generate moisture and soften the meat. After half an hour the meat was rinsed and left in a colander to drain. Meanwhile she organized her spices. Two large onions were sliced fine and lightly browned in a little ghee, ginger was ground to make 2 tablespoons and garlic for 1 tablespoon; cardamoms, cloves and cinnamon were ground to a powder, as was 1 whole nutmeg. By now the fried onions had cooled and she ground them coarsely on the stone—you can crush them in a mortar, too. She then transferred the meat to the large cooking pot and mixed it thoroughly with all these fresh ground spices, adding cumin powder, mace and roasted red chilli powder. After this yoghurt and keora water were added to the meat.

Leaving the meat to marinate a little, she took the potatoes, peeled and quartered them and fried them in a little oil. As the potatoes turned golden, she sprinkled some yellow food colouring over them (turmeric would produce an incompatible taste and odour). Originally the recipe calls for saffron, but that is so prohibitive in Bangladesh that most people use food colouring. The fried potatoes were placed over the meat and 120 ml (4 fl oz) of ghee poured over it. Once again, she left the meat to marinate and proceeded to deal with the rice, rinsing it under the tap and then draining it in a colander. She also set the water and salt to boil in a large pot. As soon as the water boiled, the rice was added to it. When it came to a second boil, she carefully poured out most of the water into another pan and then left the rice to drain. From the water she took 250 ml (8 fl oz), mixed it with 120 ml (4 fl oz) of ghee and added it to the meat, which was left covered to marinate for half an hour. Meanwhile, she set some water to boil in a medium-sized pan.

Finally it was time to cook. She spread the drained half-cooked rice evenly over the meat and potatoes and sprinkled over it some more yellow food colouring. Then she added the last 120 ml (4 fl oz) of ghee and poured some more of the salted hot rice water into the pan so that it was level—not more—with the rice. Covering the pot with a well-fitting lid, she sealed it with a thick flour and water paste, put the saucepan of boiling water on top and finally placed the sealed pot over a high flame. After about twenty minutes she reduced the heat to very low and left it undisturbed for nearly one and a half hours. Later I found you can also cook this kachchi biryani by placing it for three hours in an oven heated to 180°C (350°F, Gas mark 4). The important thing is to seal the lid to the pot and to have the heat come from above and below. By the time it was done, the entire kitchen was full of the wonderful biryani smell. Before serving, Nilufar stirred the contents of the pot so that the rice, potatoes and meat were well mixed. She regretted that that day she was all out of almonds and pistachios; otherwise she would have added them to the meat before cooking.

The other favourite served at weddings as well as private dinners is the uniquely Bengali Muslim dish, the rezala. This is made with khashi meat and, though not overly spicy, tends to linger on the palate. The milk and the saffron in the dish produce a beautifully tinted gravy, while the sharp fragrance of the green chillies combines with other elements to produce a most unforgettable bouquet. No doubt there are minor variations that good cooks bring to their rezala, but the one I was taught by my friend's mother seems fairly standard.

KHASHIR REZALA

FOR EIGHT PEOPLE

INGREDIENTS

2 kg (4 lb) of meat
250 gm (8 oz) of grated onion
2 tablespoons of ground ginger
3 teaspoons of ground garlic
5-6 whole cardamoms
5-6 pieces of cinnamon 2.5 cm (1 in) long
250 gm (8 oz) of yoghurt
1 tablespoon of sugar
3 teaspoons of salt
250 ml (8 fl oz) of ghee
250 ml (8 fl oz) of warm whole milk
A tiny pinch of saffron
20 whole green chillies

METHOD

For the eight people she had invited that evening, she had bought 2 kg (4 lb) of meat, cubed and washed, to make the Khashir rezala. This she combined in a large pot with onion, ginger, garlic, cardamom, cinnamon, yoghurt, sugar, salt and ghee. Once all of this was thoroughly mixed, she covered the pot and let it cook on a low flame for about half an hour. Then she uncovered and stirred the meat well and kept it covered again until all the moisture had evaporated and the ghee was visible. Then she took warm whole milk, added saffron to it and poured it over the meat. Next, green chillies were added, the heat reduced to a minimum and the meat left tightly covered for about half an hour before it was ready to serve. When my sister-in-law makes this rezala she always selects red, ripened chillies (fresh, not dried) for the dish. They stand out in a most pleasing contrast against the pale yellow of the gravy.

In the advancing heat of Baisakh, such rich preparations become hard to stomach, even for those who can afford them, and the diet of the have-nots, especially in rural Bengal, seems more attractive. Many of them are too poor to eat fish every day and one of the summer staples is *panta bhat*, or fermented rice. Leftover rice, when there is an adequate supply of it, will be covered with water and kept overnight in the kitchen where the heat will ferment it by morning. For the peasant who has a hard day's work ahead of him, it is a substantial breakfast seasoned with hot fried chillies, raw onions or even bits of leftover vegetables. Though my childhood was strictly urban, I was no stranger to panta bhat, for my mother and grandmother both liked having it, with hot chillies and sour pickles, on hot summer afternoons. Somehow I could never feel enthusiastic about the slightly sour taste of the fermented rice, and avoided it even when offered.

It was Bangladesh which taught me how delightful panta bhat could taste when one was ravenously hungry. I was working on a drinking-water survey and had to make several trips to nearby villages. It was around the middle of Baisakh that three of us went to a village near Munshiganj, a small town in the district of Dhaka. The Buriganga river, attenuated in the heat, and the leaden stillness of the sky made us long for a summer storm. But there were no clouds to promise relief as we trudged along the uneven, dusty village paths. In places the land had cracked open, and obviously irrigation could not be done extensively in that village. By the time we had finished our work, all of us were famished and parched. The handpump tubewells in the village gave us cool water, but there was no food in sight. Even the teashops were closed. The village seemed so godforsaken, and the people so poor and emaciated, that we did not have the heart to ask for any food. But their own permanent deprivations had made them sensitive to others' needs. After much whispering, an old man stepped forward and asked us to come to his cottage for something to eat. He would not take no for an answer and so, under his badly thatched roof, we sat cross-legged on a torn mat and ate panta bhat with some very hot vegetable dish into which a few shrimps had been added. The kindness and sincere hospitality of that man whom I never saw again were seasonings that made our meal taste better than any wedding feast of biryani. Today the taste still comes back to me like a cool shade on a very hot day.

The heat of Baisakh is turned to productive uses by the women of Bengal. The third day after the new moon of Baisakh, *Akkhaytritya*, is the appointed day for both Hindus and Muslims to make kasundi, our version of table mustard. The Bengali mustard seed is dark and pungent and is a favourite ingredient, ground with green chillies, in making dishes with certain fishes and vegetables. Kasundi is a kind of mustard pickle, where the ground mustard is combined with green mangoes or tamarind or lemon (to provide a sour taste) as well as with oil and other spices. Most Bengali pickles are made by drying in the sun, instead of being cooked or preserved in vinegar. Baisakh, therefore, is an ideal time to start. Women are particularly enthusiastic about this domestic activity. The love of sourness seems almost genetically coded into young Bengali girls. Just as children in the West hanker for candy, Bengali girls will do anything to pick all kinds of sour fruit or steal sour pickles from their mother's larder.

Making a good kasundi was considered even more difficult than making good pickles and women tended to guard their recipes jealously. It is a lost art now in the cities where commercially bottled kasundi is widely sold, but village women still make it, purifying themselves first, as for all other things that have to be preserved through the year. Some families resolutely refuse to make kasundi because they believe that if they do, a member of their family is sure to die. In my own family, another very restrictive superstition still holds sway. All pickles, kasundi and boris are inauspicious for travel. Despite the innumerable trips I have made out of Calcutta, I have never succeeded in carrying any of these with me.

While the pickles get preserved in the sun, human beings find even the slightest effort exhausting. Rain is badly needed by way of relief and if Baisakh does not have its rainstorms, land and life are both endangered. As Sharatchandra Chattopadhyay writes in 'Mahesh':

> It was almost the end of Baisakh, but not even the shadow of a cloud was visible. Fire seemed to rain down from the sky. The huge field stretching all the way to the horizon had been baked and burnt under the sun until it had cracked all over, and from these countless crevices the earth's blood seemed to dissipate endlessly into smoke. Staring too long at its reptilian upward motion made your head swim—almost like some powerful intoxicant.

Mahesh, the protagonist of this story, is a bullock owned by a poor Muslim peasant, Ghafur. During a terrible drought Ghafur finds himself unable not only to pay his dues to the landlord but also to provide for himself, his daughter and even his beloved Mahesh. Driven by hunger, Mahesh encroaches on the landlord's sacrosanct pastureland, for which he is duly punished by the landlord's henchmen. Finally the dumb beast, deprived even of water to slake his thirst, dies before his helpless master's eyes. Ghafur, stripped of whatever little he owned, like so many landless peasants before and after him, leaves his ancestral village forever with his daughter, his only prayer to Allah being that those who deprived Mahesh of god-given grass and water should receive their proper punishment.

But there are other years when Baisakh is kind and, though the pickle-makers may curse, the earth celebrates the appearance of short violent rainstorms, *kalbaisakhis*, that dramatically bring the temperatures down and leave the dehydrated earth replenished, the trees washed, the air free of dust. Destructive though they can be, flattening fruit and standing crops, the first sight of the onrush of dark clouds, like an irresistible army in the northwestern sky, only arouses feelings of joy in the beholder.

One afternoon in Dhaka when I was coming back to my house in Dhanmondi from a friend's in Tejgaon, I was caught in a kalbaisakhi. It had been an oppressive afternoon and as I got into the rickshaw I could see a familiar darkening of one corner of the horizon. Foolishly, I thought the wheels of the rickshaw could beat the demons of the sky. But a drenching in the rain was not going to be the end of the story, for soon a storm of hailstones started falling. The driver abandoned me on the deserted road, ran across the pavement and stood under a tree while I sat trapped in the rickshaw, resigned but not afraid, until the dark grey road, brick-and-cement pavement and bits of grass were magically transformed into one white expanse of cobbled ice.

The last and most terrible month of summer, Jaishtha, mid-May to mid-June, is a boon for fruit lovers. Ripening mangoes and jackfruits, white translucent kernels of the unripe palm, sweet and tangy litchis, vivid and juicy watermelon, bland *jamrul* and even astringent *kalojam* abound in the markets. The different varieties of mangoes—West Bengal's himsagar, Benares langra, chousa and dusseri from Uttar Pradesh—are served as snacks and desserts, for breakfast and for *jalkhabar*, our version of afternoon tea. And sometimes we have the rich delight of mango pulp mixed into kheer, thick, rich evaporated milk.

The heat also prompts frequent servings of yoghurt or milk mixed with *chira* (flattened rice soaked in water) and mangoes or bananas, called *phalahar*. This was most in evidence in our house every Tuesday in Jaishtha, when women other than widows had to observe the ritual of Jaimangalbar. More a folk custom than a strictly religious occasion, the purpose was to appease the goddess Mangalchandi and gain her protection for the family. All fish, meat, onions and garlic were forbidden. At lunch the phalahar would be served and in the evening you would have luchis with vegetables. Another observance in Jaishtha, once common among rural Hindu women in Bengal, was the Sabitribrata, on the day before the Jaishtha new moon. The women would fast all day without touching a drop of water in that dreadful heat. In the evening, after breaking fast, they would have to feed a Brahmin—all this in the hope of avoiding the pain of widowhood.

Obviously there is nothing like faith to take your mind off hunger and thirst. In Bangladesh the month of Ramzan in the Islamic calendar happened to fall in Jaishtha one year when I was there. I was amazed at the will and cheerful endurance of those who fasted, especially while going through a whole day's work at the office. In the evening, after saying the *maghreb* (evening) prayers, they would enjoy their light meal of *iftaar*, which always began with a cool drink—lemonade, green coconut water, or even the juice and pulp of watermelon. Though I did not fast, I always enjoyed watching the iftaar being brought in: soaked chira with ground coconut and sugar, brown local chickpeas fried with one or two red chillies, mango slices and flat discs of fried ground lentils seasoned with green chilli and onion. By contrast, when Ramzan was over and the great festival of ld-ul-fitr arrived, I was overwhelmed and almost oppressed by the weight of the rich food.

After occasional bouts of heavy meals like these in Dhaka during the summer, I used to long for my mother's light touch and some of the bland, cool summer items from my childhood. My first year in Dhaka was spent searching fruitlessly for posto, those tiny white poppy seeds which are sold after heating to neutralize the possibility of germination. Apart from being considered easily digestible in the summer heat, posto also has a uniquely delicate taste which caresses the palate without arousing it. But those were bad times in Bangladesh, the early seventies, and many ordinary things were hard to get. Today posto is available around the world, so some of the easiest and most delicious recipes can be tried anywhere too.

POSTO CHUTNEY

FOR THREE PEOPLE

INGREDIENTS

100 gm of posto
50 gm of coconut
Green chillies
A few cloves of garlic
Slices of green mango to taste
Salt and sugar to taste

METHOD

The simplest is a posto chutney made by grinding the posto together with some coconut, green chillies, garlic and green mango. The paste is seasoned with salt and sugar to taste. In the absence of green mangoes, lemon juice can be used.

POSTO BATA

FOR THREE PEOPLE

INGREDIENTS

50 gm (1.6 oz) of posto
1 tablespoon of fresh mustard oil
Chopped green chillies
Salt to taste

METHOD

Posto bata also requires no cooking and is eaten in small quantities as a starter with rice, almost like a relish. For the three of us my mother usually took posto, soaked it in water for half an hour and ground it fine on the stone. The texture should be tight, not watery. Then she would mix it with some fresh mustard oil, salt and chopped green chillies. All these ingredients can vary in quantity according to taste and in the absence of a grinding stone a mixer or food processor can be used.

POSTO BATAR CHACHCHARI

FOR THREE PEOPLE

INGREDIENTS

100 gm (3½ oz) of ground posto
1 tablespoon of oil
1 tablespoon + 1 teaspoon of ghee
1 medium onion, finely chopped
1 teaspoon of ground cumin
½ teaspoon of chilli powder
1 teaspoon of ghee
2 cardamoms
2 pieces of cinnamon
Salt and a little sugar

METHOD

As a variant on posto bata, known as posto batar chachchari, she would heat oil and 1 tablespoon of ghee in her karai, throw in the finely chopped onion, fry it brown, add the posto with ground cumin, chilli powder, salt and a little sugar. All these would be stirred with a little water being sprinkled over the mixture from time to time to avoid burning. When the posto was nicely browned, she would add 1 teaspoon of ghee mixed with some ground garom mashla (cardamoms and cinnamon).

ALU POSTO

FOR THREE PEOPLE

INGREDIENTS

100 gm (3 oz) of finely ground posto
250 gm (½ lb) of potatoes
2½ tablespoons of oil
1 large onion, finely chopped
4-5 green chillies
250 ml (8 fl oz) of water
Salt to taste

METHOD

For alu posto take potatoes and peel, cube and fry them in oil till light brown. Set aside and fry the finely chopped onion in the same oil. When this turns brown, add the potatoes, some salt, green chillies and water. Keep covered over a medium heat until the potatoes are tender. Add the posto and stir over high heat until all water has evaporated.

You can also make a more substantial dish with posto. By the time I had located the seeds in the Dhaka market, I had already tasted two Bangladeshi preparations using posto. As is only to be expected from the Muslims, they were khashi and chicken, not vegetables, and they were delicious. The chicken was made by the wife of the friend at whose wedding I had been made to participate with the family. She was a quiet, shy girl who appeared to be totally dominated by her headstrong husband until I saw her walk out on him with her month-old baby because she felt her parents had been insulted. They were reconciled later, and no doubt their daily life was sweetened by her wonderful talents as a cook.

CHICKEN WITH POSTO

FOR EIGHT PEOPLE

INGREDIENTS

3 kg (6 lb) of chicken
250 gm (8 oz) of yoghurt
250 gm (8 oz) of grated onion
1 tablespoon of ground ginger
1 teaspoon each of ground garlic and coriander
2 teaspoons of ground cumin
1 tablespoon of chilli powder
2 tablespoons of ground posto
1 teaspoon of ground fennel
½ teaspoon of ground mace
60 gm (2 oz) of almonds, blanched and slivered
60 gm (2 oz) of raisins
2 tablespoons of salt
120 ml (4 fl oz) of peanut oil
120 ml (4 fl oz) of ghee
Salt to taste

METHOD

For chicken with posto for eight people she had taken two plump medium-sized chickens. Skinned, portioned into

10-12 pieces each and washed, the birds were combined in
a large pot with yoghurt, onion, ginger, garlic and coriander,
cumin, chilli powder, posto, fennel, mace, almonds, raisins,
salt and peanut oil and ghee. The whole thing, well mixed,
was cooked tightly covered, on a very low heat for an hour.
Then she checked to see if the flesh was tender. You can add
extra water if you find the chicken tough and stringy. Once
it is done, the meat is stirred over high heat until it is nicely
coated in the oil/ghee and spices, with no moisture left.
Before serving you can sprinkle some extra almonds on
top. A polao, instead of plain boiled rice, is a good
accompaniment.

As for the other preparation, I discovered it not in Dhaka,
but in the town of Rajshahi, in the northern Bangladesh district
of the same name. To most Bengalis Rajshahi is famous for two
things: the best langra mangoes outside of Benares and the
wonderful *kanchagolla*, a kind of milk-based sweet, made in
Natore on the outskirts of the city. But for me, the trip had
more romantic associations. During my girlhood one of the
most famous romantic Bengali poems we read was about the
fabled heroine of Natore, Banalata Sen, she whose eyes promised
all the warmth and sanctuary a fledgeling finds in its nest.
Wandering around the ancient royal palace of Natore, near
Rajshahi, I was told by one of my guides that the deserted
areas all around were prime land for the cultivation of poppy
and marijuana. During each of the three evenings I spent in
that realm of poetic fancy and poppy seeds, my host's cook
produced the most unforgettable dinners. He served this khashi
and posto creation on the last night of my visit.

LAMB WITH POSTO

FOR FOUR PEOPLE

INGREDIENTS

1 kg (2 lb) of lamb
2 large onions, finely chopped
5 cm (2 in) long piece of ginger
An entire head of a small garlic
120 gm (4 oz) of ghee
4-5 sticks of cinnamon
6 whole cardamoms
4 bay leaves
60 gm (2 oz) of posto
6-7 whole dry red chillies
3 teaspoons of sugar
2 teaspoons of salt

METHOD

For lamb with posto for four people, take the lamb, cut it into small pieces (keeping the bones in), rinse it in water and set aside. Chop onions, ginger and garlic as finely as possible. In a thick-bottomed pot melt a stick of sweet butter or heat ghee over a medium flame. Add cinnamon, cardamoms and bay leaves. When these have been fried for a couple of minutes, add the chopped onion, ginger and garlic and fry them until brown. Add the meat, salt and sugar, and keep stirring over a medium heat. As the meat is being browned, put posto in a bowl, cover it with hot water and set aside. Keep stirring the meat until it is very dark and starts sticking to the pot. Add whole dry red chillies and the posto and water. Add some more hot water, enough to cover the meat, cover the pot tightly and leave on a low flame till the meat is absolutely tender. Uncover and taste for salt and sugar balance, adding whatever is necessary. The sweetness should be somewhat pronounced. Finish over a high flame. All water should evaporate and the meat should be coated with the butter/ghee and spices. Though no ground spices are used, the chillies provide sharpness of taste and the minute graininess of the posto counters the tenderness of the meat very well.

Among the Hindus of West Bengal, the most memorable domestic ritual in Jaishtha is Jamaishashthi, on the sixth day after the new moon. There are many shashthis, sixth days of the moon, through the Bengali year which the Hindus have loaded with significance, all of them for the benefit of their children. On this one, sons-in-law are blessed by the parents-in-law, given gifts and ceremoniously fed a huge meal, obviously a relic of the times when women were totally dependent on their husbands and the parents would do their best to appease the mortal god who held the happiness of their daughter in his hands. When I was a child, my grandmother would give new clothes to all her sons-in-law, including my father, and there would be a general bustle leading to the special elaborate meal. Though tradition demanded a whole head of rui fish for each son-in-law, I do not think we were so particular.

Years later, I was quite amazed at the care my mother took to please my Muslim husband when she entertained him for Jamaishashthi. There was no traditional fish head, for she knew he could not stomach it. But apart from the obligatory dal and fried vegetables, there was a wonderful dish made with green jackfruit whose firm flesh has given it the nickname 'tree-goat' in Bengali. It was one of his favourite vegetables and my mother had managed to find that out. On that hot stifling day, there was no meat, but a variety of carefully selected fish preparations instead. The first to be served was a peculiar specimen called the topshe or tapaswi, a small fish about 20 cm (8½ in) long, which is served whole, first marinated in onion–ginger paste, then coated with egg and breadcrumbs and deep-fried in oil. Bengalis consider this a delicacy and my husband was very fond of it, the more so because it was a rarity in the Dhaka markets. The name tapaswi means one who meditates, and is supposed to have arisen from the ample whiskers, like those of a holy man, sported by the fish. The British called it the mango fish, perhaps because the season for the two coincide. One Englishman is supposed to have said that all his financial losses and his mental and physical sufferings in India were amply compensated by his good fortune in having tasted the mango fish of Bengal. The ones my mother served that day were plump with roe.

After the topshe came rui in yoghurt sauce, followed by fishballs made out of a bony fish called chitol. My mother learnt to make the fishballs from one of her Bangal colleagues, and I must say, they were a great success from day one. We call them *koptas* or *baras*, but they are also given the charming name of *muithya*—something made in the *muthi* or fist—by some East Bengal people. I think both recipes are likely to be appreciated everywhere. Usefully, they can be duplicated with whatever large fish is available.

DOI MACHH

FOR THREE TO FOUR PEOPLE

INGREDIENTS

500 gm (1 lb) of fish
250 gm (8 oz) of yoghurt
1 tablespoon of sugar
3 medium onions, finely chopped
1 tablespoon of ground ginger
4-5 tablespoons of oil
1 teaspoon of ghee

3 sticks of cinnamon
4 cloves
4 cardamoms
2 bay leaves
5-6 green chillies
1 teaspoon of turmeric
Salt to taste

METHOD

To prepare doi machh, cut the fish (we like the carp varieties for this) horizontally into long 2.5 cm (1 in) thick pieces. The peti portion is specially suitable for this. Wash the fish, dust it with a little salt and turmeric and fry it lightly in oil. Remove and set aside to drain off all excess oil. Meanwhile whip yoghurt and mix sugar in it. In a karai heat oil, add ghee, and throw in whole garom mashla (cinnamon, clove, cardamom) and bay leaves. After a minute, add the onion and ginger with turmeric. Fry these until brown, add the yoghurt and a little salt. As soon as it comes to boil, add the fish and green chillies, reduce the heat to low and keep covered for six to eight minutes. Uncover, check for salt and sugar balance and remove. If you wish, you can garnish this as the Bangals would, with chopped coriander leaves.

CHITOL KOPTA

FOR FOUR PEOPLE

INGREDIENTS

500 gm (1 lb) of fish
2 medium potatoes
½ teaspoon of ground ginger
1 medium onion, finely chopped
1 beaten egg
120 ml (4 fl oz) oil
Salt to taste

METHOD

For chitol kopta, the flesh is scooped away from the skin of the bony back portion with a spoon, but you have to be careful to move the spoon the way the bones are laid. If it moves against them, the bones will come away with the fish. To make the fishballs, first boil potatoes and mash them finely. Mix these thoroughly with the lump of fish. Though chitol, being very sticky, does not need this as a binder, I find the potatoes make the texture soft and fluffy. To the fish and potato mixture add some salt, ginger, and finely chopped onion and egg. Mix all of these together to make a tight dough-like lump. It should not be thin or watery. Divide it into 20 round or oval balls, patting each smooth between the palms. Then heat oil in a karai, and deep-fry the fishballs in it. In the hot oil they will swell up like little balloons, though they shrink later when taken out. These koptas can be served by themselves as an appetizer or snack, or just as an item with rice and dal. But mostly they are put into a thick gravy before serving with rice. For this, you need:

2 medium onions, finely chopped
½ teaspoon of ground ginger
1 teaspoon of chilli powder
½ teaspoon of turmeric powder
2 bay leaves
3 pieces of cinnamon, 4 cardamoms, 4 cloves for whole garom mashla
2 teaspoons of sugar
500 ml (16 fl oz) of water
2 teaspoons of flour
Salt and sugar to taste

If the oil in which you have fried the fishballs has been

reduced too much, you can add some fresh oil to it and heat it. Then throw in the bay leaves and garom mashla, fry for a couple of minutes, add the onions and fry till golden brown. Add 2 teaspoons of sugar and wait till it turns to a caramel colour, after which add the other spices. Fry these well, add the water and salt as needed. When it comes to the boil, add the fishballs and keep covered for five to six minutes. Taste for salt, add flour to thicken the gravy and remove. Once again, you can use less or more water, depending on how much gravy you would like, and the spices will have to be adjusted accordingly. This, too, can be garnished with coriander leaves. Or you can mix in a small handful of fresh chopped mint to the fish mixture before making the fishballs.

True to form, my husband was unable to eat anything near as much as my mother would like. As I watched the battle of wills between mother- and son-in-law, I realized how odd poor people would have found this reluctance for food. I remembered a one-time maid who used to sniff and recite a proverb whenever she saw such carryings on among her betters. 'The son-in-law now refuses the delectable head of rui we have given him; but one fine day he'll have to go down on his hands and knees to look for what the rice thresher left behind.' The other side of the coin is the typical Bengali male, like my father, who feels affronted unless his wife serves him with every item on the table.

Four days after the adoration of the son-in-law, it is Dashahara, the day on which bathing in the Ganga is said to clean one of the ten deadly sins that besmirch mankind. It is also said that if it does not rain on Dashahara the family of serpents will multiply rapidly to the detriment of human life in the monsoon. Unfortunately there are many Dashaharas when it does not rain. Many whole Jaishthas, in fact, go without rain. The unimaginable suffering of men and animals can only be relieved by the saviour monsoon. In some villages life comes to a standstill; even with irrigation the crops suffer; and anyway, it is mostly the rich farmers who have access to irrigation pumps. People, especially women, have to trek miles to find a source of drinking water, since very often the modern handpump tubewells are in a state of disrepair. A passage from 'Mahesh' gives us a real sense of the killer heat that leaves all creation panting, waiting for the rainclouds of Asharh like the proverbial chatak bird:

> Jaishtha was almost over. It was only by confronting the sky today that one could comprehend how much greater the sheer ruthlessness of destructive nature could be than during Baisakh, terrible as that had been. No hint of mercy was to be perceived. It was almost frightening to think that the shape of things could ever change, that this same sky could show itself one day clad in tender, moisture-laden clouds. Rather, it seemed that the fire which rained down day after day from this ignited sky was infinite, endless—that it would not rest till all was consumed.

But life does go on regenerating itself, and the shape of things does change. In time, or unbearably late, the monsoon does come to Bengal, the utter deathly stillness of the summer heat broken by the roll of thunder and the onrush of wind and cloud from the Bay of Bengal. Until then, excruciating though it is, land, crops and living creatures expand their beings to the last point of waiting.

BARSHA
monsoon

During the last few days of summer, each longer than the previous one, the endurance of man, land, animals and vegetation is stretched to breaking point. As the people of Bengal live through this scorching, humid hell, waiting for Barsha, the monsoon, some find comfort in quoting the opening phrase of *Meghadootam*, a Sanskrit love poem by the Indian poet Kalidasa: *'Asharasya prathama dibase'*, on the first day of Asharh. For this is the month which will bring the relief of rain, gentle and violent, to an exhausted earth.

Nature, of course, does not always conform to calendar dates. Though the first of the mystic month of Asharh falls in the middle of June, Barsha is sometimes delayed by as much as two or three weeks. In some years there is the welcome presage of a short but violent pre-monsoon downpour, after which the silent summer oppression returns with renewed force for many more days. When the monsoon does finally set in, it too is the most deceptive advent, arriving with sweet succour from the parching heat and showing nothing of the later fury which will swell the rivers to cause ruinous floods.

But then who can think of future disaster while enjoying the immediate relief of life-giving showers? As children, even the first sight of dark clouds rolling towards us from the distant southeast would set us skipping with excitement. The anticipation intensified as the winds gathered force, as the low rumble of thunder was heard and the first streaks of lightning rent the sky. It is hard to remain unresponsive to what Rabindranath Tagore called the 'terrible rapture' of the oncoming monsoon. As the first drops fell, we would rush clamorously out, onto the streets or up on the roof, for a ritual drenching.

The first day of Barsha is generally honoured with the eating of a special meal, made more enjoyable by the drastic drop in temperature created by the rains and cloud-covered sky. The most well-known Bengali dish associated with the monsoon is *khichuri*, rice and dal cooked together with certain spices. This is the housewife's response to the sudden arrival of the monsoon rains, or heavy rain at any other time of the year. Though simple, it is a superb dish which requires care and does not survive neglect or inattention. It is probably one of the oldest dishes in the Bengali repertoire. From wandering mendicants who begged for their food, to various religious orders that observed a strict simplicity of diet, countless people have depended on khichuri to give them a balanced meal. Without any trimmings, it can be even rice and dal boiled together in a pot. Slum dwellers in Indian cities can still be seen doing that on the sidewalks. With the delicate refinements of certain spices, it becomes a delicacy which is not too rich for frequent consumption. After 200 years of colonial rule, the British also took it back with them as kedgeree. Like the 'curry', kedgeree probably was a contribution of the Indian (often Muslim) chef working in the British officer's home. The simplest form of khichuri was probably a welcome addition to the heavily laden breakfast table, a departure from the usual kinds of porridge.

There are of course many kinds of khichuris, depending on what kind of dal is being used. The consistency may be thin, thick, or dry and fluffy like a pilaf, plain or with seasonal winter vegetables like new potatoes, green peas and cauliflower added to the basic rice dal mixture. The one constant factor is the use of atap rice, usually of the short-grained variety. The other characteristic of khichuri is that, whatever the consistency, each grain of rice and dal has to be fully cooked but not soft enough to lose its identity. This is why, although it is quick and easy to make, it needs careful watching. As the rice and dal get cooked and the water lessens, the khichuri tends to stick to the pot and can easily burn.

SIMPLE KHICHURI

FOR FIVE PEOPLE

INGREDIENTS

500 gm (1 lb) of atap rice

500 gm (1 lb) of roasted moong dal

60 ml (2 fl oz) of mustard or any other cooking oil

2 teaspoons of ghee

4 sticks of cinnamon, 2.5 cm (1 in) long, 4-5 whole cardamoms
*   and 4-5 whole cloves for garam mashla*

2 bay leaves

A liberal pinch of whole cumin seeds

A piece of ginger 4 cm (½ in) long, chopped fine

2 whole green chillies

1½ teaspoons of turmeric powder

Salt and sugar to taste

METHOD

The rice and dal, rinsed separately under running water in
a colander, are left to dry on a flat surface for about fifteen
minutes. This process makes them easier to cook and,
anyway, in Bengal, we never cook anything without rinsing
it first in water. While they dry I put on the kettle so that I
have ready the hot, though not boiling, water I need to add
to the khichuri. I heat the oil in a medium-sized, heavy-
bottomed deep cooking pot, add the garom mashla and bay
leaves and wait for a couple of minutes, without stirring
them, for the fragrance to be released by the heat before I
throw in the cumin seeds and chopped ginger. These I stir-
fry for a couple of minutes, then add the half-dried rice and
fry it for two to three minutes. Finally I add the roasted
moong dal and the turmeric and stir the mixture for another
two to three minutes before pouring in the hot water. The
level of water should generally be 4 cm (1½ in) over the

rice and dal. If necessary, more hot water can be added towards the end, depending on how thin you like your khichuri or if the rice and dal are sticking to the pot. But a lot of water at the beginning will make a mishmash of the grains. Once the water comes to a boil, I add salt and sugar, reduce the heat to low and cover the pot. Generally it takes about twelve to fifteen minutes for the khichuri to be ready. To avoid sticking and even the slightest burning, which ruins the flavour, I keep checking from time to time and stir the mixture thoroughly with a spatula. If needed, I add a little more hot water. After ten minutes of cooking, it is a good idea to test the grains of rice and dal. When they feel nearly ready, I throw in the green chillies, check for salt and sugar, wait till the consistency is just right, add ghee and remove the pot from the stove. The earlier you add the chillies, the hotter the khichuri will be, for the stirring will blend them in.

This plain khichuri does not require much preparation and is quick and easy to make. Since leftover khichuri, both hot and cold, is also delicious, nobody worries too much about the quantities. A more sophisticated version, called the *bhuni khichuri*, which requires more frying and has the texture of a pilaf, is made either for guests or for the family when the cook has more leisure. The colour of simple khichuri is always yellow from the turmeric, but this version can be made without it, so that the natural whitey-brown tones of rice and roasted moong dal are kept. Richer in taste than plain khichuri, one cannot have too much of it.

BHUNI KHICHURI

FOR THREE TO FOUR PEOPLE

INGREDIENTS

500 gm (1 lb) of rice
250 gm (½ lb) of roasted moong dal
4 medium onions, finely chopped
2 teaspoons of ground ginger
2 tablespoons of chopped ginger
Garom mashla as for the simple khichuri, but crushed lightly
3 bay leaves
1 teaspoon of freshly ground cumin
1 teaspoon of whole cumin
7-8 ground chillies
120 gm (4 oz) of raisins
175 ml (6 fl oz) of ghee
Salt and sugar to taste

METHOD

Rinse and dry the rice and dal as for simple khichuri. Then heat the ghee in a pot and throw in the whole cumin with 2 bay leaves. As soon as they turn brown, add the crushed garom mashla and, a minute later, the chopped onions and ginger. Stir-fry till brown and add the rice . Lower the heat to medium and keep stirring until the rice makes popping noises. Then add the dal, fry for some more time and pour in the hot water, enough to cover the contents and stay almost 2.5 cm (1 in) above. Again, one has to be careful with the water, particularly because this khichuri has to be dry and fluffy, not soggy and mushy. A little more water can always be added if needed. As soon as the water comes to a boil, add salt and sugar and the green chillies, then lower the heat and cook, covered, for about five to six minutes. Check the salt and sugar balance at this point, adding more if needed, before adding the ground ginger and ground cumin as well as the raisins. Then add the remaining bay leaf, cover the pot tightly and reduce the flame to the barest minimum. If the khichuri looks too dry, this is the time to sprinkle more hot water over it. From time to time over the next four to five minutes, shake—never stir—the covered pot carefully, so that the grains will not stick to the bottom. When done, the bhuni khichuri will be very fluffy and should give off a complex aroma, heavier than that of the simple khichuri.

Many people love to add extra dollops of ghee to their platefuls of simple khichuri, although in these days of cholesterol fears, lemon juice squeezed over the top is also used to add zest. The bhuni khichuri, however, has too much ghee and spices to need any extra seasoning.

Although khichuri is almost a complete meal in itself, most Bengalis would be disappointed not to have certain well-loved accompaniments: slices of brinjal or halves of patol deep-fried in oil, potatoes sliced thin and fried with a seasoning of panch phoron, dry red chillies and salt. On the non-vegetarian side there is the ubiquitous omelette and pieces of fried fish. Some people boil eggs and then deep-fry them crispy brown to serve with khichuri. And in Muslim Bangladesh, where the bhuni khichuri (many versions of it) is very common, a dry but highly seasoned meat dish will be served with it.

As the rains of Asharh continue—sometimes violent, at other times steady, or even stopping from time to time—the leaves of plants washed clean of summer dust and grime display their vigorous greenery. But the welcome greyness of clouds shielding the sun reminds you that this is no second spring. Rows of red-blossomed Krishnachura trees throw into relief the dense masses of clouds, whose lowering darkness is said to be the colour of the skin of Krishna, the Hindu deity.

Fairly early in Asharh comes *Ambubachi*, three days which mark the beginning of the monsoon proper according to ancient myths. Even if the monsoon has not appeared before this, even if the rains have begun and stopped, the skies have to open and mingle with the earth during these three days, for legend says that the fluid flow of red or brown earth mingled with rainwater at this time is a ritual bleeding of the earth presaging fertility.

Ambubachi is serious business to orthodox Hindus. In times gone by, even the two primary activities of the elite and the peasantry were forbidden. Brahmins were not allowed to pursue their study of the Vedas and the peasants had to refrain from ploughing the land, a practical directive since the three days of rain would leave the earth soft and receptive to cultivation. The change in the appearance of the land, from the gaping, fissured cracked earth of late summer, to the spongy, moist darkness of soil is amazing. Farmers can hardly wait to take their ploughs and oxen into the fields and get ready to sow their crops.

Hindu widows were not allowed to cook any food during Ambubachi and rice was absolutely forbidden for them. I used to see my grandmother and several other elderly widows in neighbouring houses make their preparations for these three days. They would prepare luchis and several vegetable dishes in advance and lay in a stock of fruit and home-made sweet yoghurt to be eaten with chira, flattened rice. Puffed rice *(muri)* and popped rice (*khoi*) were also permitted, as home-made sweets. East Bengali Hindus are, however, more rigorous about widows' rituals. For them even pre-cooked food is taboo during Ambubachi. The widowed grandmother of a school friend of mine used to sustain herself for three whole days on the pulp and juice of mangoes and ripe jackfruits, together with milk, yoghurt, muri and khoi. The occasional salted slices of cucumber or soaked chickpeas with chopped ginger provided some variety.

The only positive aspect I could find about Ambubachi for widows was that they could drink milk, usually reserved for children and very old people in the average middle-class household, with some freedom. Milk is rarely drunk chilled in Bengal. I always found it interesting to see my grandmother add handfuls of khoi to the bowl of hot milk and see them float with mild popping sounds, or squeeze in the juice and pulp of a mango which turned the milk a vivid saffron yellow. The heat of the milk accentuated the strong smell of mango and I would inevitably stand over the bowl and sniff as hard as I could to enjoy the heady fruitiness to the full. Folklore also says that drinking milk during Ambubachi provides immunity from snakebites, no mean advantage in rural Bengal where the fields and the villages can be luxuriant death-traps with lurking cobras and kraits. Not that such considerations operate any longer in the cities where milk is consumed purely for its nutritional qualities.

Soon after Ambubachi comes Rathajatra, the first religious festival of the monsoon. Literally translated, Rathajatra means a chariot trip or journey. The story goes that when Lord Jagannatha, a later incarnation of Krishna, was a child, he and his brother Balaram and his sister Subhadra decided to visit their aunt to convalesce from a bout of monsoon fever. After a week's visit, the three returned home, fully restored to health. The most elaborate celebration of Rathajatra takes place in the state of Orissa, where there is a huge temple of Jagannatha. A gigantic wooden chariot is constructed each year, the images of the three deities placed inside and priests and devotees combine to hold the huge rope attached to the chariot and pull it along to a predetermined destination. In the past, many people would often be trampled to death under the wheels of this moving contraption, not just by accident, but also because people believed that to die that way ensured an entry into heaven and freedom from the cycle of rebirth. The English word 'juggernaut' is not only a transliteration of Jagannatha but derives its meaning from such incidents of self-immolation. Neighbouring Bengal has also adopted the chariot festival as her own, partly because the story of the gods as children echoes the other Bengali folktales about the childhood of Krishna. This is another day when it is supposed to rain, but no one minds because rain on Rathajatra presages a good monsoon.

At home the mandatory item of food on this day is papor or papadam, thin pale yellow or creamy white sheets of dried powdered dal (sometimes spiced) or rice flour, fried and served at lunch with khichuri and vegetables. The rice papors, creamy white in colour, were meant more for children than for adults because they were quite bland and absorbed less oil. I always liked to watch them being fried and would stand in the kitchen to watch my mother pick up the thin desiccated slices of papor and throw them in the hot oil. They immediately puffed up and crinkled into fascinating curves and she would lift them out carefully to avoid breaking or browning them too much. In our house fish, meat or eggs were strictly forbidden on this day, but it was no hardship. We would sit in front of our platefuls of steaming, fragrant khichuri, the green chillies and the brown cinnamon or bay leaf standing out against the yellow background, waiting for Keshto, the cook, to come and serve fried slices of brinjal, potato, patol or even pumpkin. These I would arrange ceremoniously on my plate around the khichuri, the orange pumpkin, the dark brown brinjal and the greenish brown patol forming a lovely unity of colour. As I squeezed lemon juice over the khichuri, Keshto would come again with a huge bowlful of crisply fried papors which disappeared almost in a flash.

The excitement of Rathajatra is mostly for children. In the evening, after the thrill of pulling our own mini chariots up and down the long verandas, my cousins and I would be taken to the nearest mela, or fair, which began on the evening of Rathajatra and continued for nearly two weeks. Normally, food cooked at fairs or roadside stalls was strictly forbidden in my well-guarded childhood. But this was an evening for indulgence and we were usually taken out, not by parents, but by Patolmama, an old friend of my uncles, a confirmed bachelor with a heart of gold, who could refuse a child nothing. Tingling with anticipation, we would walk through the bright lights, past the rows of men sitting in front of their clay stoves with huge black karais on top, for heart-stopping rides on various merry-go-round contraptions. Later we would come back and join the jostling crowd shouting out orders for their tele bhajas, crispy snacks fried in oil: *beguni*, brinjal slices dipped in a batter of spiced dal powder and deep-fried, or *alur chop*, rounded balls of spiced mashed potatoes covered in the same batter. As I peeped from behind Patolmama's back, the hissing and bubbling of the oil, and the heat, smell and smoke in the inadequate light of hanging lanterns and kerosene lamps almost lifted the scene out of reality. With a delicious shiver I would stare hypnotized into the karai full of hot oil, remembering popular descriptions of hell where sinners are supposed to be fried in cauldrons of oil exactly like begunis or alur chops.

Away from the hot and sticky frying smell of the food stalls, the fragrance of beli and jui, two jasmine-like flowers, would lie heavily in the deep evening air. For the fair is traditionally one of the year's biggest gathering of plant sellers, with specimens ranging from rare or beautiful flowering plants for pots to specially bred cuttings of mango, lime or litchi trees.

In part it is this wave of lush, abundant vegetation produced by the rains which gives the monsoon, more than any other season, associations of romance. In part, though, it is the rain itself—refreshing, coy, earnest, disappearing altogether for days on end, returning reluctantly and bursting anew to provide cover for lovers' assignations. A memorable passage in the works of the sixteenth-century poet Gobindadasa describes Radha practising her steps for the nocturnal *abhishar*, or the setting forth of the woman to meet her lover at a secret trysting place. To duplicate the conditions she will face on her way to meet Krishna, the delicate woman deliberately pricks her lotus-like feet with thorns. To avoid waking her husband and in-laws, she muffles the sound of her anklets by wrapping them in cloth. And to walk firmly on the slippery paths, she practises walking on the floor of her room where she has poured out a pitcherful of water. But all these tensions were worthwhile, for they ended in a union with the beloved. For the Bengali heroine, the nights of separation, *biraha*, were far worse, even in the safety of the bedroom. As the rain fell around her in curtains, she would stay wakeful and sad, thinking of the beloved who was also alone. Food, as can be imagined, is the most unimportant consideration for such victims of passion who grow pale and thin with obscure longings. Though much of these sensibilities and associations are dying under the pressures of modern urban existence, and the increasing impact of the West, the evenings when the monsoon weddings take place and the air is redolent with the perfume of jasmine garlands entwined in the hair of women, still evoke a sense of romantic nostalgia.

For all the fanfare and trumpet that accompanies the arrival of the monsoon, it is only in its second month, Shraban, when it has begun to taper off to periods of quiet and steady rain, almost like a honeymooning couple settling down to the quieter business of living, that you really start believing in it. The ground soaks up the water to the point of sogginess. There is mud on the streets and the drains overflow. This lack of poetry about the monsoon in the cities belies Tagore's vision of Shraban as the month of mystery and adventure as well as of unremitting rain.

The true beauty of Bengal in Shraban is to be found only in the villages where the fertility of the earth coexists with the threat of engorged rivers that can later become wantonly, cruelly destructive. Amazingly, neither the rural landscape nor the pattern of agricultural life has changed much over time. Once the earth has been softened by the Asharh rains, the farmers plough their fields and plant the most important crop of the year, the Aman rice crop. The scanty summer planting, the Aush rice, has also benefited from the rain and stands firm in the fields to be harvested quietly around August. But most of the land is devoted to the all-important monsoon planting, around which rural life and economy revolve.

The two primary categories of cooked rice are the siddha, or parboiled rice, and the atap rice, untouched by heat. Each will include rice of varying degrees of fineness and length. Parboiled rice keeps better and is more nutritious, which is probably why it is commonly used for lunch and dinner. The harvested rice is parboiled, dried in the sun and husked before marketing and storage. Atap rice is used for specific purposes such as the cooking of polao, khichuri and *payesh* or rice pudding, as well as being made into rice flour with which the Bengali makes a host of pithas, sweet and savoury. Among Hindus atap rice is also considered more appropriate for widows who are forced to be vegetarians and are constrained by numerous rules. The finer varieties of atap rice are usually saved for payesh and pilafs and Muslim biryanis, while the coarser ones are used for plain rice. In Chittagong, in Bangladesh, for instance, the local preference is for atap rice, even for daily meals.

Differences of soil, altitude and other factors also produced variations in the quality of rice from district to district in Bengal. The terrain in Bangladesh, say experts, is such that you can grow 10,000 varieties of rice there. While such potential is far from being realized, certain strains of rice acquired a special reputation. Barisal became famous for its *balam* rice, which is one of the tastiest and longest-grained varieties of parboiled rice in Bengal. But one has to be a Bengali, nurtured on rice for generations, to appreciate this rice. For the uninitiated, there might well be no difference between packaged rice grown in the US or imported Patna rice or the balam which is growing rarer with time or the many kinds of fine-grained ataps.

Another important consideration behind the cooking of daily rice is texture. Traditionally, Bengal cooks drain the water in which rice has been cooked and parboiled rice is preferred because it is firmer than atap rice and also because it loses less of its nutritional value. Bengalis also have a distinct preference for old, stored rice, both parboiled and atap. Newly harvested rice is found to be more sticky and less firm. For khichuri or polao, where the rice is first fried, old atap rice is preferred because the grains, having lost all moisture, absorb the oil better. This greater fluffiness of texture also gives it a more voluminous appearance. Hence the Bengali saying, 'Old rice increases in the cooking'—applied also to tried and trusted servants and friends.

The abundance of the rice crop has also led to the other mutations that had their own place in daily life and ritual. Puffed rice, muri, became a favourite occasional snack as well as breakfast food served with milk and brown sugar. Popped rice, khoi, apart from being eaten with milk, is used to make a favourite winter sweet, *moa*. It also has a distinctly auspicious significance, unlike puffed rice, for it is poured into the sacred fire in front of which Hindu wedding takes place, as a special offering to the gods. This, of course, is not peculiar to Bengal, but part of the pan-Indian Aryan culture.

To most outsiders, however, the most interesting mutation is the flattened or flaked rice, chira. Like muri and khoi, this, too, is made all over India, the unhusked rice being boiled longer than for parboiling and then flattened by being pounded forcefully. The husk separates from the grain during the pounding to reveal a paper-thin white grain with irregular edges. The fineness of the chira depends both on the quality of the rice and the art of the people making it. Probably no other region does as much with the chira as Bengal does. Soaked in water and softened, it is eaten with sugar, fruits, yoghurt or milk as phalahar. Combined with the coastal bounty of coconut, ground fine, it provides the most delicate of tastes. It can be fried very quickly in hot ghee or roasted in a dry pot, to be eaten as a savoury item seasoned with salt, pepper and chopped ginger. In winter it is combined with vegetables to make a quick polao, or with sticky-sweet date-palm sugar to make another kind of moa. Mixed with yoghurt and milk-based sweets, the chira becomes part of the offering for the gods, and brides and bridegrooms go through the ceremony of *dadhimangal* very early on their wedding day when they are given this to eat before the day's fast begins.

Given the all-pervasive presence of rice, the mother of all these inventions, it is easy to understand with what eagerness the Bengali peasant looks forward to the monsoon when he can put all his energy and labour into the sowing of this crop. The seeds are broadcast by hand over the receptive land and shoot up thickly in no time. Then comes the meticulous, backbreaking labour of transplanting the seedlings in carefully spaced rows. Men and women forget their differences as they stoop, ankle-deep in water, pressing in the seedlings with the ease of much practice. Though the monsoon helps to make the land ready, too much rain or violent winds can cause infinite disasters. So the farmers who long for the rain also pray for moderation. By the end of Shraban or a little later, the fields are full of the vivid emerald green of the standing rice crop, and then the beauty and promise of the sight is compensation enough for all their labour.

Once, around this time, I made the overnight journey by steamboat from Dhaka to Barisal, from where we took the boat to my husband's home village of Dapdapia in Nalchite thana. On my previous visit in the winter, we had travelled on from the landing jetty by kutcha roads, but this time the roads had all disappeared under water. As we glided along the numerous little canals, the well-grown rice plants on both sides nodded and shivered as the moving water touched their feet. In places the water almost disappeared and the boat somehow scraped through a mass of vegetation. The green leaves and budding ears of rice touched my face sharply, sometimes replaced by the softness of the luxuriant *kalmi*, a water-reed that is a favourite monsoon vegetable.

For me, it was a journey made magic by the sound of oars in the water, the rustle of leaves as we advanced through them, and the intensity of a green earth under a threatening sky. The slow journey seemed of infinite duration, evoking all the fairy tales my grandmother used to tell me of the rakkhashi, demon queen, whose vital spark lay in the shape of a black hornet inside a box, below the waters of a huge lake. I would sit enthralled as she told me of the nights when the queen assumed her true shape and went out of the palace to devour horses and elephants and even unwary human beings; of the prince, her stepson, who discovered her identity and fled from her pursuing hands and tongue; of his watery journey down, down to the hornet which he brought up to the land and killed, all in one breath, thus finding deliverance for himself and his father's kingdom.

Once we had arrived at the homestead of Kadam Bhai, a landowner farmer and longtime family friend, we had a simple and delicious lunch. The high point of the meal was a dish combining *dhenki shak*, a feathery fern-like green quite unfamiliar in Ghoti households like ours, and tiny shrimps.

Rarely seen in the markets of Calcutta, dhenki shak grows mostly in East Bengal, Assam and the northern hilly areas of West Bengal.

Its beauty lies in the head, where the 30 cm (1 ft) long stem bends forward gracefully into a hook and coils to an end. In many places this appearance has earned the shak the name of *boudaga* shak, *bou* meaning bride and *daga* being the tip. The analogy obviously derives from the blushing Bengali bride, her head covered with her sari, demurely bending forward.

Kadam Bhai's daughter, Shefali, had added tiny cubed potatoes and shrimps to the chopped dhenki shak and seasoned it with pungent ground mustard—complemented by mustard oil—fresh ground coconut, green chillies, turmeric and salt. Although dhenki shak may be hard to get in urban markets, the other ingredients can be combined with spring onions.

SPRING ONIONS WITH SHRIMPS AND COCONUT

FOR FOUR PEOPLE

INGREDIENTS

500 gm (1 lb) of spring onions
2 medium potatoes
3 tablespoons of mustard oil
1 tablespoon of ground mustard
3 tablespoons of ground coconut
2-3 green chillies
Salt to taste

METHOD

Chop spring onions into 2.5 cm (1 in) lengths (including the onions at the bottom) and keep them aside. Dust a handful of shrimps with turmeric and salt and fry lightly. Peel and cut potatoes into 2.5 cm (1 in) long, thin slices and brown them lightly in oil. Heat mustard oil in a karai, throw in the spring onions, add a teaspoon of salt and keep covered for a couple of minutes. When you uncover the karai, a lot of moisture will have oozed out. Keep on a high flame, add the ground mustard, stir for a minute or so, add the fried shrimp, browned potatoes, coconut and green chillies, stir thoroughly for three to four minutes and keep covered over a low flame until the flavours are blended, the potatoes are tender and all the moisture has evaporated. Before removing, stir over high heat so that the dish becomes very dry and check the salt, adding more if needed. As a side dish, this can be eaten with rice along with other items.

In our watery land, Barsha is the time for eating all kinds of other lush leafy greens. The kalmi growing beside the water is a common favourite. Chopped fine, it is stir-fried with panch phoron, dry red chillies and lots of chopped garlic. Spinach can be made the same way with or without the panch phoron, but the mustard oil is essential. In the fields can be seen stretches of *shushni* shak, whose deep velvety green soothes the eye just as the shak itself is supposed to soothe you to sleep. Another succulent green, the *pui* shak, seems to have no substitute that can emulate its slightly slippery, slightly astringent taste. Yet another strange vegetable that Bengalis go crazy about is the *kachu* shak, the long, hollow stems (not leaves) of a kind of colocasia which, when cooked, become a pulpy mush and readily absorb the flavour and taste of other ingredients added to them. Kachu shak is an ideal combination for small shrimp or the head of a fish, and there is also an extraordinarily delicious vegetarian dish made by spicing the boiled shak with whole bay leaves, ground cumin, chilli, turmeric and some coconut, the whole being flavoured with ghee before being removed from the fire. Little brown pre-cooked chickpeas are usually added to this preparation.

Though available round the year now, the pumpkin is at its most prolific during the rains. It is so commonplace that most Bengalis consider it a native vegetable, but in reality it is probably a seventeenth-century import resulting from the Portuguese trade. The supposition finds some confirmation in the fact that in colonial times the pumpkin was referred to as the *biliti* or English *kumro*, just as the tomato was called the biliti begun (English brinjal). The indigenous kumro, similar to the white gourd, acquired the name of *chal* kumro, pumpkin on the roof, to distinguish it from its orange cousin.

A variety of tasty pumpkin dishes can be eaten with impunity by the strictest Hindu vegetarians. One very easy way to deal with it is to fry whole cumin seeds, chopped onions and green chillies, add the cubed pumpkin to it and saute it till soft and edible. Fried shrimp can also be added to this.

PUMPKIN WITH COCONUT

FOR SIX PEOPLE

INGREDIENTS

1 kg (2 lb) pumpkin
Half a coconut
1½ teaspoons of ground coriander
1 teaspoon of ground cumin
1 teaspoon of chilli powder
120 ml (4 fl oz) of milk
3-4 bay leaves
1 teaspoon of garom mashla
4 tablespoons of cooking oil
2 teaspoons of sugar
Salt to taste

METHOD

Pumpkin with coconut is more laborious since the

pumpkin needs grating. Grate the entire portion of the pumpkin. Grate the coconut and set aside. Heat some oil in a karai and put in the grated pumpkin. When it is half-fried, add the grated coconut. When the mixture turns brown, blend all the ground spices except garom mashla with the milk and add to the pumpkin. Keep stirring until all the moisture evaporates. Add the garom mashla before removing. If the oil seems inadequate for the frying, a little more can be added before the spices are put in.

Among the other monsoon vegetables that Bengalis love are varieties of kachu or colocasia. The king of the kachu kingdom is the *maan* kachu, often called just maan, which also means prestige or repute in Bengali. An enormous tuber, sometimes weighing as much as 15 kg (30 lb), it is treated with the respect deserved by its repute. This has been strengthened by Ayurvedic theories ascribing to the maan the capacity to purify the blood, thus curing common afflictions like boils, sores and skin diseases. In our house for many years the pieces of maan bought from the market were simply boiled and mashed with salt and mustard oil. Green chillies could be added too, and, occasionally, the spiced oil from the pickle jar. Later, a Bangal friend showed us the greater novelty of eating it uncooked. The portion of maan was ground on the stone coarsely and the juice discarded. The fibre was then ground a second time with coconut, mustard seeds, green chillies and salt. The smooth paste was seasoned with pungent mustard oil.

Thankfully, some Bengali vegetables are better travelled. The banana tree, so loaded with myth and symbol in the folk life of Bengal, provides two of Bengal's most cherished vegetables: the blossom, *mocha*, and the inner core of the trunk, *thor*. Medieval Bengali literature is full of references to both thor and mocha being cooked and presented to Chaitanya (founder of the Bhakti cult) by his disciples. The tactile and visual pleasure of watching the magenta spathes of the mocha being pulled back to expose the baby bananas nestling underneath, of removing them in bunches and pulling out the hard central stem and the translucent fibre in front, is lost with the canned product, but much time is saved and one avoids having one's fingers blackened with the juice which has to be discarded by boiling the chopped mocha before cooking.

MOCHAR GHANTO

FOR FOUR PEOPLE

INGREDIENTS

500 gm (1 lb) of freshly chopped mocha, cooked and drained
60 gm (2 oz) of chickpeas soaked overnight or cooked lightly
175 gm (6 oz) of ground coconut
2 medium potatoes, peeled and cubed
1 teaspoon of whole cumin for phoron
1 teaspoon of ground garom mashla
4 tablespoons of oil
1 tablespoon of ghee
120 ml (4 fl oz) of water
4 teaspoons of sugar
2 teaspoons of salt

METHOD

Mix half of all the ground spices except the garom mashla thoroughly with the cooked mocha and set aside. Heat the oil in a karai or pot (aluminium, not iron, since that reacts adversely with mocha), fry the potatoes light brown, remove and set aside. In the same oil throw in the phoron, fry for a couple of minutes and add the pre-soaked chickpeas and the rest of the ground spices minus the garom mashla. Keep stirring for two to three minutes, and add the spiced, cooked mocha. Stir again for a few minutes, add the potatoes, stir for three to four minutes more, and pour in the water. Keep covered over medium heat. When the water has almost evaporated, add the ground coconut, salt and sugar. The sweetness has to be a little pronounced. Stir well, taste, and mix in a pinch of flour before removing from the stove. Mix the ghee with the garom mashla, add to the mocha, stir thoroughly and leave covered until it is time to serve. In a traditional meal, the mochar ghanto is eaten with rice after the fried vegetables and dal have been eaten and before any fish or meat dish is served.

After the attenuation of summer, the myriad rivers of Bengal swell joyously under the copious rainfall of Asharh and Shraban. Replenished, they cast off their previous lethargy and flow merrily on, the waves glinting in the occasional sunlight from behind the clouds. It is an invitation to the fishermen, Bengal's boat people. As the evening shadows lengthen, they start off, usually in pairs or small groups, in their fishing boats to haul in the silver catches all through the night. The Bengali *majhi*, boatman, has existed as a theme figure in many folktales and folksongs through the centuries and he is also the hero of Manik Bandyopadhyay's classic, *Padmanodir Majhi* (*Boatman of the Padma*). Like his predecessors and successors, Bandyopadhyay's boatman comes back in the early hours of the morning under the faint light of a crescent moon in a sky filled with broken clouds. The light from the boatman's lantern illuminates the hold where the night's haul of hilsa—the monsoon's most prized and available fish—lies dead. This delicate fish does not live long out of water, but even in death its beauty is not destroyed. The silver scales gleam in the lamplight and the unblinking eyes resemble blue gems.

The monsoon is so associated with the *ilish*, called hilsa by the British, that Bengalis have given the name *ilshe guri* to the lacy mist of rain which replaces the heavy downpour of the first month, ilshe being the adjectival derivative of ilish and guri meaning grain or powder. The hilsa's life cycle is something like that of the salmon. After starting life in the sea, the fish comes to spawn in the estuarine waters where the rivers meet the Bay of Bengal, and slowly moves upwards along the rivers to the northern regions of India, growing in size up to 2.5 kg (5 lb). Many of the hilsa caught during the monsoon are big with roe, which is a delicacy in its own right and considered a caviar of the tropics. When taken out of the fish, the roe resembles two elongated kidneys, joined at the top, brownish in colour with innumerable black veins showing in the enclosing membrane. It can vary in length according to the time and the size of the fish, but is rarely more than 15 cm (6 in). When fried or whipped and cooked with spices, it has a lovely, chewy graininess imbued with the characteristic hilsa flavour. But the bigger the roe, the less tasty the fish.

All the differences between Ghotis and Bangals, between Hindus and Muslims, disappear in an agreement of amity— that there is nothing to rival the hilsa. Friendly disputes arise again over which is the superior: the hilsa from the Ganga which West Bengalis swear by, or the hilsa from the Padma which Bangladesh drools over. Padma specimens can be much bigger than those from the Ganga, but in terms of flavour and softness of texture, due to the proportion of oil in the fish, the Ganga variety is the superior of the two to my mind. But perhaps that is my Ghoti bias.

For the real pleasure of eating this 'darling of the waters', as a Bengali poet called it, you have to come to Bengal, East or West. When you do, you must be prepared to eat with your fingers, for the hilsa's treacherous bones can lodge themselves in the throat of the unwary. I once heard an American in Dhaka compare Bengali women to the hilsa: 'Very tempting on the outside, but try to get close and you choke on the bones.' His comment prompted me to reflect that some people deserve their bones.

In its preparation, too, the hilsa breaks all rules. All other fish are repeatedly washed and cleaned thoroughly of blood and slime before they are cooked. Blood, in fact, is anathema in food. For the Muslims, blood is haram, or absolutely repugnant. They make sure that even their meat is drained of blood by severing the arteries in the neck of animals and birds before actually killing them. And though the Hindus slaughter their animals without such refinements, they too are careful to wash all traces of blood from their fish or meat before cooking. But when it comes to the hilsa, many Bengalis will wash the fish only once, after the head and guts have been removed, even though a lot of blood oozes out subsequently as the fish is cut into pieces. By some strange logic, the blood is supposed to confer added delectation. What amazed me most was the sight of a Bangladeshi Muslim friend of mine in Dhaka treating her hilsa this way. Even her mother, a devout Muslim lady, stood looking on as if nothing extraordinary was happening.

Once the head and guts have been removed and the body scaled, the hilsa is halved along the spine lengthwise. But the cut stops 10 or 12.5 cm (4 or 5 in) above the tail where the body becomes too narrow. The tailpiece is then separated and set aside. The two longitudinal halves are cut horizontally into pieces as thick as you want, usually 2.5 cm (1 in) or so. The peti has large bones and the flesh is more oily, which makes it the more prized portion. But the daga or back portion is very good crisply fried or in a jhol combined with vegetables. It is much more bony though, and requires concentration to eat without a mishap.

There are recipes enough for the hilsa to fill an entire book.

Individuals, families and regions have all developed their special styles, spices and combinations for this delightful fish. Here I will mention only a few that are my favourites and also very easy to make.

The simplest and one of the best ways to have hilsa is to fry it. Once the pieces are washed and cleaned, they are dusted with salt and turmeric powder and left for a few minutes before being fried to a rich, deep brown in mustard oil. A good hilsa will release almost 120 ml (4 fl oz) of oil in the process of frying. Herring fried in this way is particularly good, though it may not yield as much oil. Bengalis treasure the hilsa oil, pouring it over piping hot servings of rice and mixing it in thoroughly so that the fish can be eaten with this reinforced flavour. All you need to accompany this is a pinch of salt on the side and one or more green chillies (according to your taste for hot food) from which you take occasional bites. If, however, you are serving the fish with khichuri, or if there are lots of other items for which you want to save the rice, then you store the fish oil carefully; for it is an invaluable flavouring agent for vegetables, especially those cooked together with the hilsa head. Another classic Bengali preparation for the hilsa, *shorshe ilish*, is simple and depends on a single predominant taste, that of mustard.

SHORSHE ILISH

FOR FOUR PEOPLE

INGREDIENTS

500 gm (1 lb) of peti pieces (a big fish will give you eight or nine pieces)

1½ tablespoons of pungent black mustard

7-8 green chillies

4 tablespoons of mustard oil

½ teaspoon of turmeric powder

250 ml (8 fl oz) of water

METHOD

For shorshe ilish wash and clean the peti pieces thoroughly. Grind pungent black mustard (white or brown mustard is no acceptable substitute) with a touch of salt and a green chilli. This will dispel the bitterness of the mustard. The whole point of the dish is its pungency which complements the rich oiliness of the fish. Mustard seeds can be ground in a blender, though not as finely as on a grinding stone. Take green chillies (2-3 if you cannot tolerate too much) and slit them down the middle. Rub the pieces of fish with salt and turmeric. Heat mustard oil in a karai and add the mustard paste together with turmeric powder. Stir for a couple of minutes and add water. As soon as it comes to the boil, gently put in the hilsa pieces and the green chillies. Cover and cook for ten minutes over a medium flame. Uncover and taste to determine how much extra salt is needed. The water should evaporate sufficiently to leave the fish coated in a thick, grainy, yellow gravy when you remove it. If you want a thinner gravy, you can add some more water. Remove from the stove and add a little fresh mustard oil to the fish. Leave covered for a few minutes. When you serve it with plain boiled rice the sharp taste of the mustard will hit the palate. The important thing to remember, I find, is not to overcook the fish. The stomach pieces, in particular, are very soft and oily and too much heat will destroy the texture, if not the flavour. As with most Bengali dishes, there is always room for experiment and adjustments. Some people prefer more of the mustard paste than others, while some love to drown their fish in mustard oil.

A similar way of preparing the fish—more common in East than in West Bengal—is called a *paturi* from the word *pata*, which is Bengali for leaf.

ILISH PATURI

INGREDIENTS

500 gm (1 lb) of hilsa peti
½ teaspoon of turmeric powder
2 tablespoons of ground mustard
Green chillies
2 tablespoons of mustard oil
Salt to taste

METHOD

For this ilish paturi, take the fish pieces, clean them and mix them thoroughly with salt, turmeric, the ground mustard, green chillies and a liberal helping of mustard oil. The whole mixture is then wrapped in banana leaves and the packet tied with string before it is thrust among the dying embers of a clay oven, or toasted on a tawa or flat pan over a low heat. The packet is turned over several times. By the time the top layer of leaf is burnt black, the fish should be ready. The process can also be duplicated in an oven set at 150°C (300°F, Gas mark 1). In the absence of banana leaves, aluminium foil can be used. Once the fish is cooked, it should be removed from the wrappings and all the sauce scraped out with a spoon. The moisture and oil from the fish combined with the mustard paste and oil will produce quite a bit of gravy.

During my childhood and college years in Calcutta, I had heard my relatives speak of the 'strange' ways the East Bengalis sometimes treated their hilsa, but I had never encountered any recipes that seemed particularly outré. It was only after I went to live in Bangladesh that I came across some of the less usual forms of preparing hilsa. A cook I hired in Dhaka, who came from the Bangladesh district of Mymensingh, was the first person to serve me hilsa with coconut milk. Though Sabu the cook had the maniacal appearance of true genius and though he had already proved his worth in the kitchen, even I was at first a bit sceptical about how this dish was going to turn out. The daring idea (or so it seemed to my timid West Bengali mind) of combining unlikely items like onions and ghee with hilsa (fish is always cooked in mustard oil, and Ghotis never use onion with hilsa) seemed to me fraught with disastrous possibilities. But when it was served, I was charmed with the novelty and richness of the taste.

HILSA WITH COCONUT MILK

FOR FOUR PEOPLE

INGREDIENTS

500 gm (1 lb) of hilsa peti

1 lemon

A whole coconut to extract milk from, approximately 250 ml (8 fl oz) coconut milk

7-8 medium onions

4 cm (1½ in) piece of ginger

4-5 green chillies

2 dry red chillies

120 ml (4 fl oz) of ghee

Garom mashla consisting of 3 sticks of cinnamon and 4 whole cardamoms

Salt to taste

METHOD

Wash the pieces of hilsa, but do not add salt or turmeric. Extract the milk from the coconut by cutting out pieces from the shell, grinding them in a blender, mixing it with some hot water and squeezing out and discarding the fibre. Peel 2 of the onions and the piece of ginger and grind them to a paste with the red chillies. You can use only one chilli if you want. Chop the remaining onions finely. Squeeze all the juice out of the lemon into a bowl. Heat the ghee in a karai and add the garom mashla. After a couple of minutes, add the chopped onions and the green chillies. Fry till the mixture becomes reddish brown and add the ground onion and ginger and 2 teaspoons of salt. Add a quarter of the coconut milk and fry a little longer. When the contents start sticking to the pot, pour in the rest of the coconut milk and add the pieces of hilsa. Reduce the heat to low and simmer covered for twelve to fifteen minutes. Uncover to see if the fish is done and the salt is right. You may need to add some more. Pour in the lemon juice, stir gently and remove from the stove. This dish tastes much better with fine atap rice than parboiled rice. Wedges of lemon can also be served so that each person can adjust the tartness to his own taste.

Bangladesh also has its own recipes for hilsa roe. There I have seen the uncooked roe being put in a bowl and mashed thoroughly with a spoon or fork. The membrane disintegrates and is discarded and the granulated substance of the roe is seasoned with salt, turmeric and a little chilli paste or powder. One large potato is then peeled and chopped into tiny cubes and browned with mustard oil with one large onion, chopped fine. Then the seasoned roe is added together with several slit green chillies. The entire mixture is stirred thoroughly until it turns into a brown-mustard grainy mass with the potatoes showing as tiny lumps. This increases the quantity of roe which can become a side dish for a family of four or five. My feudal friend from Tangail, Farhad Ghuznavi, also described the preparation made in his village by combining the hilsa roe with *karamcha*, a very sour local berry which has a semi-magical status, for a rural Bengali rhyme invokes karamcha with the leaves of lime trees as the potent combination for driving away rain.

A Bengali family can sometimes make an entire meal out of the different preparations of hilsa during the monsoon and find nothing strange about it. Sometimes we start with a chhanchra of hilsa head with green leafy vegetables served with the initial helping of rice. Then we take a fresh supply of hot rice, pour hilsa oil over it and have pieces of fried hilsa daga. This will be followed by the fried roe portioned out between family members. The peti, cooked in a pungent mustard sauce, will be the *pièce de résistance* that finishes the meal; or one can start straightaway by pouring the hilsa oil over rice and eating portions of the roe with it. This may be followed by a thin hilsa jhol with brinjals and potatoes after which the richer taste of hilsa peti with coconut milk will taste wonderful.

Hilsa is not the only fish that produces its roe during the monsoon. The carp family—such as rui, katla, mirgel—all swell with eggs at this time, and in the bazaars both the fish and the roe are sold in separate portions so that you can buy only as much of each as you wish. The roe of the rui is a favourite monsoon dish, as much because it is so easy to cook and so very tasty as because it is a substantial source of not-too-expensive protein. Once the translucent covering membrane has been peeled away before cooking, the inner granules are seen to be slightly bigger than the hilsa roe's, grey and lumpish. Its texture, too, is dissimilar and needs a binding agent to hold it together in any definite shape. In these *boras*, fried balls made of carp roe, a little mashed potato lends a fluffy softness to the grainy roe and flour acts as a binder.

CARP ROE BORAS

FOR FOUR PEOPLE

INGREDIENTS

250 gm (½ lb) of carp roe
2 teaspoons of freshly ground ginger
1 medium onion, finely chopped
2 teaspoons of turmeric powder
4-5 green chillies, finely chopped
A small bunch of mint leaves, finely chopped
1 large potato
1 tablespoon of lemon juice
2 heaped tablespoons of flour
60 ml (2 fl oz) of mustard oil
½ teaspoon of salt

METHOD

Take carp roe, wash away all traces of blood on the outer membrane and carefully peel it away and discard it. Put the roe in a bowl and mix it with ginger, onion, turmeric powder, green chillies, mint leaves, lemon juice and salt. Whip the roe very thoroughly until it is frothy. Boil the potato and mash it to a fine smooth paste. Add this to the roe together with flour and mix thoroughly. Heat mustard oil in a karai and drop in the roe mixture, a large spoonful at a time. As the spoonfuls form into round balls, fry them brown on all sides before removing them.

These boras can be eaten fried like this as a savoury snack, appetizer, or as a side dish with rice and dal.

Freshwater crabs are also plentiful in Bengal during the monsoon and usually bought for lunch on a Sunday or other holiday, when one can have a leisurely meal and spend time prying the white flesh loose from the body and the claw. The

Bengali crab is never very big, the entire body being no more than 7-10 cm (3-4 in) in diameter, the claws providing added dimension. They are medium grey in colour. During the monsoon we prefer to buy a lot of females for the coral and a few males for the greater quantity of flesh in their claws. The flesh is flaky and quite soft, unlike that of crabs and lobsters from the ocean. Since we do not throw live crabs in boiling water to cook them, the fishmonger generally wrenches the claws from the body and cracks them in several places. The top shell is also removed by pounding it on a hard surface with a hammer. Before cooking, the bodies are cut into two or four pieces (according to size) and washed thoroughly, with the claws, in very hot water.

CRAB JHAL

INGREDIENTS

Crab 500 gm (1 lb)
Onions (chopped fine or ground to a paste)
Ground ginger
Chilli powder
Turmeric powder
Ground mustard
8-10 green chillies
Mustard oil
Salt to taste

METHOD

Dust the crabs with salt and turmeric and fry in hot oil first. The pieces of the body are put in so that the unshelled portions face downwards. This will help congeal the coral. A couple of minutes after putting in the bodies, the claws and legs are added and fried until they are bright red in colour. Then they are removed and set aside. The onions are then browned in the same oil, all the ground and powdered spices put in and the crabs returned to the pan. They are stirred over high heat for six to eight minutes, then salt and green chillies are added with enough water to cover the crabs. The pan is covered and the crabs are cooked over a medium heat until they are done. Finally, the dish is finished over a high flame so that all the moisture evaporates and the spicy gravy coats the crabs. Ideally the spices should penetrate the cracks in the claws and flavour the flesh inside. This is usually served with plain boiled rice. Garom mashla can sometimes be substituted for the ground mustard for variety.

All this bounty from the rivers can make it easy to forget, especially in the safety of a daily urban existence, just how threatening the rivers can be during Barsha. But the same laughing waters that ensure the livelihood of numerous fishermen and are a source of the piscine variety which is the mainstay of Bengali cuisine, can become a ruthless, destructive force, demonic in its mirth as it sweeps away everything in its path. Once, in Bangladesh, at the end of Shraban, I was confronted with the full potency and terror of the rolling, raging waters. The rains had been fierce and unremitting and there were reports of floods from the southern districts. We, however, were going north, taking the ferry at Aricha where the rivers Jamuna and Padma meet. By the time the ferry appeared and all the waiting vehicles had got on, the August sky had darkened ominously, a gale-like wind had begun to tousle the surface of the river and the junction of the rivers seemed as wide and turbulent as the sea.

As we made our way, the storm intensified and the huge ferry rocked like the frailest of banana boats. Like the medieval heroine Behula who had placed her husband's corpse on a raft made of banana tree trunks and journeyed down the rivers to placate a vengeful goddess, I too felt I needed all the faith I could muster to reach my destination. Perversely, I got out of the jeep and stood on the deck of the ferry, wrapped in a flimsy sheet of plastic. Under my feet I was aware of the engines vibrating hard and fast, while the sheet of rain enveloped me, rent from time to time by furious streaks of lightning. Echoing through my panic, I could hear one of East Bengal's famous folksongs about a boatman and a merchant who carrying valuable merchandise in a leaking boat got caught in a storm. Reproachfully, the merchant laments that had he known how damaged his friend's boat was, he would never have entrusted himself and his goods to it. For now the heartless river was speaking in many tongues, each spelling doom, and all that could be seen in front was the dancing golden girl who played with the bolts of lightning.

Bhadra, mid-August to mid-September, the last month of the monsoon, is by traditional reckoning part of early autumn or Sharat. Tagore depicted Bhadra as hovering between a dense, brooding melancholy and tumultuous outbursts before disappearing in a haze of sultry heat, but the reality is more an all-pervading humidity. Still the rains continue, sometimes inexorable, sometimes intermittent, sometimes violent. No chanted incantation about lime leaves and karamcha berries has any effect on the dreaded moisture falling, falling, falling. By now everyone is exhausted by the monsoon that was once so eagerly awaited. Even the poets give up. For them, Bhadra arouses only images of melancholy and despair. Radha, as depicted by the sixteenth-century poet Vidyapati, bemoans the emptiness of her world in Bhadra for Krishna has gone forever.

Everything is either coated with mildew or soggy with moisture and the few hours of sunshine here and there are utilized to air sheets, clothes and bedding. Even the bazaars are no longer much joy as customers jostle each other on wet, muddy floors and try to pick out vegetables that are not rotten or riddled with worms and fungus. Job Charnock, the intrepid British trader who is credited with founding Calcutta, had his first experience of the place in Bhadra. He arrived by boat on 24 August 1690 and the entry in his diary describes the monotonous dripping rain, the grey gloom and the men falling sick with tropical fever and dysentery.

In the villages, where the huts have holes in the roofs, the interiors invariably have a dank smell. During the day the leech lies in the watery fields, while after dark the persistent attentions of the mosquito cause epidemics of malaria. Sometimes the monotonous rain is transmuted into cyclonic storms and for days on end the wind will howl and moan through the groves of bamboo, flattening them to the ground. The peasants in their thatched huts and the fishermen in their paltry boats are left vulnerable and isolated.

From being the provider the river now becomes the pitiless destroyer. Most of the major rivers overflow their banks, the spate sometimes so violent that the banks crumble, while the angry torrent reaches to swallow the nearest village. Even the most sceptical urban dweller uneasily tries to remember which day of the week each bout of rain sets in, for folklore has it that rain beginning on a Tuesday or Saturday will not let up for an entire week. As radio and television issue repeated warnings, people's minds echo with the names of the swelling rivers: Ajoy, Mundeshwari, Kolaghai, Ganga, Padma, Jamuna, Meghna, Dhaleshwari, Madhumati, Arial Khan . . . rivers rising, swelling and threatening. The Padma in Bangladesh has the unenviable soubriquet of Kirtinasha, destroyer of deeds, because of the numerous times she has changed course and obliterated lives and achievements of human beings. Later, of course, this same wayward force will throw up a new shoal of land in the middle of the water—land that is soft, alluvial, rich with fertile silt, land that will bear gold, land for which man will not stop at murder.

Like the heat of the summer, the damp and humidity of the monsoon also take their toll on the system. Indigestion and diarrhoea are common as are colds and fever. Cups of hot, sweet tea are much in demand. At the slightest hint of a sniffling nose or sore throat and cough, the Bengali will demand tea, sometimes with the juice of ginger added as a remedy for colds. Like all popular remedies for illness, the cup of tea has become the pivot around which a whole series of images about the lazy Bengali babu has evolved. Since the drink is a direct result of our colonial experience, it is not surprising that many of the images come from stories about the British boss putting up with the inadequacy of his tea-loving clerk. The fellow is never found when needed; he has always just stepped out for tea. He never has time for work; he's too busy sneezing and coughing. And when there is a particular rush of jobs to be done, he's sure to have disappeared for the day, ostensibly laid up in bed with a fever, but actually enjoying the cosiest of *addas* in his favourite teashop.

The adda is not a food but one of the great Bengali institutions. The nearest definition would be a regular gathering of friends or cronies, where everything under the sun is discussed threadbare. And no adda, at home or in the teashop, can be complete without tea, even in the height of summer. The Bengali teashop is usually an unpretentious place. In the villages or poorer urban neighbourhoods it may be nothing more than a tarpaulin or piece of bamboo matting stretched over four posts. Under this rude shelter will be a table, a couple of rickety benches and a portable stove with the kettle permanently on. The more respectable places will be like small one-room restaurants where groups of men will spend hours smoking and drinking cups of tea. The occasional loner will also be there, absorbed in his newspaper, and no one will hurry him over his tea and perusal. One of my favourite teashops, on the pavement running along a major thoroughfare in south Calcutta, is more a stall than a shop. The two portable stoves are almost next to the kerb and the small counter with shelves below has trolley-like wheels so that the owner can take it back home with him at night. Beyond this there is only provision for shelter over the owner's head and over the two stoves behind him, and two stools for the customers. But the lack of seating comfort means nothing and the steady crowd grows from afternoon onwards, the customers standing thickly around this makeshift contraption or sitting on the steps of nearby houses, each enjoying small glasses of this man's special beverage—lemon tea with sugar and a pinch of *bitnoon*, a dark, pungent salt.

Sometimes, during Bhadra's oppressive rains, tea is all that you want and the loss of appetite is such that even hilsa loses its charm. This is when various chutneys are made frequently, as much for taste as for therapy. Coconut, posto and mint leaves, ground with green chillies, tamarind, salt, sugar and fresh mustard oil, are used for fresh-tasting raw chutneys. The karamcha and the juicy kamranga or star fruit are cooked with roasted, powdered panch phoron and a couple of dry red chillies, yielding their tartness into a thin sauce. One of the most delicious chutneys, served to the family as also to guests at weddings, parties and funerals, is made with pineapple, which is a monsoon fruit in Bengal.

PINEAPPLE CHUTNEY

FOR FOUR PEOPLE

INGREDIENTS

1 nice ripe pineapple
250 gm (8 oz) of sugar

Half a coconut
2½ tablespoons of ghee
3 sticks of cinnamon
3 cloves
8-10 whole cardamoms
60 gm (2 oz) of raisins
1 l (1¾ pints) of water
1 teaspoon of flour
1 teaspoon of salt

METHOD

Among the many recipes for pineapple chutney, I particularly like this one. We take a nice ripe pineapple and peel and cut it into tiny cubes. The important thing is to throw out the hard central portion and to gouge out the eyes with a sharp knife. Half a coconut is grated. In a medium-sized aluminum karai ghee is heated and garom mashla consisting of cinnamon, cloves and whole cardamoms are thrown in. (Some people grind the garom mashla coarsely before using it.) When the fragrance is released, the cubed pineapple, raisins and salt are added. These are stirred over a medium heat for four to five minutes before the water is added. A lot of water is needed to cook the pineapple and to leave some for the gravy. When the pineapple is tender to the point of being almost shredded, the coconut is added along with sugar. The chutney is then cooked over a high heat for about five minutes. The salt and sugar are tested (more salt will probably be needed at this stage) and a teaspoon of flour blended with a little water is mixed into the chutney to give it a smooth gravy. After a couple of minutes the chutney is removed from the stove. It is either chilled or served at room temperature, never hot. Bengalis do not eat chutney as a relish with other items of food. It is eaten at the end of a meal, sometimes with papor on the side, before dessert.

To relieve the aches and pains of monsoon flu, and prevent the monsoon sniffles, many traditional housewives, especially among the Bangals, swear by a concoction made with *kalo jeera* or nigella seeds. Folk wisdom endows these little black seeds with miraculous qualities, from repelling moths in silk and woollen clothes to curing all kinds of digestive and bronchial ailments. This particular preparation, a little round pulp of spicy-hot relish, is also delicious with rice.

KALO JEERA BHARTA

FOR THREE PEOPLE

INGREDIENTS

1 teaspoon of kalo jeera
A little ghee
1 or 2 whole green chillies
Mustard oil
Salt to taste

METHOD

To make kalo jeera bharta, a teaspoon of *kalo jeera* is toasted on a flat pan or tawa. Then an entire head of garlic is taken, all the cloves peeled, rinsed and crushed roughly on the grinding stone. The garlic is then fried in a little ghee, together with green chillies. Afterwards, the garlic, chillies and roasted kalo jeera are all ground together into a paste and fresh mustard oil and salt added. The relish is divided up between two or three people to be eaten with hot rice as a starter.

Despite the rain, gloom, debility of disease and threat of

flood, the irrepressible Bengali spirit manages to find some occasion for joy and festivity in Bhadra. Even the heaviest rain acquires a benign significance on Janmashtomi, early in the month, because the birth of Krishna in prison on that date took place on a night of pouring rain, and ever since it is believed that it will inevitably rain on Janmashtomi. I grew up listening to my grandmother telling me the thrilling tale of Krishna's father Vasudeb smuggling his infant son out of prison. The world outside was full of water, below and above. But Vasudeb struggled on, miraculously sheltered by the thousand-hooded king of serpents, Vasuki, and reached Gokul where he left the baby in the keeping of a childless dairy farmer, Nanda, and his wife, Jashoda. Had Krishna's whereabouts been discovered, he would have been killed by his Herod-like uncle Kangsa, who had been forewarned of death at the hands of a nephew.

For the devout Hindu, particularly the Vaishnavs, Janmashtomi is a day of total fasting. In the old days affluent households would organize nonstop singing of devotional songs for eight or twenty-four hours. As if to compensate for the rigours of such a day, custom decrees that one of the most glorious offerings of nature, the ripe palm or *taal*, should be eaten after Janmashtomi. The ripe taal cannot be eaten directly because of its fibrous content and the bitter element in its pulp. Once peeled, therefore, the fibrous sections of the fruit are rubbed against a woven surface to extract the thick saffron pulp and juice. It has a very strong, almost intoxicating aroma which fills the house and alerts the neighbours as well as the flies. The extract is then loosely tied up in a cloth and left hanging for as long as five or six hours, until the bitter juices have dribbled out.

The pulp is too cloyingly rich to eat by itself, so Bengalis have devised two methods to deal with it. One is to cook it slowly with milk and grated coconut to make a creamy kheer, one of the classics of East Bengal. The other, familiar to me from my own West Bengal childhood, is to mix it with both rice flour and wheat flour, as well as a bit of grated coconut, and fry it in the form of little round boras. There are no near equivalents for the extraordinary taste and flavour of taal pulp. Its full-bodied fruitiness resembles that of the mango, but has an extra honeyed quality which can make it oppressive if you absorb it for too long. But those lovely crunchy boras, brown on the outside and saffron inside, did not linger long enough to oppress anyone. I could well understand why a popular Vaishnav song visualized Nanda, the dairy farmer and Krishna's adoptive father, dancing gleefully as he consumed his taal boras.

For the last few days of Bhadra the sun tends to blaze in the sky and the earth gives up its moisture. The only clouds visible are the white and fleecy ones of autumn. The last Hindu festival of the season, appropriately, takes place on the sankranti, or last day of Bhadra when Bishwakarma, patron deity of artisans, skilled labourers, mechanics and all those who live by their hands, is worshipped in Bengal. His name literally means the maker of the world, and all factories, presses and artisans' workshops remain closed in his honour, no matter how much the babu or the factory-owner may grumble. The women of the artisan communities observe Bishwakarma's day as *arandhan* (without cooking). No fires are lit in their kitchens. Instead, all the festive foods are prepared the day before in a fever of activity. And no matter how meagre their means, each family will buy and cook a hilsa, whose taste and quality is the subject of much discussion over the following days.

For children, Bishwakarma puja means kite-flying, the traditional expression of the conviction that the monsoon has really withdrawn. For real enthusiasts, this is no less serious than worshipping the god. Yards and yards of string are painstakingly coated with lethal powdered glass before being rolled on to double-handled spools. Once the kites are up, honour demands the hounding of all rivals, locking threads with them and trying to dislodge them with the superior abrasion of your thread. Victory, when it comes, is greeted with the resounding cry of '*Bho-katta!*' By the afternoon of the sankranti the multicoloured kites chase the clouds and each other with all the fresh enthusiasm of liberated energy.

early and late autumn

An old Bengali proverb says that if the *kash* has started flowering, you know the rains are over and the autumn has begun. More than spring, it is this season, compounded of early autumn or Sharat and late autumn or Hemanta, that is a time of unalloyed hope. One more monsoon has been lived through. One more harvest awaits the grower of rice. In the countryside the white, broom-like kash flowers grow beside the ponds and rivers mirroring blue skies with fleecy white clouds.

The humid lushness of monsoon is slowly replaced with a gradual evaporation of moisture and the overwhelming, almost dank greenness of the landscape is transformed to a mixture of green, gold and brown. The *ata*, a fruit available specifically during this short and delightful season, symbolizes the qualities of the Bengali autumn in appearance and flavour. Its hard, knobbly, green and black exterior is a surprising contrast to the fragrant creaminess of its flesh wherein nestle glossy black seeds. So tasty is the flesh that Bengalis do not mind the bother of having to spit out seeds after every mouthful.

While the fields gleam with the ripened rice crop, in the cities there is the splendour of the festive autumnal rites to come. The *kumors*, or potters, build the life-sized straw-and-clay images of the goddesses Durga, Lakshmi and Kali, toiling to make each more brilliant in colour, each more vibrant with life. For the hour of the goddesses is now at hand and Bengal awaits them expectantly. Stepping daintily on rose-tinted feet, they come, one by one, to be worshipped in a blaze of light and sound and colour.

First comes Durga, goddess of deliverance, on the seventh day after the autumn new moon. Daughter of Himalaya, Lord of the Mountains and of his wife Menaka, she is depicted by the kumors as a resplendent golden figure standing on a lion's back, each of her ten arms bearing a particular weapon as she triumphs over the demon Mahishasura, thus delivering all creation from the dark forces of evil tyranny. Not content with picturing her as a shining figure of deliverance, the folk imagination of Bengal has woven a touching story around her. Married to Shiva, the ascetic deity, Durga has a hard and comfortless life with her husband and four children in the far-flung mountain kingdom of Kailash. Just once a year, in the autumnal month of Ashwin, she comes home to her parents, together with her children, and enjoys all the love and attention lavished on her. Unfortunately this visit lasts only three days. On the fourth, the sadness of separation overwhelms everyone.

Thus the potent mother goddess was transformed into the archetypal daughter, married off as a young girl to a bridegroom who lived such a distance away that frequent visits were impossible. The parallel between daughter and goddess still holds today. Some of the tenderest Bengali songs are the *agamani*, heralding the arrival of the daughter-goddess, and some of the most poignant are the ones sung on the day of her departure.

Between these days, the goddess lives in her mortal shell created so lovingly by the kumors, and benignly accepts the homage and worship of her people, promising in return the fulfilment of desire, long life, good health and deliverance from trouble. In feudal rural Bengal and in nineteenth-century Calcutta, Durga puja was usually performed with great pomp and splendour in the houses of the big landlords or wealthy babus. Today, such private ceremonies are rare. Instead, neighbourhoods raise money, buy the images of Durga and her children, complete with lion and demon, and install them in canopied enclosures called pandals. A priest is hired for the entire festival and he conducts all the rituals as set down in the holy texts.

But the festival still brings with it feverish excitement. New clothes are bought, the streets leading to the pandals blaze with decorative lights and loudspeakers start blaring popular songs. On the eve of the first day, the images are consecrated in a special ceremony, *bodhan*, that infuses life into the clay. The following morning, Saptami, we would bathe and troop out to visit the nearest pandals. Each image would be subjected to careful scrutiny and there would be much discussion on the artistic merits of each sculptured form, the ferocity of the demon, the expression on the goddess's face, her clothes and decorative jewellery. The stance and form of the various attendant animals—the peacock, the rat, the white owl and the white swan—often provoked humour and admiration.

Ashtami, the second day of Durga's visit, is the most important day of the festival. In the morning everyone is supposed to fast, bathe and go over to the nearest place of worship where the priest chants special prayers to the goddess and the devotees repeat them while holding a small offering of flowers and leaves that have to be thrown at the feet of the goddess. The entire ritual is repeated three times before you are free to go home and break your fast.

Even those who are short on observance during the year tend to obey the vegetarian restrictions of Ashtami. Not that these mean austerity. For lunch we would have khichuri and at dinner, after a whole afternoon and evening of tramping around the city, visiting the goddesses in their pandals, there would be round golden luchis, puffed up like balloons. The evocation of Ashtami with the drums beating and the bell ringing for the evening ritual of arati performed before the goddess by the priest, has a special association in many Bengali minds with luchis and various tasty vegetarian dishes.

Luchis are a kind of fried bread specially loved in Bengal even though we are primarily rice eaters. In northern India a similar bread is known by the name of *puri*. The main difference between the luchi and the puri is that the former is made out of the finest white flour while puris are made with coarser flour which retains a portion of the husk from the wheat. In appearance a luchi is a round golden disk, 12.5-15 cm (5-6 in) in diameter, and puffed up like a balloon with hot air. The flour is mixed with water and some ghee and kneaded thoroughly before being separated into small portions which are rolled out into flat disks for frying. However, if a lot of oil or ghee is added to the dough while kneading, the luchi also absorbs a lot of oil in the course of frying. It becomes flaky instead of puffy and is known as a *khasta luchi*. These are much too rich to eat on a regular basis. There are many variations in the size of luchis. Some people like making tiny ones, 7.5 cm (3 in) in diameter. In our home we prefer them slightly bigger, about 12.5 cm (5 in). Small or large, they need to be served as soon as possible after being made. The ideal way is to have a supply of hot ones coming from the kitchen as you eat, although that means a rough deal for the cook. The frying pan is no substitute for the karai, for luchis have to be deep-fried. A Chinese wok might do, although being more shallow than the karai, it will need more oil to start with. As the oil lessens with the frying, the cook adds more. But it must always be heated well before the next luchi is put in.

LUCHIS

FOR SIX PEOPLE

INGREDIENTS

500 gm (1 lb) of flour
2½ teaspoons of ghee or peanut oil
300 ml (10 fl oz) of water.
1 teaspoon of salt

METHOD

I usually take 500 gm (1 lb) of flour, which makes five or

six luchis for each person. For big eaters you need more. I put the flour on a large tray or platter, preferably with raised sides, add salt and ghee or peanut oil and mix them well. (You can make sure that the oil is sufficient by taking a handful of the flour and pressing it tightly in your fist. If the flour adheres in a lump, the oil is right; if it falls apart, mix in just a little more oil.) After the oil has been well mixed in, the flour has to be kneaded into a dough with water. I generally start with 300 ml (10 fl oz) of water, which I keep adding slowly to the flour as I gather it in from all sides of the tray to make one lump. If you find you still need a little more water, then carefully sprinkle some over the dough. Too much will ruin the dough, making it too thin. Once the flour has become a neat lump, the hard work of kneading starts. The more you do this, the better the quality of dough and the puffier the luchi. Usually ten to twelve minutes of forceful kneading with both palms, pressing down with the base of the palm, is good enough. At the end, the dough should feel elastic when pulled apart. It is then divided into the little round portions called *nechis.* Each one is smoothed over between the palms and pressed to flatten it, then rolled out on the board as thin as possible to make a 12.5 cm (5 in) luchi. The traditional way is to dip the nechi into a bowl of oil and then roll it out so that it does not stick to the rolling board. However, the oily surface can be slippery, and the easier way out is to dust each nechi very lightly with flour before rolling. A perfect circle is hard to achieve, but this is the ideal. As I roll the luchis out, I keep them side by side on a large dry platter or sheet of newspaper spread on the kitchen counter. It is best not to let them overlap too much because they might start sticking to each other. Once seven or eight have been rolled out, I put the karai on the stove, heat 120 ml (4 fl oz) of peanut oil in it and start frying. To do this well, hold one side of a luchi, lower it gently into the oil—still holding it—and set it afloat like a paper boat. This way you avoid a splash and prevent the thin disk of flour from crumpling up. As it puffs up like a balloon, turn it over with a spatula, fry for a minute more and gently lift it up along the side to drain off all excess oil. A good luchi should not be too brown, but creamy-beige in colour. I keep rolling the rest of the nechis in between bouts of frying. Hot luchis should never be covered, or they will go limp.

Though you can eat luchis with almost anything, even by themselves, on the evening of Ashtami they would always be served with two classic vegetarian dishes associated with ceremonial occasions: a potato dish called *alur dam* and a dal made with yellow split peas and tiny pieces of coconut. There are many variations of the alur dam, but usually on Ashtami this light version, flavoured with a pinch of asafoetida, used to be made in our house. A *dam* usually means something cooked covered for a long time over a low heat. However, potatoes do not have to be cooked for a very long time. Alur dam has, in Bengali, come to mean a dish of potatoes, usually whole or quartered, coated in a thick spicy sauce. It is usually eaten with luchis or wheat-flour chapatis, not rice.

ALUR DAM

FOR FOUR TO FIVE PEOPLE

INGREDIENTS

500 gm (1 lb) potatoes
3-4 dry red chillies
3-4 teaspoons of whole cumin seeds
3-4 teaspoons each of cumin and chilli powder
1½ teaspoons of tamarind

3 tablespoons of mustard oil
2-3 bay leaves
1 teaspoon of panch phoron
A tiny pinch of asafoetida
¼ teaspoon of turmeric powder
400 ml (13 fl oz) of water
Salt to taste

METHOD

To make alur dam, boil and peel the potatoes—in that order—and quarter them. Take dry red chillies and whole cumin seeds. Toast them in a dry frying pan over a medium flame until the chillies are dark brown. Remove and grind them as fine as you can in a pestle or on a grinding stone. (If, however, this seems too much trouble, take 3-4 teaspoons each of cumin and chilli powder and roast them together in a frying pan. The taste and flavour will be pretty good, though not as good as that of freshly ground spices.) Next, take tamarind extract and mix it smoothly in a bowl with 60 ml (2 fl oz) of hot water. Set aside. Heat mustard oil in a karai and throw in bay leaves, panch phoron and a tiny pinch of asafoetida crumbled between your fingers. As the panch phoron stops sputtering, put in the potatoes and sprinkle the turmeric powder over them. Stir repeatedly until they turn golden brown and pour in the water. Once it comes to the boil, reduce the heat to medium and simmer for four to five minutes. Then add salt to taste, 2 teaspoons of the roasted spices and the tamarind paste. Stir thoroughly for another three to four minutes and taste to find your balance of salt and sour. You can add more or less of the roasted powder depending on your tolerance for hot food. If the gravy becomes too thick, or too sour, more water can be added.

The dal that was served together with this was a little more laborious. In the days before the pressure cooker it was a pain to cook, for these yellow split peas could take more than half a day to get done, but now most middle-class families, even those with working women, can easily serve this kind of dal by cooking it in the pressure cooker.

CHHOLAR DAL

FOR FOUR PEOPLE

INGREDIENTS

250 gm (½ lb) of yellow split peas
3 bay leaves
3 whole red chillies
One half of a whole coconut
2 tablespoons of sizzling mustard oil
1½ teaspoons of whole cumin seeds
½ teaspoon of ginger paste
½ teaspoon of ground chilli
1 teaspoon each of fresh ground cumin and coriander
400 ml (13 fl oz) of water
3 teaspoons of sugar
1 tablespoon of ghee
2 teaspoons of ground garom mashla
Salt to taste

METHOD

For chholar dal to feed four people, my mother would weigh out the yellow split peas and cook them in the pressure cooker with double the amount of water, bay leaves and whole red chillies. She left the cooker for about fifteen to twenty minutes on a high flame. By then the cooked dal would be of a thickish consistency and the individual grains would be soft but unbroken. This she would empty out in a bowl and set aside. Then she would take one half of a whole coconut and pry out half the flesh from the shell. The brown skin at the back would be painstakingly peeled with a sharp knife. If you find this too hard, you can try soaking the coconut for ten minutes in a bowl of hot water. Once peeled, the coconut would be chopped into tiny pieces and fried in the sizzling mustard oil in a large karai until they turned pink. She would add whole cumin seeds to the coconut and fry them for a couple of minutes before adding ginger paste, ground chilli, fresh ground cumin and coriander and salt to taste. Once all this had been fried for two to three minutes, she would pour the dal into the karai. (On bad days when there were no freshly ground spices and she had to fall back on powdered spices, she would pour in the dal after frying the coconut and the whole cumin, adding the other spices later.) The dal would be checked for salt, water added, and the whole mixture assiduously stirred until the grains were mashed. Some sugar would be added; this is a dal in which the sweetness should be a little pronounced. Just before removing the dal from the fire, she would add ghee and ground garom mashla.

To finish off the Ashtami dinner, there was usually the simplest of desserts, kheer, of which we never tired. This was milk, evaporated slowly over a low flame. Though it must originally have started as a measure to preserve and utilize excess milk in the days before refrigeration, kheer remains a great favourite in Bengali households. When made as a chosen dessert, 1 l (1¾ pints) of milk, reduced to about 600 ml (1 pint), was considered to be of the right consistency. Once that was done, sugar, the amount varying according to the cook's preference, would be added and the pan removed from the stove and left to cool. Sometimes tangerines from the rare first crop, an expensive treat, would be peeled and the inner pulp from the segments stirred into the cool kheer. If it is added before the kheer has cooled, the acid in the tangerine can cut the milk and destroy the thick, creamy texture of the kheer. Mop this up with luchis or eat in sensuous spoonfuls, and you will come very close to absolute bliss.

Navami, the last day of Durga's stay, is gastronomically the opposite of Ashtami; meat-eating is the order of the day. This practice dates from the time-honoured custom of offering live sacrifices of goats and buffaloes to the goddess and eating the holy sacrificial meat the same day. The priest who killed the animals had to be a strong man, for ritual demanded the severance of head and body at one blow. Failure on the part of the priest was looked upon as an ominous sign that the goddess was displeased and had refused to accept the sacrifice. The meat would then be cooked following special recipes without any onion or garlic, which were regarded by the Hindus as heathen spices.

The huge courtyards in the houses of the wealthy where the sacrifice was made must have been a gory sight. If goats were the offering, as was most often the case, several would be slaughtered one after the other and the entire courtyard would reek of blood while heads rolled around. There are gruesome stories of nineteenth-century Calcutta where young men would hold wrestling matches on the bloody courtyards in the afternoon. Each time they fell, they would be covered with holy blood and slime until they all looked like the figures in a nightmare. Finally, as the evening fell, these bloody apparitions would set out with torches and march triumphantly through the neighbouring streets.

Today, no community puja will organize the sacrifice of animals and the meat eaten on Navami is, except in a very few houses, bought from the markets as on any other day. For those who do not wish to sacrifice animals, vegetables like pumpkins, gourds and coconuts are used as substitutes. This is probably due to the influence of the Vaishnavs who abhor violence. It must also be linked to the increasing economic difficulties of buying sacrificial animals. As a result, the terrifying and trauma-ridden ceremony of sacrifice has been almost reduced to comedy where the earnest priest has to decorate the sacrificial pumpkin with the obligatory vermilion, turmeric and oil and split it with one blow of the knife. The one thing that remains from the old days is Navami meat, often cooked without onion or garlic. In our house, my parents did not avoid those spices. But my grandmother, before she was widowed, always cooked her meat without these heathen ingredients. Instead of the heavy, almost oppressive aroma of those alliums, her cooking filled the house with a delicate flavour of cumin and coriander. After all these years and the taste of so many meat preparations, I can still recall the taste of the Navami meat of my childhood with nostalgia. On rare occasions, my mother, whose nostalgia is even stronger, still cooks meat her mother's way. When trying this recipe, you might need to add more water or cook the meat longer, depending on its quality.

MEAT WITHOUT ONION AND GARLIC

INGREDIENTS

500 gm (1 lb) meat

60 gm (2 oz) of yoghurt

3 teaspoons of turmeric

1 tablespoon + 2 teaspoons of mustard oil

*Garom mashla, consisting of 2 cardamoms, 4 cloves and 2 pieces
    of cinnamon, 2.5 cm (1 in) long, ground with water*

6 teaspoons each of freshly ground cumin and coriander

4 teaspoons of ground ginger

4 teaspoons of ground mustard

2 teaspoons (you can use less) of ground red chillies
4-5 teaspoons of ground posto
60 ml (2 fl oz) of oil
3-4 bay leaves
500 ml (16 fl oz) of hot water
Salt to taste

METHOD

We have always called this dish *Didar mangshor jhol* or
grandmother's meat without onion and garlic. At home it
would be made with goat meat, but lamb can be easily
substituted. The front leg or lamb chops can provide suitable
meat. My mother takes the meat and cuts it into small cubes,
rinses it in cold water and mixes it with yoghurt, turmeric,
a little salt and 1 tablespoon of mustard oil. This marinaded
meat is left covered in room temperature for an hour.
Meanwhile, she organizes her spices: garom mashla
(cardamom, cloves, cinnamon) ground with water, freshly
ground cumin and coriander, ground ginger, ground
mustard and ground red chillies. Some days I have seen her
add 4-5 teaspoons of ground posto as well. Once the meat
is marinaded, she heats the oil in a thick-bottomed pan and
throws in the bay leaves. As they turn brown, she adds the
meat with its marinade. This is stirred for three to four
minutes, covered and left on a medium flame. Within five
to six minutes a lot of moisture is generated and she adds
all the ground spices except the garom mashla. Then the
meat is stirred vigorously until all the moisture evaporates
and it almost starts sticking to the bottom of the pan. Often
good meat can become quite tender by this time. She then
adds hot water for the gravy, and leaves the meat on the
stove until it is absolutely tender. Finally, she heats 2
teaspoons of oil in a small saucepan and blends the garom

> mashla in it. This is added to the meat, the pot left tightly
> covered until mealtime so that none of the fragrance escapes.
> Sometimes this is served with luchis, at other times with
> rice.

Though I have never seen animals being sacrificed to the
goddess, I have witnessed a religious festival where sacrificial
blood and meat are pivotal elements. This is the great Muslim
festival of Id-uz-zoha or Bakr-id, observed in commemoration
of the prophet Abraham's willingness to sacrifice his son in
devotion to the Lord. Cows and khashis, castrated goats, are
fattened before being brought to the market and bought by the
devout according to their means. Cows being expensive, it is
only the wealthy who can afford to offer one. Sometimes several
families pool their resources to buy one.

The first time I witnessed the ceremony in Dhaka, Bakr-id
happened to fall in the winter and by the end of the day I was
very glad it was cold. We happened to live in an affluent
residential area and almost every family around us offered
animals for sacrifice. By mid-afternoon, the stream of blood
from our wealthy landlord's offering of one cow and two khashis
had almost covered the front entrance. Hordes of beggars were
besieging every gate because Islam demands that you donate a
portion of your sacrificial meat or *korbani* to them.

Since the amount of korbani left, even after distribution, is
too much to consume at one time, Bengali Muslims have devised
a way of cooking the extra meat, especially beef, with onion,
garlic, ginger, salt, bay leaf and oil. When the meat is half-
cooked, some garom mashla is added. Heated once every day
in the summer and on alternate days in the winter, this meat
keeps quite well for a month. Towards the end, the repeated
heating tends to make some of the meat flaky. But the unique
taste, produced by the very slow cooking, proves that making

a virtue of necessity is not as bad as it sounds.

The three days of Durga puja are over only too soon and the last day, Bijoya Dashami, the tenth of the new moon, finds everyone preparing to say farewell to the goddess and her children. The daughter has to leave her indulgent home and go back to the reality of life with her ascetic husband. The married women of each neighbourhood go to the pandals to offer sindur. They smear it on the forehead of the goddess and her feet and then on each other's foreheads and partings to protect themselves from the misfortune of widowhood.

I once happened to have lunch on this day with a very traditional East Bengali family and they served an ambal made with *shapla*, the stalks of water lilies, a dish that I have never seen elsewhere. The elderly mother told me that in the old days this would be offered to the goddess together with fermented rice soaked overnight in water. Both these items, inexpensive and easily available in any rural household, were primarily eaten by women who not only enjoyed their tangy flavour, but also ate them to save more of the 'important' items like fresh rice, fish or meat or milk for the men. The fact that the goddess is offered such humble items along with expensive fruits, milk-based sweets and sacrificial meat is an indication of how much the women of Bengal have identified themselves with her. The distance between deity and devotee disappears in the closeness between mother and daughter, in the bond between woman and woman.

On the evening of Bijoya Dashami, the images in the community pandals are loaded on to trucks and taken to the nearest river, the Hooghly in Calcutta, for the final rite of *bhashan*, throwing them into the water. It is then, in the wake of the departed goddess, that the most beautiful aspect of Bijoya Dashami comes—the discarding of all ill-feelings of hostility, anger and envy. Within the family, younger people touch their elders' feet in *pronam* and receive their blessings, while contemporaries embrace each other with good wishes. As the evening deepens, relatives, friends and neighbours drop in to convey their Bijoya greetings. They must be offered sweets, which cannot be refused—I have even seen diabetics put fragments into their mouths to honour the custom. And so the visits go on until the day of the full moon, the visitors bringing along more sweets to add to the household stock. The commonest sweet is the sandesh, because it is dry and easy to carry. But there is nothing to stop you from bringing an earthen pot of rosogollas swimming in syrup, or even variations like rajbhog or pantua. None of these are made at home, for most people do not wish to rival the moira, the professional sweet-maker.

Some years, when my mother happened to be in the mood, she would spend part of her Bijoya afternoon making two home-made sweets which were a refreshing change from the cloying commercial products that would flood our house at that time. One of them was the *patishapta*, a delicious Bengali variant of sweet, stuffed crêpes. With a bit of practice, it becomes one of the easiest of desserts.

PATISHAPTA

FOR FOUR TO SIX PEOPLE

INGREDIENTS

½ of a good large coconut

250 gm (8 oz) of brown sugar, gur or white sugar

2 whole cardamoms

250 gm (½ lb) of flour

2 tablespoons of peanut oil or ghee

250 ml (8 fl oz) of water

2 tablespoons of sugar

METHOD

First she would make the filling. She would grind the flesh
extracted from one half of a good large coconut on a special
coconut grinder and mix it with brown sugar, gur, or if that
was not at hand, white sugar. The mixture would be cooked
in a karai over a medium flame. Usually a separate karai is
used for sweet preparations, so that none of the strong
lingering smells of spices can invade the delicate flavour of
sweets and milk. After ten to twelve minutes of constant
stirring, the sugar and the coconut would be evenly blended
and a lovely caramelized smell would fill the air. Sometimes
she would need to add more sugar, and if it was white, she
would also grind cardamoms and add them to the coconut
mixture at this stage. As soon as it was cool enough to
touch, she would divide it into twelve to thirteen portions,
shaping each into a roll about 10 cm (4 in) long. These
would be covered and set aside.

To make the crêpes, she would take flour and mix it
thoroughly with peanut oil or ghee. If they were not to be
eaten immediately, she would use a mixture of flour and
cream of wheat to keep the crêpes soft. Then she would
add water and sugar and mix it carefully to form a liquid
thick enough to roll over the surface of a tilted frying pan.
When she was satisfied with the consistency, she would
take the medium-sized frying pan, heat it slightly and grease
it carefully with peanut oil. In Bengal the usual way to do
this is by taking the discarded stem of a brinjal and rubbing
the pan with the flat end that is attached to the brinjal. The
important thing is not to add too much oil. The pan would
then be put over a medium flame, a large serving spoon or
a cooking ladle full of the liquid poured in, and the pan
tilted to spread the liquid evenly. As soon as the batter started
cooking into a golden skin, she would wedge a spatula under

the surface to loosen it from the pan. Then she would take one of the coconut rolls, place it close to one edge of the crêpe and roll the two together up like a stuffed mat. Pressing down on the patishapta gently with her spatula, she would flip it over until both sides were brown, remove it from the pan and start on the next crêpe, greasing the pan carefully. When this was being served as a dessert for special guests, my mother would go one step further. She would evaporate some milk to make a thick kheer. Some chopped almonds would be cooked in this kheer and a flavouring of ground cardamom would be added. Then it would be poured over the waiting patishaptas, much as chocolate sauce is poured over desserts in the West.

The other home-made sweet that appeared on Bijoya Dashami, this one primarily for my benefit, was the *malpo*, flat, round fennel-seed dumplings in syrup. This is quite simple to make and appears often in our house.

MALPO

FOR FOUR TO SIX PEOPLE

INGREDIENTS

250 gm (8 oz) of sugar
5 tablespoons of water
1 teaspoon of lemon juice
250 gm (8 oz) of flour
2 tablespoons of peanut oil
250 ml (8 fl oz) of whole milk
1 teaspoon of whole fennel seeds

METHOD

To make malpo, first the syrup has to be prepared. The consistency is important for if it is too thin, the malpos tend to fall apart. I find that 250 gm (8 oz) of sugar with 5 tablespoons of water and a teaspoon of lemon juice is about right. Once the syrup has boiled, my mother sets it aside. Then she mixes flour with peanut oil and when they are blended smoothly, adds whole milk and a teaspoon of whole fennel seeds. These give the malpos their distinctive taste. Then she heats oil in a karai, lowers the flame to medium and, taking large spoonfuls of the flour mixture, drops them in, one at a time. Each round malpo is fried carefully until both sides are brown and the edges curl up crisply. Nothing can be worse than half-done malpos. Once all of them are fried, she dips them in the syrup, turns them over and lays them out on a flat serving dish. Then the rest of the syrup is poured over them. These keep well without losing their taste—there is nothing like the surreptitious pleasure of quickly eating a malpo in the middle of your day's work when you are sure nobody is looking.

Durga's departure is hardly over before it is time for Lakshmi, her daughter, goddess of wealth and prosperity, to arrive. Though much removed from their past lives in the villages, urban settlers have not forgotten what they owe to this prim golden goddess. Durga might deliver you from crises and unforeseen dangers, but without Lakshmi's blessings the wherewithals of life would be sadly lacking. Women, particularly, are her devotees and daughters and wives are often referred to as the Lakshmi of the home. Their beauty, or grace, too, is attributed to her generosity. So it is that her seat is right in the centre of every Hindu home. Each family, whether rich or poor, has its own little niche where a picture or image of Lakshmi is ensconced to be worshipped by women every Thursday. Symbolically, a basket decorated with cowries, which were used as currency at one time, is kept by the image.

It is on the autumn full moon that Lakshmi is worshipped with special rites and ceremony. One popular song eulogizes the state of grace the world has achieved because of her blessings: the rivers are full of gently burbling waters that reflect the stars in the sky, the fields are full of golden grain and each household has one or more of the plump brown cows whose copious flow of milk is like a tidal wave of white flowers. Perhaps it is this association of milk with plenitude that makes payesh, or Bengali rice pudding, one of the most important offerings for Lakshmi in Bengali homes.

But in Bengal, wealth and prosperity are not easy to come by and Lakshmi demands more than rituals, offerings and compliments from her followers. The autumn full moon is called *kojagori* and thereby hangs a tale. The word is derived from the Sanskrit *ko jagarti*, meaning 'who's awake?', and legend says that on this night the goddess flies all over the earth, carried on the back of her faithful white owl, asking who is awake. Those who can fight lethargy and stay up are the beneficiaries of the goddess's good graces for the coming year. And while you stay up, you have to play dice with your spouse—the game being particularly appropriate for the occasion, for the goddess is almost as fickle in her favours as the dice. In their eagerness to hold her to their homes, Bengali women paint outlines of her little feet on their floors in a line from the front door to where the image of the goddess has been placed, as if she has just walked in and gone and sat down in her niche. Fancifully, they believe that if the footprints are only depicted going into the house, then she will be unable to leave.

Payesh, made in Lakshmi's honour is always distributed among neighbours or relatives. It is usually cooked outside the kitchen in specially sanctified surroundings. Usually a portable stove and special pots and utensils are used. Payesh is derived from the Sanskrit word *paramanno*, which means the ultimate or best kind of rice. With time, of course, the ingenious Bengali has devised many kinds of payesh that do not have any rice. But one fundamental rule remains: payesh is something that has to be cooked in milk. And there are no shortcuts to it, like using any kind of canned evaporated milk or condensed milk. For the very special taste of payesh (as of kheer) comes from the milk being very slowly reduced in volume over a low flame. Cream, which is such an important thing in the West, is hardly used in Bengal. Probably the tropical climate makes it difficult to skim the cream from the milk. And cold or chilled milk is never drunk, it is always boiled to kill the bacteria. However, when hot milk is left uncovered, a thick skin will form and that is often skimmed off to be heated over low temperatures and yield ghee. In payesh the sweetening agent is usually plain sugar except in the winter when date-palm sap is available and lends its own distinctive flavour to the milk. Brown sugar from sugarcane is never used because it tends to ruin the creamy texture of evaporated milk.

In our family the rice used for payesh is usually one of the small-grained fragrant varieties like Gobindabhog. When that is not available, Basmati is the next best option. Payesh can be served either at room temperature or chilled, but it tends to thicken as it gets colder. Personally, I find a little goes a long way since it is so rich, but some people can gobble up enormous helpings.

PAYESH

FOR SIX PEOPLE

INGREDIENTS

75 gm (2½ oz) of Basmati rice
2 teaspoons of ghee
2 l (3½ pints) of whole milk
120 gm (4 oz) of sugar

2-3 whole cardamoms

3 pieces of cinnamon 2.5 cm (1 in) long

METHOD

Rinse the rice in a colander and spread it out on a tray to dry. Mix it thoroughly with the ghee. This will prevent it from becoming sticky and forming lumps when it is being cooked in the milk. Some cooks even fry the rice in ghee, but that is needless labour. Set aside the rice. Take the whole milk in a deep, thick-bottomed pan. This, like the karai for patishapta, has to be uncontaminated by spices. Usually in Bengali homes a couple of pots are set aside for boiling the milk and to cook kheer or payesh. Bring the milk to a boil over a high heat and immediately reduce the flame to low. Now comes the painstaking part of evaporating it, stirring constantly so that it does not stick to the bottom of the pan or boil over. After about an hour, or when the milk has been reduced to about 1.5 l (2½ pints) add the rice and keep stirring until it is cooked. You need to check the grains repeatedly, otherwise the rice will become a mush. If the milk is absorbed too fast, you can add a little more. Once the rice has been cooked, start adding sugar. Pour in 120 gm (4 oz), then keep adding until you reach the sweetness to your taste. Some of my friends prefer very sweet payesh, but I find it too cloying. If you wish to add almonds and pistachios for garnishing, they will have to be soaked in a bowl of hot water to soften. Hard nuts are not acceptable in Bengali food. Peel and chop the soaked nuts before you start on the payesh. Throw them in at the end and cook for a couple of minutes. You can also add a heaped tablespoon of raisins to this. Finally, grind the whole cardamoms and add for flavouring before removing from the heat. If you do not like cardamoms you can add a little keora water once the payesh has cooled. Or you can put the pieces of cinnamon into the milk as it evaporates. Make sure to throw them out before serving.

Two weeks after the worship of Lakshmi, on the dark night of the new moon, Bengal invokes the terrible Kali, the dark goddess of power. Naked, ornamented only with a necklace of skulls and a skirt made of severed human arms, she is the dark side of Durga, the destructive fury who can rage through all creation unconscious of the havoc she wreaks. In her rampaging fury she stepped on her husband Shiva, the detached ascetic, which finally brought her to her senses—we see her biting her tongue in shame.

The devotees of Kali are supposed to drink some kind of alcohol, usually brewed from rice (often referred to as *karan bari*), on this night, but that practice is no longer much in evidence. Drinking is not really part of the traditional Bengali's life. However, there are many hilarious stories of the feudal days when Kali was worshipped at home by wealthy people, particularly those of the Shakto sect or who considered themselves Tantrics. As the night progressed, master and servant would lose all sense of respective status because of the unusual quantities of alcohol in the system. The servant could be seen ordering his master about and the latter busily trying to carry out those orders, but unable to do so because he could not even walk straight!

The only observance in our house was on the eve of Kali puja. Since that is the fourteenth day after the full moon and since Kali is supposed to be attended by fourteen demonic attendants, the number fourteen assumes mystical significance. Fourteen dots of vermilion and oil paste are painted on the walls of the house to protect the inhabitants from the supernatural forces. And fourteen varieties of leafy greens (small samples, tied together, are sold in the markets) have to be eaten with rice at lunch. In the evening fourteen candles or oil lamps are lit and placed on window seats and balconies.

By the end of the month of Kartik, the first month of Hemanta or late autumn, urban Bengalis resume the normal pattern of life in school, college and office. But in rural Bengal this is a time of great expectations. For the following month, Agrahayan, is also the time to harvest the rice that gave the region its soubriquet, 'golden Bengal', in the first line of the national anthem of Bangladesh. The name itself, Agrahayan, is compounded of two words—*agra*, best or foremost, and *hayan* or unhusked rice. Many scholars believe this was originally the first month of the Bengali calendar, not only because it would be natural for ordinary farming people to calculate a year around major agricultural events, but also because Agrahayan is considered the best of all months for weddings. Of course, this is partly a practical matter; the mellow temperatures make the rich food for the guests and the heavy brocaded silks and jewellery for the bride more bearable. But there is a special aura of auspiciousness too about the first month of the year. For the second most important month for Bengali weddings is Baisakh, the current first calendar month when the heat of the summer is on full blast.

In the countryside, Agrahayan is a time of hard work outdoors. In good years, when the monsoon has been just right, the fields are full of the standing rice crop that needs to be harvested and brought home. Most of that is still done by hand, as it has been for centuries. Under the bearable autumn sun, the peasants cut the rice with their sickles and tie it in golden bunches to be transported by bullock carts. Slowly, as the days progress, the once golden fields become stretches of stubble, the dead remnants of the plant being later gathered for animal feed and supplementary fuel. In the evenings, as the first chill of oncoming winter is felt, some of the rice straw is used for small fires in front of which people can sit and warm themselves. Once the rice has been harvested and stored in covered bins of woven straw, the work of threshing, husking and milling begins. Women help with the threshing, beating the bunches of harvested crop against the beaten earth floors of village courtyards. Rice which will be parboiled is cooked in the husk in huge vats of water and set out to dry in the sun before being taken to the nearest mills.

In the old days, before mills or any kind of technology, it was the women who did the back-breaking job of husking the rice. The traditional Bengali instrument for taking the husk off the rice is called a *dhenki*, a long wooden board mounted on a short pedestal in the middle, much like a see-saw. One end of the board has a short pestle-like attachment underneath and that is positioned over a large shallow depression in the ground where the unhusked rice is kept. It requires two women to handle the dhenki. One stands near the end without the pestle and presses it down with her foot. As soon as she releases her foot, the board dips down to the other end, the pestle hitting the rice with force, thus separating the husk from the grain. As she presses with her foot and lifts the board from the rice, the other woman turns the rice over with her hand, so that all the grains can be hit evenly. It is an infinitely time-consuming process, and is no longer viable. But some food aficionados claim that rice husked by a dhenki is far superior in taste to rice processed in a mill. This may be based on the fact that the dhenki always leaves some of the inner husk on the grain, whether parboiled or atap, thus making it more nutritious. The long hours of monotonous labour with the dhenki has made the word a symbol for unquestioning drudgery. A Bengali proverb says that even if a dhenki is transported to heaven, it will find some rice to husk.

In the unlucky years, of course, this happy intensity of work is less visible. Sometimes the late autumn comes with the most disastrous rainstorms and vicious cyclones. Agrahayan, then, is a time of despair. Apart from destroying the rural settlements and killing human beings and livestock, these angry visitations can also decimate fields of standing rice. In Bengal we have a whole body of sayings supposed to have come down from the legendary wise woman, Khana, daughter-in-law of the equally legendary scholar/astrologer, Barahamihir. Most of these sayings are centred around the weather, cropping patterns and different aspects of rural life. It is said that so correct were Khana's pronouncements that her father-in-law cut off her tongue in a fit of male jealousy. But well before she was silenced, Khana had made her prediction: if it rains in Agrahayan, even the king will have to go begging. The fields of Agrahayan then are not acres of golden bounty, but a miserable expanse of underdeveloped or rotting crop.

Aside from expending energy in garnering and processing the Aman rice, some Bengali peasants also start working on their winter crops, or preparing the land for them. In areas where the date-palm tree is plentiful, late autumn is the time to start tapping the juice from the trunks. This juice or sap, called *khejur ras*, is one of the most delightful gifts of nature, like the maple syrup in the United States. The first few tappings do not provide the best juice, though the pale and fragrant liquid can be a refreshing morning drink. But later tappings through the winter produce a rich, thick liquid which is slowly boiled to make various kinds of gur, liquid, grainy liquid or solid. The wonderful fragrance of gur on the fire spreads far and wide, and is one of the most pleasing aspects of Bengali rural life in autumn/winter.

For rural Hindu women and even their urban counterparts as late as the 1950s, Agrahayan was also the month for a quaint ritual in honour of the sun called Ritu or Itu puja. My mother and all her younger sisters who were born and raised in Calcutta observed this ritual with great regularity until they were married. And there were some attempts to induct me into this practice too. Entirely feminine, it combines beautifully women's awareness of nature and a celebration of fertility. On the last day of Kartik (the month preceding Agrahayan), a large open-mouthed earthen pot, *malsha*, would be filled with moist earth and five kinds of grain, including rice, would be scattered over the top. A little pitcher, usually copper, would then be filled with water and set firmly into the mound of earth. The women would fast, bathe and chant the relevant mantras, make an offering of seasonal fruit, and water the earth in the pot. Then one of them would tell a well-known story about the Sun-god. Finally, the earthen pot would be placed in a special corner of the house. As the days of the month went by, the seeds in the pot would germinate into sprouts and long green leaves. Every Sunday—Rabibar, the day of the sun in Bengali—the ritual of fasting, chanting, watering and story-telling would be repeated. By the end of the month, some, if not all, of the rice in the field had been harvested and brought home. So, on the final day of Agrahayan, the Sun-god would receive a final offering of rice pudding made with the new rice and sweetened with the earliest gur. After this, the whole pot would be immersed in the nearest pond, water tank or river.

Once the rice has been harvested, rural Bengal propitiates the gods for their bounty through the joyful festival of *nabanno*, which literally means 'new rice'. Radha Prasad Gupta, a chronicler of many aspects of Bengali life, once recounted to me his childhood memories of nabanno with something close to ecstasy. The mingled fragrance of the uncooked offering for the gods—a combination of milk, gur, pieces of sugarcane, bananas, and above all, the new rice—was unique enough to linger in his memory throughout his life. Even in Bangladesh, where the majority of the people are Muslims and do not have the Hindu pantheon to propitiate, some cultural commonality can be seen in the celebration of the new rice. Once the gods have received their dues, the new rice and the season's first gur are cooked in milk to make payesh which has to be distributed among the neighbours. Rich farmers are obviously in a position to be more punctilious and generous in this respect than landless peasants and sharecroppers.

Unlike the summer in the West, autumn, early or late depending on the Puja holidays, is the time when the urban Bengali takes his vacation. Schools and colleges are closed for a month or so and the weather is ideal for travelling within Bengal or to any other part of India except the northernmost areas. After the establishment of an extensive and efficient railway system by the British, train travel *en famille* during the autumn vacation became an institution. Despite the presence of dining cars, the best part of these journeys usually consisted of opening up your 'tiffin carrier' and consuming the luchis, alur aam, dry curried meat and the mishtis you had brought from home.

The tranquil fullness of nature in the autumn also imbues the waters of Bengal and rural people can sometimes indulge themselves with amateur fishing, spending contemplative afternoons with bait and line. There is a wonderful variety of fish to choose from. Iswarchandra Gupta, the nineteenth-century Bengali poet who glorified food in his poems with eulogy, mischief, humour and ecstasy, used one of them to celebrate the fish found in autumn: small fish like punti, mourala, tangra and bele, the round-bellied pomfret, the pankal, baan and gule of the eel family, shingi and magur of the catfish family, estuarine delectables like parshe, bhetki, bhangar and, of course, the earliest specimens of king prawn, the galda chingri.

Many of these fish are cooked in strong, pungent gravies

because they themselves have strong flavours and very firm flesh. The eel-like creatures have the advantage of having no bones apart from the spine. Nor do they have any scales. So they can be easily cut up into 5-8 cm (2-3 in) pieces and cooked with a ground mustard sauce like the hilsa during the monsoon, or just a fiery red chilli sauce. Green chillies are added for extra zest and the phoron is either kalojeera or panch phoron. The magur and the bhetki are treated differently. They are more expensive and are generally bought for guests or on special occasions. Magur, quite apart from its taste, has the distinction of working wonders on the invalid's system, if plainly cooked. And if you are not ill, what more wonderful than a kalia made of magur, the rich dark gravy spiced with freshly ground cumin, coriander, ginger, turmeric, red chilli and garom mashla? Bhetki, called 'bekti' by the British, can be made into a kalia too, but I tend to prefer it more lightly cooked with chopped garlic, ground mustard and green chillies. The British in Bengal doted on bekti, because it was boneless and could easily be cut into fillets to be cooked in a Western style. Perhaps the flavour, too, reminded them of fish at home. The years of cohabitation also taught the wily Bengali the potential of bhetki. Even the word fillet has become part of the Bengali language, with the final 't' well pronounced. At weddings and other formal occasions, these fillets of bhetki are made into 'fries', another instance of the adoption of a foreign word. The fillets are marinaded in an onion, ginger and red chilli paste to which salt and lemon juice have been added. They are then dipped in egg, coated with breadcrumbs and deep-fried in oil. Those who like fish and chips can try this variant.

Of course such anglicized preparations are mostly urban. Small towns and villages, even in the early part of this century, were quite innocent of elaborate culinary practices based on the food of the ruling race. My father spent several years during his boyhood in a residential school in Bankura district in northern West Bengal, a quiet provincial place where the only technology was probably the presence of the railroad. Here even ordinary things like biscuits or commercially baked loaves of bread were unknown in those days before the Second World War. Instead, the standard breakfast fare during the autumn season was a clutch of homely *bhabras*, hot crispy fritters, made from besan or chickpea flour, mixed with water, salt, ground chilli and a little rice flour for crispness. The thick batter was left overnight in the kitchen to ferment a little, and in the morning the cook would heat a lot of oil in his large karai. Then he would take some of the fermented mixture and put it in a bit of cloth with a small hole in it. Holding the cloth bundle over the hot oil, he would squeeze the mixture out through the hole to form separate collections of concentric circles. The crisp, hot fritters would be gobbled up with great relish by the hungry hordes that sat waiting. For those schoolboys, the famous Calcutta bakeries, Firpo's—now closed—and Flury's, were as unimaginable as the fancy pastries and loaves they sold. All over the northern Bengal districts of Bankura, Birbhum and Puruliya, these homely bhabras were common breakfast items. Now, however, even the most godforsaken village will have a teashop selling biscuits and buns.

In the countryside Agrahayan is also the traditional month for making boris, little pellets made from dal soaked in water, ground to a fine paste on the grinding stone and then dried in the sun. Salt and appropriate spices are added to the paste. The white kalai dal (sold as *urat dal* in most grocery stores in India), for instance, is often flavoured with ground asafoetida. Once the dal paste is spiced, a clean cloth is spread out on a large plate or tray, little blobs of the paste placed on it in rows and left to dry in the sun for several days until all the moisture has evaporated. Once thoroughly dried, the boris are packed in large tins and stored for the coming year.

Bori-making has always been an exclusively feminine art, traditionally associated with elderly women, widowed grandmothers and aunts, one of the reasons perhaps being that such women had already reached menopause and were free of the 'unclean' days of the month during which younger women were not supposed to do anything requiring cleanliness or purity. Bengali literature abounds with references to a whole army of cosy older women turning out boris. Many rituals grew around this domestic duty. Even if a young married woman set out to make boris, she would first bathe and purify herself. Once she had the paste ready, she would take a portion and shape them into two huge boris, called buro and buri, old man and old woman. These would be crowned with unhusked rice paddy and *durba* grass (a part of any puja ritual from ancient times) and the woman would pray to them for the success of her bori-making.

As with all art, the boris reflected the hand that made them. The consistency of the dal, the degree of spicing and the intensity of whipping the paste before making the pellets, all varied from woman to woman. Kalai dal, for instance, is used to make a variety called phulboris, which are featherlight and melt in the mouth once fried in oil. The woman who could whip the dal hard enough to make the lightest phulboris acquired a reputation. In one famous novel, *Arogyaniketan*, a character is even identified by the memory of the phulboris made by his grandmother.

By now, of course, much of the mystique of bori-making is over. They are made commercially on a large scale and dried in ovens. Even in our home, which is very traditional, boris have rarely been home-made. Nor are commercial boris ritually made in Agrahayan. Inevitably, mass production means some diminution in quality, but the great advantage is that packaged boris are now available in Indian grocery stores around the world. The larger ones are fried and used in fish or vegetable stews, while the smaller ones, fried crisper, are crumbled over cooked leafy greens as well as other vegetables. One of my most favourite applications of bori is slightly unorthodox. But it is very easy to make and lends an extra dimension to a Bengali classic, begun pora, or spiced roasted brinjal.

BEGUN PORA

FOR FOUR PEOPLE

INGREDIENTS

2 large fat purple brinjals
1 small onion, finely chopped
1-2 chopped green chillies
1 small handful of coriander leaves
4-5 teaspoons of pungent mustard oil
Salt to taste

METHOD

Select big, round, fat purple brinjals for begun pora, the rounder they are, the better. Cut each one into four sections, but leave them joined near the stem. Now rub some oil on the outer surfaces of the brinjals. The best way to make begun pora is to roast them over a gas flame. In the absence of a gas stove, heat the oven to 230°C (450°F, Gas mark 8), place the brinjals on a foil-covered baking dish and roast them evenly on all sides. They will have to be turned around several times until the skin turns completely black and peels off easily. Some of the juices will run out on the foil. Check if the flesh is cooked by inserting a fork into the portion closest to the stem, which is the firmest and takes longest to cook. If they are roasted directly on a flame, as is the tradition in Bengal, the outer skin is charred to a crisp and falls off in crackling pieces. The final product tastes better, but it also makes a mess to be cleaned up. When the brinjals are done, take them out and let cool. Meanwhile, take a handful of small boris and fry them in oil over a high heat until they are very brown. Chop the onion as fine as possible. Then chop the green chillies and a small handful of coriander leaves. By this time the brinjals should be cool. Peel off the blackened skin carefully. If they have been done in an oven, the skin will not be so crisp and will come off with some of the flesh adhering to it. Scrape the flesh away with a spoon before discarding the skin. Dipping your hands in a bowl of cold water helps when you are peeling the skin. Cut off the stems, mash the flesh thoroughly with a fork and mix in the chopped onion, chilli and coriander together with salt to taste and the pungent mustard oil. Crumble the boris and add them to the mixture. This tastes equally good with rice or chapatis or even by itself. Like the Middle Eastern baba ganoush, it can also be served as an appetizer, with small bits of unleavened bread.

As the autumn ripens to its own fullness, the days shorten, the twilight lessens and intimations of mortality whisper in the smoky evening air, I always feel a subdued melancholy. Perhaps this is because both my grandfathers died in the autumn, one early and one late, in successive years, and death among the Hindus, like birth and marriage, has a protracted set of rituals which surround one with its oppressive presence.

Thankfully, being a grandchild, I was spared the sight of the crematorium and the funeral pyre. Only the sons of the dead have to be present at the cremation, which usually takes place near a river. Once the body is reduced to ashes, the mourners bathe in the river, don new dhutis and cover their upper bodies with a chadar or light shawl. Stitched clothing is absolutely forbidden and mourning women are supposed to wear their saris without blouses. Once they have bathed, a small piece of iron (a key, for instance) is strung round the neck of each mourner. This is supposed to act like a barrier and protect the living from the dead.

The period of mourning varies. In our family it lasted eleven days because we were Brahmins. Other castes have lesser restrictions. And during all this time my uncles and their wives had to wear their unstitched clothes, walk barefoot and sleep on the floor on a blanket. The men could not shave and neither men nor women could oil or comb their hair. The absence of oil extended to food also. Cooking was permissible only at lunchtime when rice and green bananas would be boiled in an earthen pot over a wood fire to make the prescribed *habishanno*. The only seasoning the mourners could use was ghee and a bit of coarsely ground sea salt. Once in a while, a bit of ground dal would be thrown into the pot of rice to make it more nutritious. Dinner invariably consisted of fruits and milk.

On the tenth day my uncles went for a ritual bath in the Ganga and threw away the iron round the neck. Afterwards another set of clothes, unstitched again, was given to them. The old ones were given to the barber waiting there to trim their nails and shave their beards and heads. Women only have their nails trimmed.

On the morning of the eleventh day the priest conducted the *shradhdha* or final rituals. The offerings for the dead are many: food, clothes, utensils, even pieces of furniture like beds. But it is also mandatory to serve the dead man's favourite dishes as part of the offerings. Once the rituals have been completed, the priest takes all the non-perishable items as his booty.

Apart from the general collection of offerings, there is a special one of cooked rice and fish, called *pinda*, without which the spirit of the dead person cannot be satisfied. Once again, it is an indication of what Bengal considers its basic staples to be. The pinda, usually cooked by the wife or the daughter-in-law of the deceased, is set out in separate lumps on banana leaves for all the ancestors that can be recalled. Since the denizens of the other world cannot visibly partake of mortal rice and fish, members of the subcaste of *agradani* Brahmins had to eat some of the pinda. Despised, considered fallen, the agradani appeared at the rituals for the dead like some material ghost, and one stark story tells of an agradani so driven by poverty that he cannot resist gobbling up the pinda offered to his son. The leftovers are dumped in the nearest river after some have been scattered on the ground for the crows, who are considered the representatives of ghosts.

Once the religious rituals are taken care of, the dead person's family is obliged to invite a certain number of Brahmins and serve them with a good vegetarian lunch. Satisfying the Brahmins has been a compulsory part of many Hindu ceremonies from ancient times, as the evidence of literature shows. No Brahmin, if invited, can refuse to come. But some will eat only token mouthfuls of fruit and sweets, believing that if they eat well, they will have to share in the dead person's sins. In the evening there is another vegetarian meal to which relatives, friends and neighbours are invited. It is longer, and more formal, although the children of the dead continue with their austere meals and sleep on the floor till the thirteenth day.

Though strictly vegetarian, the shradhdha meals are no less tasty than those served at weddings. There is no austerity in cooking. Fried vegetables like brinjals or patols or even spinach form the first course. Then comes dal, usually made with yellow split peas, followed by a fish–meat substitute—a rich dish made either with chhana, pressed cottage cheese, or with dhonka, squares of pressed, ground dal. The meal ends with the usual chutney, sweet yoghurt and mishtis.

Chhana is made into spicy curries all over India, but the dhonka is probably more typical of Bengal. The name itself is intriguing for it means hoax or deception. And the squares of dal are meant to deceive you into thinking you are eating meat; or at least they are meant to puzzle the eater. Of course those heathen spices, onion and garlic, cannot be used in a meal cooked for a funeral feast. But the spicy richness of dhonka leaves no sense of lack. Though it is quite time consuming, it is worth the time and effort spent on it. The main trick is not to break the dhonka pieces. My first few attempts were disastrous because I insisted on stirring them; however shaking the pan gently is good enough.

DHONKAR DALNA

FOR FOUR TO SIX PEOPLE

INGREDIENTS

250 gm (½ lb) of yellow split peas soaked overnight
½ a coconut, finely ground
Salt to taste
A little sugar for the dal and coconut mixture
1 teaspoon of ground ginger
250 gm (½ lb) of potatoes
120 ml (4 fl oz) of oil
1 teaspoon of whole cumin
2 bay leaves
3 teaspoons each of ground ginger, cumin and coriander
A little salt
2 tablespoons of yoghurt
2 teaspoons of sugar
250 ml (8 fl oz) of water
120 ml (4 fl oz) of coconut milk
2 teaspoons of ground garom mashla
3 teaspoons of roasted chilli-cumin powder

2 teaspoons of ghee
A few chopped coriander leaves

METHOD

Start dhonkar dalna a day ahead by soaking the yellow split peas overnight. The following day drain the water, let the dal dry a little, and grind it to a very smooth paste. Coarsely ground dal will be a mess. Grind half a coconut, again very finely, and mix with the dal. The important thing is to make sure that the amount of coconut is half that of the dal. Season this mixture with salt, a little sugar and 1 teaspoon of ground ginger. Put it in a frying pan over a low flame and stir until it is quite dry. Transfer to a greased tray or dish and press and shape into a large, flat square 2 cm (¾ in) in thickness. Cut this into small 2.5 cm (1 in) squares or rectangles with a sharp knife. Set aside. Take the potatoes and peel, cube and fry them in oil heated in the karai. Remove and fry the dhonka squares in the same oil carefully until they are brown. Remove and set aside. Throw in the whole cumin and the bay leaves as phoron. As soon as they turn brown, add the ground ginger, cumin and coriander, a little salt, the yoghurt and 2 teaspoons of sugar. Fry these over a high heat for two to three minutes. Add the fried potatoes, stir for another two to three minutes and pour in the water. Bring to the boil and keep covered over a medium heat until the potatoes are cooked. Uncover, turn the heat to high and add the coconut milk. As the gravy thickens, add the dhonka. As soon as this comes to the boil, add the ground garom mashla with the roasted chilli-cumin powder and ghee. Gently shake the pan and let all the flavours mingle before removing from the stove. Check the salt and sugar balance and add if necessary. In East Bengali households they garnish this dish with chopped coriander leaves. Less chilli-cumin powder can be used if it seems too hot.

Having been a child at the time, I do not remember the taste or appearance of shradhdha food. But I do remember finding the whole experience of death, lamentation and ritual curiously incomprehensible and frightening. This fear and uncertainty made me close my mind to thoughts of the dead. I did not even think that I missed the grandfather in whose house I had lived since my birth. But many years later I learned that the affection of his autumnal years had left its mark deeply. One evening my mother came in and left two ata fruits on my desk. As I broke open the first one, I suddenly remembered a story, written by the Bengali comic genius Rajshekhar Basu, which my grandfather had told me.

A group of schoolboys and their tutor went to a small town outside Bengal for their autumn holidays and stayed at a country bungalow with a huge orchard. When they discovered that several of the trees bore large ripe atas, the boys decided to buy a large quantity of milk the next morning and make some atar payesh. Meanwhile, they decided to explore their new neighbourhood and were delighted to come upon a large villa with a huge garden. Near the wall was a guava tree loaded with beautifully ripe fruits. While their tutor turned a blind eye, they promptly climbed the tree and filled their pockets with guavas. Before they could escape, however, the owners of the property, a plump old gentleman and a thin old lady, came back, the latter carrying a large red bundle. After a suitable display of righteous indignation by the old gentleman, a retired judge, the boys were forgiven and the old lady served them freshly made, delectable atar payesh. The boys thanked them profusely for the treat and went back to their bungalow only to find their ata trees bereft of all the ripe fruit. When the gardener was asked for an explanation, he disclaimed all responsibility, saying that a plump old gentleman, accompanied by a thin old lady, had appeared a short time back and had taken away all the ripe fruit from the lower branches, not heeding the gardener's protests. Once the laughter had subsided, the boys decided to wait for a few more days until more of the ata fruit ripened before cooking atar payesh themselves and inviting the old couple for a treat.

Though I smiled at the memory of this story, I also went back to that other autumn of loss. After all these years I cried, not in fear or anguish, but in welcome remembrance and affection.

SHEET
winter

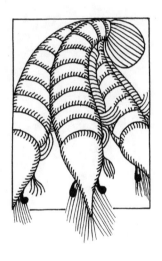

Brief, invigorating, with vibrant colour standing out in a dry and rough landscape, winter in Bengal is like the perfect love affair. It is our season of mists and mellow fruitfulness, two short months of bliss. The flowers of winter are not like the demure white blossoms of the monsoon and the autumn. Crimson roses, yellow and bronze chrysanthemums, blazing marigolds and multicoloured dahlias clamour for attention. In the country you can feast your eyes on fields of mustard awash in yellow blossom, on patches of maroony-red *lal shak*, on the subtle greens of cabbages in the earth and the climbing vine of the lau spreading over thatch roofs and bamboo frames. In the city markets the rich, purple brinjals are offset by snowy-white cauliflowers peeking from within their leaves; carrots, tomatoes, beets, cucumbers, spring onions and bunches of delicate coriander leaves invite you to stop cooking and make salads. And the infinite variety of leafy greens—spinach, mustard, lau shak, beto shak, lal shak, methi shak, mulo shak—makes you wonder if the impoverished Bengali widow is to be pitied or envied for her vegetarian diet.

All this should have inspired an artistic frenzy of still lifes on canvas. But somehow we are still waiting for our Cezanne. Perhaps because we are too busy eating. For the most important and joyful thing about winter to a Bengali is the opportunity and ability to eat far more abundantly than during any other season, to indulge in all the rich meats, prawns, eggs and fish dishes that sit too heavily on the stomach at other times of the year. The colonial years have left behind the festivities of Christmas and New Year which the Bengali has enthusiastically adopted and the early winter month of Poush sees the *pithaparban*, a folk festival designed specifically for the making and eating of large quantities of sweets. And even if he cannot afford too much of these, he still has a wonderful array of vegetables and fruits from which to choose.

This is also the time for the indolent, outdoor-shy Bengali to venture out for a day in the zoo or a day at the races, or a day in the country where picnic lunches are sedately eaten in the fashion of an impressionist painting. The dry, almost too dry grass is a welcome change after the sogginess of the monsoon and village children often get a fire going under a large tree and cook themselves a rough meal of rice, dal and vegetables, all cooked in the same pot, a meal called *choruibhati*, literally rice for the sparrows. The lambent sunshine is quite a contrast to the searing heat of summer and after a meal eaten in the open, it is only natural for the indolent Bengali to have a little snooze under the light-and-shade canopy provided by the branches of large trees.

For all the continuity of the Bengali eating tradition, many of those vegetables which signal winter to us did not feature in the Bengali diet three or four centuries ago. Mukundaram Chakrabarti's sixteenth-century narrative poem, *Chandimangalkabya*, contains a passage in which Shiva, on a winter morning, asks his wife Gouri to cook him an elaborate vegetarian meal. The menu of his desire consists of a bitter shukto made with brinjals, *shim* (a kind of buttery-textured bean) and neem leaves as a first course; a combination dish of brinjals, our native pumpkin, *sari* (a kind of elongated colocasia), jackfruit seeds and phulboris, all seasoned with the juice of ginger; mustard greens and beto shak fried in pungent mustard oil; fried phulboris soaked in syrup; two kinds of dal, one slightly sweet, made with yellow split peas, the other, lentils with lime juice; a sweet chutney of sour karamchas; a ghanto made with maan, jackfruit seeds and boris, all flavoured with a phoron of cumin fried in ghee; and finally, spinach cooked with a sour fruit, *amra*.

Shiva's menu is extraordinarily elaborate, but it does not seem alien because the ingredients are still around and the basic methods of cooking vegetables have not changed all that much. Where, however, are the cabbages, cauliflowers, potatoes, tomatoes, beets or green peas? Nowhere in sight, and the Bengali managed very well without them. As I have said earlier, many vegetables which are now part of the daily diet were imported into Bengal during the sixteenth and seventeenth centuries by Dutch, French and Portuguese traders. Though it is hard to determine which vegetable was brought in by whom, potatoes, most scholars concede, were the contribution of the Portuguese. When the British became the rulers of India, their eating preferences also influenced the cultivation and the marketing of these 'foreign' vegetables. Tomatoes, called 'English' brinjal, used in fish and vegetable recipes to create a sweet-and-sour taste, can be attributed to the British presence. The concept of serving raw vegetables as salad too was introduced by our colonial rulers. Throughout the eighteenth and nineteenth centuries, the culinary genius of Bengal slowly developed the modern vegetarian classics by combining the old and the new. Cabbages, potatoes and peas became the base for a spicy winter ghanto which rivals the mochar ghanto that has been a favourite since medieval times. Cauliflowers, combined with potatoes, were made into a rich and fragrant dalna that was a wonderful variation of the summer speciality, the patol and potato dalna. As for green peas, the Bengali spurned the plain boiled version served on the dinner tables of his British ruler and made delectable savouries like matarshutir kachuri or chirar polao or the fillings for samosas with them, aside from adding them to other vegetable dishes.

The most amazing import of course is the potato. Next to the Irish, Bengalis are probably the largest potato eaters in the world, and yet this is such a relative upstart in the hierarchy of our food. Along with rice, it is an inevitable daily ingredient in the diets of vegetarians and non-vegetarians alike. And at no other time does the Bengali do as much with the potato as in winter, when the small new potatoes are available in addition to the old ones. In my grandfather's house, the dry potato bhaji, tiny cubed potatoes fried with panch phoron and whole red chillies was a compulsory item served with chapatis at dinner. In my parents' home, we would sometimes have bati chachchari made out of julienned potatoes. This is a simple and delicious preparation, ideal for the cook who does not have much time or attention to spare. My mother would cut and wash the potatoes, mix them thoroughly with salt, a tablespoonful of finely chopped ginger, a couple of green chillies and a tablespoonful of mustard oil. The mixture would then be put in a small aluminium pot and left tightly covered on a very low flame until the potatoes were cooked and the oil and the ginger juice had mingled to add their flavours to the vegetable. Fish, meat, eggs as well as other vegetables are combined most often with potatoes.

But of course no bhaji or bharta can bring out the full glory of winter's new potatoes. Small, round, pale-skinned, these tubers would never be wasted in such preparations. Instead, they are made into different kinds of dam. Served with puffy, golden luchis, the alur dam transports even the most carnivorous Bengali to celestial bliss. As with the hilsa, there are many recipes for the potato dam, and families have their special combinations of ingredients, all of which are delicious. Apart from the simple recipe mentioned in the previous chapter, I would like to mention another one of my favourites.

ALUR DAM

FOR FOUR PEOPLE

INGREDIENTS

500 gm (1 lb) of potatoes
3 medium onions, grated
10-12 cloves of garlic, ground into a paste

1½ tablespoons of tamarind extract mixed with 250 ml (8 fl oz)
  of hot water
1½ teaspoons of red chilli powder
1 teaspoon of turmeric powder
Garom mashla (3 cinnamon sticks, 4 cardamoms, 4 cloves)
2 bay leaves
60 ml (2 fl oz) of oil
1 tablespoon of ghee
Salt and sugar to taste

METHOD

To make alur dam for four, I take 500 gm (1 lb) of potatoes, boil and peel them and cut them into cubes. New potatoes are left whole. Then I heat the oil mixed with 1 tablespoon of ghee, fry the garom mashla and bay leaves in it and add the grated onion and garlic. When these are browned, I add chilli and turmeric powder and after a minute, the potatoes. These are stirred briskly until they turn brown and the spices cling to them. Then I add the tamarind water, an extra 120 ml (4 fl oz) of plain water, salt and sugar to taste, bring it to a boil and simmer over a low heat until the flavours blend and the gravy thickly coats the potatoes. Finally, I check and make sure that the sweet-sour-salt balance is right. If not, I adjust it.

The new potatoes were also used by my mother, a working woman, to make a very tasty but very quick dish during the winter. She would boil and peel the potatoes. Green peas would be shelled and washed. Then she would heat some oil in her karai, sauté the potatoes for a few minutes, add the peas, sauté a little longer and then add several large tomatoes coarsely chopped, 3-4 green chillies and salt to taste. This would be left to simmer with a little water until the tomatoes gave up their juice and a thickish sauce coated the vegetables. Chopped coriander leaves would be added and, when the karai came off the fire, she would sprinkle some fresh mustard oil on the vegetables and leave them covered until it was time to serve them. Meanwhile, hot chapatis would be made.

The new potatoes of winter also figure in a dalna with cauliflowers, but I always preferred a lighter combination of the two which is easy to make anywhere.

CAULIFLOWER BHAJI

FOR THREE TO FOUR PEOPLE

INGREDIENTS

1 medium cauliflower
120 gm (4 oz) of green peas
2-3 medium potatoes or 7-8 new potatoes
1 medium onion, finely chopped
3-4 spring onions, finely chopped
2 tablespoons of mustard oil
3-4 dry red chillies
1 teaspoon of whole cumin seeds
2 bay leaves
Salt to taste

METHOD

To make this cauliflower bhaji, take a medium-sized cauliflower and chop it into very small florets. The hard stem at the bottom has to be cut into tiny pieces. Cook green peas and drain them. Peel potatoes and cube them small. Heat some mustard oil (start with 2 tablespoons, add more later if needed) and fry the potatoes golden brown. Remove and set aside. In the same oil, throw in a phoron of dry red chillies, whole cumin seeds and bay leaves. After a couple of minutes, add the onions, fry till golden brown and throw in the cauliflowers. Stir once or twice, add a little salt and reduce the heat to medium. Sauté gently for three to four minutes, add the peas and fried potatoes and simmer covered over a low heat until the florets are tender. Uncover, check for salt, adding if needed, turn the heat to high and stir until the vegetables are browned. Just before removing, add the spring onions. Despite being dry, it tastes good with both rice and luchi.

The green peas, unknown to Shiva, are one of the most prized winter vegetables today; partly because they are limited to the season, unlike the potatoes. Apart from being combined with a host of other ingredients, they are made into a wonderful savoury preparation which is a universal Bengali favourite. This matarshutir kachuri also bridges regional and national distances very easily. I have yet to find anyone who does not like it. Though it is often served with a dry alur dam, it is good enough to eat by itself. A kachuri is basically a stuffed luchi and there are two steps to all kachuris, the filling and the dough.

MATARSHUTIR KACHURI

FOR THREE TO FOUR PEOPLE

INGREDIENTS

120 gm (4 oz) of uncooked green peas
A little water for the matarshuti paste
250 gm (½ lb) of flour
Water for the dough
1 teaspoon of roasted chilli-cumin powder
2-3 teaspoons of mustard oil
2 tablespoons of peanut oil
Salt to taste

METHOD

To make the filling for matarshutir kachuri, take shelled uncooked green peas (matarshuti) and grind them to a paste with a little water. Add a little salt and roasted chilli-cumin powder and fry the mixture lightly in a frying pan with mustard oil. When the paste cools, divide it into 12-14 little balls.

Mix flour with peanut oil and a pinch of salt. Slowly add enough water to make a sticky dough which has to be kneaded for ten to twelve minutes until it is elastic, like that for luchi. Divide this into twelve to fourteen portions, pat each between the palms and press to form thick flat discs. One portion of the filling goes into the centre of each disc and is carefully covered by stretching the dough over it from all sides like a pouch. Once all the discs are filled and set out on a large tray, start rolling them out carefully so that the kachuri is as thin as possible, without the filling bursting out. This requires much practice to do well. When four or five have been rolled out, put a small karai on the stove and heat some mustard oil (some people prefer to fry their kachuris in ghee or peanut oil). Once the oil is hot, reduce the flame to medium and start frying the kachuris as you would luchis. Slide them gently along the side of the karai, so that they do not land with a splash in the hot oil. As each one swells up, turn it over with the spatula, press gently so that the inside will be done, and lift it out on a holed spatula so that no excess oil lingers on it. Keep rolling and frying the rest of the kachuris until all are done. If the oil in the karai turns too dark, replace it with some fresh oil. Fried kachuris, like luchis, must be left uncovered on trays. If they are heaped together in a bowl, or covered, they will generate moisture and lose their lovely crispness.

Flattened rice, chira, is combined with winter vegetables to make another delightful savoury, which is served as often at breakfast as at teatime. This chirar polao is far less laborious, and can be made anywhere since packaged chira is sold in grocery stores.

CHIRAR POLAO

FOR THREE TO FOUR PEOPLE

INGREDIENTS

250 gm (8 oz) of chira
2 medium potatoes
A small head of cauliflower
120 gm (4 oz) of green peas
120 ml (4 fl oz) of oil
2 sticks of cinnamon
3 cardamoms
3 cloves
2 teaspoons of posto
2-3 whole green chillies
Salt to taste

METHOD

To make chirar polao, take chira, throw out any impurities and wash it in a colander by pouring hot water over it several times. Leave this softened chira covered until it becomes dry and fluffy. Meanwhile, take the potatoes, peel and cut them into very small cubes. Cut the cauliflower head into tiny florets, discarding the hard stem. Finally shell green peas and steam them for a few minutes till they are done. Heat oil in a karai, fry the potatoes and cauliflower until brown, remove and set aside. Add the cinnamon, cardamoms, cloves as well as the posto and the whole green chillies into the hot oil. Add the chira and steamed green peas. Fry these for two to three minutes before adding the cauliflowers and potatoes with some salt. Stir the whole thing for about five to six minutes before removing and serving it hot. In some families a garnishing of *kari* leaves, normally used in South Indian cooking, is used for chirar polao.

Spinach, however, is one leafy green that has been around for centuries. All the medieval and even pre-medieval literary passages that contain descriptions of food, mention many different ways of cooking spinach. And even today, the Bengali prizes this as the chief shak of the winter. When it is time to bid goodbye to the season it is the spinach that is eaten in a symbolic meal. This is on the day after Saraswati puja, a festival which is the official harbinger of spring. It is the sixth day, shashthi, of the spring moon, and is qualified by the adjective *sheetal* or cool. In our house, a compulsory item of food was the *gotasheddho*. The simplest of dishes, its flavour depends not on spices or the hand of a master, but on natural ingredients. The term literally means boiled whole, and that is exactly what it is. New potatoes in their jackets, green peas in pods, tiny brinjals, sometimes shim, and above all spinach that has grown old enough to put out a budding stalk are all boiled in salted water with whole green chillies. When done, spoonfuls of pungent mustard oil are lavishly added to it.

Throughout the season, however, the fresh, young leaves of the spinach are eaten in countless different forms. But one of the most interesting dishes requiring spinach was introduced to our house by Sadhubaba, an old man venerated as a guru by my grandfather. One of his favourite items was an unusual khichuri which in our family went by the name of *bhoutik khichuri*, *bhoutik* meaning supernatural. Spinach was added to the basic rice and dal of the khichuri. The green astringency of the spinach was accentuated by a little sliced karola, bitter gourd, some green peas and cubed potatoes, all seasoned with ground ginger and ground black pepper. The greenish khichuri was a great contrast to the golden look of all other kinds of khichuri. The mild bitterness, occasionally interrupted by the bitingly sharp green chillies, also made a welcome change from our richer version of winter khichuri where cauliflowers, green peas, potatoes and the shim were cooked with the rice and dal and where lots of ghee, cumin and garom mashla were used. Both kinds of khichuri provided wonderfully nutritious meals for our vegetarian guests. But in our family we seem to have a greater inclination for the supernatural, and thirty years after Sadhubaba's death, my mother and her sisters still make bhoutik khichuri with pleasure and nostalgia.

Many of the guests who came to our house during Sadhubaba's visits were devout Vaishnavs and strict to the point of being vegetarians. Though khichuri and other vegetables were commonly served to them, sometimes luchis would be made for dinner and some special vegetable dish would be the accompaniment. In the winter, one of the prized items was the ghanto made with cabbage, *bandhakopi*. There are many variations in phorons or the proportion of spices used in different families. But years of trial and error have made each variation delicious.

BANDHAKOPIR GHANTO

INGREDIENTS

500 gm (1 lb) of cabbage
3-4 small potatoes
120 gm (4 oz) of shelled green peas
Garom mashla (3 sticks of cinnamon, 3 cardamoms, 4 cloves)
1 teaspoon each of turmeric and chilli powder
1½ teaspoons of ground ginger
1 teaspoon each of ground cumin and coriander
3 tablespoons of mustard oil

1 teaspoon of whole cumin
2 bay leaves
2 teaspoons of ghee
3-4 teaspoons of sugar
Salt to taste

METHOD

To make bandhakopir ghanto take the cabbage and discard the top 3-4 leaves. Quarter it and chop each quarter very fine, almost shredding it. Discard the hard stem portion in the centre. All ghantos require finely chopped vegetables. Put the cabbage in a pot with a little water and steam it over medium heat for three to four minutes. Take the small potatoes, peel and cube them. Heat the mustard oil in a karai and fry the potatoes golden brown. Remove and set aside. Then throw in a phoron of whole cumin and bay leaves. This can be substituted by a phoron of asafoetida or panch phoron. After a minute or so, add the ground spices, fry for a few minutes and add the cabbage, carefully pressing out the water before putting it in. Cook with spices for three to four minutes and add the potatoes, green peas, salt and sugar. Stir thoroughly and leave covered over a medium heat until the potatoes are tender. Taste for salt and add the ground garom mashla and ghee. Sometimes my mother adds tomatoes which lend their colour and tartness to the dish.

This ghanto is also very good with rice. Sometimes, for a change, we would have cabbage very lightly fried with a phoron of kalo jeera and seasoned with salt, sugar and green chillies. Chopped coriander would be added at the end. At other times cabbage would become non-vegetarian (though never for Sadhubaba's devotees) and be cooked with meat or with a large head of carp. Needless to say, it was the men in our family who clamoured for these complicated preparations.

Though all these vegetable dishes are common among the Hindus and though most of them are our family favourites, I cannot talk about winter vegetables without mentioning a brinjal recipe made for me in Dhaka by my friend Nusrat. Brinjals are available round the year, but it is in winter that you find the largest and fleshiest purple ones. These are often made into begun pora which I have described before. But it is in Bangladesh, in a village called Gaffargaon in the district of Mymensingh that the tastiest brinjals appear during the winter. So bursting with flesh are they, that the normal elongated shape is changed almost to a round one.

BEGUNER TAK

INGREDIENTS

A large purple brinjal
1 + 3 teaspoons each of turmeric and chilli powder
360 ml (12 fl oz) of oil
10 small onions, finely chopped
2 tablespoons of garlic paste
4 tablespoons of thick tamarind pulp extract
120 ml (4 fl oz) of water
2 teaspoons each of roasted cumin and coriander powder
6 tablespoons of sugar
Salt to taste

METHOD

To make beguner tak, Nusrat took a large purple brinjal and cut it vertically into thick portions, leaving them joined at the end, the same way we do for begun pora. About 10 cm (4 in) of the stem was also retained to facilitate handling. She rubbed the brinjal inside and outside with salt and

1 teaspoon each of turmeric and chilli powder. Then she heated oil in a large pot and fried the brinjal so that all sides were equally fried, and parted the slices with a spatula several times to fry the inner flesh. Once the whole thing was soft and brown, she lifted it out and kept it in a large serving bowl. She blended tamarind pulp and water to have 4 tablespoons of thick extract. Whole cumin and coriander seeds had been roasted before and kept in bottles and she was going to use some of it at the end. When all these spices were ready, she heated the same oil in the pot and sautéd the onions until light brown. Then she added turmeric and chilli powder, the garlic paste and a little salt and fried the mixture for about five minutes, stirring constantly. To this was added water and the mixture kept on the flame for five more minutes, being stirred from time to time. Then she added the tamarind pulp and water. As soon as it came to a boil, the brinjal was lowered into the pot and left to cook on a medium flame for about twenty minutes. During this time she would let the juices enter evenly. When she judged the brinjal to be ready, she added the sugar and let it cook uncovered for five more minutes. At this stage the sauce tends to stick to the bottom and she kept gently scraping the pot without dismembering the brinjal. Finally, she tasted the salt and removed the pot. If you find your sauce still watery at this time, you can keep it on the fire a little longer. And if it becomes too dry, a little water can be added. A final addition of roasted cumin and coriander powder, and the dish was ready. This tart and spicy dish is served usually at lunchtime together with polao and various meat and hilsa dishes.

Apart from major vegetable dishes featuring in main meals, winter vegetables are also used as filling for a round-the-year favourite savoury snack, the *shingara*. These triangular creations of a thin shell enclosing seasoned, fried vegetables are to be found in every neighbourhood teashop. Elsewhere, they are better known as samosas, a term we reserve for shingaras with meat filling. You can also find them in some sweet shops for the perfect idea of a quick tea is hot shingaras and sweet, spongy rosogollas accompanied by several cups of hot sweet tea. In Dhaka my husband and his friends reminisced to me often about their college and university days. One of the things that provoked great nostalgia was the shingara sold at Madhu's Canteen, a teashop inside the university campus. For the traveller, the best places to try shingaras would be not the big sweet shops or the restaurants, but the roadside teashops. The only thing to watch out for is whether there are plenty of customers there, for that is a sure sign of good food. And if he chooses his time well, early in the morning when the first pot of tea is brewed, a few hours later when it is time for a mid-morning break, or at teatime in the afternoon, he will find the shingaras being fried right in front of him. Nothing can equal the taste of freshly made shingaras. Sometimes, small-town teashops will make better shingaras than those in large cities like Calcutta. I will always remember the extraordinary taste of the shingaras served in two small towns—Bolpur in West Bengal, where I found them in the student canteen on the campus of Shantiniketan, and Barisal in Bangladesh where I was taken to the legendary sweet shop called Gharbaron where both shingaras and rosogollas came in magnum sizes.

Like all savouries, the shingara also varies a lot depending on who makes them. The shell for an ordinary shingara can be made with a dough similar to that for luchi. Each disc is cut into half and a portion of filling is placed on each half, which is then folded over and sealed at the edges to resemble a triangle. In winter the filling consists of tiny cubed potatoes, green peas, peanuts and raisins, or potatoes, green peas and tiny bits of cauliflower, all fried together either with panch phoron or with a bit of chopped onion or some cumin seeds. These are then deep-fried like kachuris. Of course, the shell can be very rich and flaky too, like a good pastry shell. Sabu, the bald, irascible, paan-chewing, maniacal cook I had in Dhaka, used to make meat-filled shingaras for my guests when he happened to be in a good mood. But he always guarded the recipe jealously, so I could never learn how the shell was so many-layered and flaky, how the meat inside was so finely shredded yet juicy, and what combination of spices he used. But even after so many years I can honour those shingaras in remembrance.

In this tropical region winter is not only the time to eat well, but also to sleep well. The beautiful days of lambent sunshine tempt anyone who has leisure outdoors. Quilts and blankets are spread out over balcony rails to collect the warmth of the sun all day. Even the midday sun is so merciful that it is no longer the proverbial mad dogs and Englishmen who will brave it but mild old people and hardworking housewives who will sit on balconies or porches and soak up the sun. At night, there is the happiness of snuggling under the warmed quilts after a relished hot meal. And though there is nothing like the pleasure of sleeping late on a chill winter morning, there are compensations for foregoing that. I can still remember waking up very early and going up to the roof of my grandparents' house. Everything would be shrouded in a pale mist through which the dim sunlight filtered through. Noise of the city traffic seemed strangely absent, the silence punctured from time to time not by the birds but by the distant foghorns of ships in the harbour. Though different from the magical evocations of a monsoon day, the shrouded silence of such mornings has its own undeniable sense of mystery. Once on the steamer coming back from Barisal to Dhaka, I happened to wake up at four o'clock in the morning and went out on the deck to find that we were completely becalmed by an impenetrable white fog. I experienced the true meaning of isolation and silence as the chilly white fog enveloped me, and it was hard to believe that this was tropical Bangladesh, not some cold northern country.

In my grandparents' house winter was the time to really enjoy all the 'hot' foods which were taboo in the summer. Eggs being 'hot' featured prominently in the diet in many different forms. For a long time Hindu Bengalis ate only duck eggs. Chicken being a heathen bird, the prohibition extended to its eggs. But duck eggs had a pronounced odour which made it difficult to eat them boiled or fried or poached. So it had to be an omelette at breakfast and a gravy-based dalna when they were served at lunch or dinner. The Bengali omelette bore no resemblance to the soft, fluffy French ones, so tremulous in the middle, which Europeans savour with ecstasy. Ours were fried in pungent mustard oil to an almost leathery consistency and flavoured with chopped onions and fiery green chillies.

By the time I was old enough to have distinct preferences, the chicken and its egg had become part of our household diet. Hen's eggs went on acquiring greater popularity over time not only because of increased availability and growing size, but also because of a strange conviction that they were less 'hot' than duck eggs. Later, when I was living in Bangladesh, I found a curious application of the same belief. Duck eggs were absolutely forbidden for nubile young girls in many villages because of the conviction that the 'heat' would turn their innocent thoughts in dangerously lascivious directions. But as poultry farming has made both chicken and its eggs more affordable, the mythical properties of duck eggs have begun to fade from people's memories. One of the most striking instances of indigenization of foreign foods that I have come across in Bengal is the French toast. I, like so many other Bengalis, had known it to be a savoury snack, golden slices of bread, dipped in a mixture of whipped egg, salt, onion and green chillies and fried in our usual mustard oil. Imagine my surprise when I found a meek, mild and sweet preparation masquerading under that name at the American breakfast table.

The pleasantest surprise I had with eggs was in Bangladesh, during my first experience of the great Muslim festival of Shab-e-barat, night of destiny. On this night, all devout Muslims are supposed to visit the cemeteries where their family members are buried, to light incense sticks and say special prayers. These observances are important because on this night the fate of every believer is determined in heaven for the coming year. For an outsider like myself the most memorable aspect of Shab-e-barat was the quaint custom of eating bread (mostly made with rice flour) with different kinds of *halua* on the following day. Most households will make huge quantities of bread (flat discs like chapatis) and distribute them to beggars who come in droves. This obligatory sharing of food on festive days with those who possess nothing is one of the most beautiful aspects of Islam. It was only on that occasion that I realized what infinite variety and skill goes into the making of halua. It could be made out of flour, arrowroot, ground yellow split peas, eggs, carrots, gourds and even meat. Some of this bewildering array was on display in the houses I visited on that day, and the taste of them, eaten in succession, was like an ascending scale of notes. But to my mind the tastiest and one of the easiest haluas was that made with eggs.

DIMER HALUA

FOR FOUR PEOPLE

INGREDIENTS

8 eggs

2 teaspoons of milk

175 gm (6 oz) of sugar
120 ml (4 fl oz) of evaporated milk
120 ml (4 fl oz) of ghee
3 whole cardamoms
3 pieces of cinnamon, 2.5 cm (1 in) long
A pinch of saffron
Chopped almonds and pistachios

METHOD

To make this dimer halua, first soak the saffron in 2 teaspoons of milk in a cup. Break the eggs into a large bowl and whip until the yolks and the whites are smoothly blended. It should not be frothy though. Then pour the rest of the ingredients except the almonds and the pistachios slowly into the bowl. Mix smoothly. Taste a little for sweetness, adding sugar if needed. Then transfer the mixture to a thick-bottomed pan or karai and put it on a low flame. Stir constantly, making sure the halua does not stick or burn. Gradually the whole thing will be transformed into tiny yellow granules. As soon as all the moisture has evaporated and the sheen of the ghee is visible, remove from the stove. Delay will make the halua harden with heat. Garnish the halua with chopped almonds, pistachios and the soaked saffron. Some people even add raisins to the mixture before cooking. If you do not like saffron, you can add a few drops of rose-water.

My sister-in-law would sometimes make a variant of this which was firmer in consistency and could be shaped into diamonds or squares. It tasted divine on a wintry morning with parota. It is also an ideal tit-bit to serve the occasional guest, for it keeps better than the halua.

DIMER BORFI

FOR FOUR PEOPLE

INGREDIENTS

8 eggs
500 gm (1 lb) of sugar
250 ml (8 fl oz) of ghee

METHOD

For dimer borfi she would take the eggs and separate the
whites from the yolks. Then she would whip the whites
until they were absolutely stiff. The yolks would also be
whipped into creamy smoothness and the two would be
mixed together. To this she would slowly add sugar. Next,
ghee would be heated in a pan and the egg mixture, flavoured
with rose-water or saffron, would be poured in and kept
over a low flame. After that it was a matter of stirring and
stirring until your arm was ready to fall off. This one has to
be cooked much longer than the other one, until it really
starts sticking to the pan. The colour too will be different.
When she found she could not cook it any longer without
burning the mixture, she removed it from the stove and
transferred it to a flat tray or serving dish. First it would be
shaped into a rectangular piece, 0.6 cm (¼ in) thick, and
then crisscross cuts would be made to form diamond-
shaped borfis.

Such memories of rich food in winter also take me back to
the Bangladeshi village during this season. Going to Dapdapia,
my husband's home village in Barisal, was a whole different
pleasure during the astringent crispness of the Bengali winter.
None of the magical lushness of the monsoon was in evidence.
No river in full spate, nor ponds brimful of water and water
weeds. The kutcha roads were dusty beneath our feet as we

walked from the landing place to the family home. This of course was not a traditional thatched cottage but a concrete structure built by one of my brothers-in-law for occasional visits to the village. The ancestral home stood close by, though it was in very poor condition. Next to it was an overgrown plot of land where my father-in-law lay buried. But no ghostly presence marred my pleasure in that wintry landscape where the large trees had lost some of their leaves, the earth looked dry and brown and yet burgeoned with various crops, and the khejur trees stood in rows with earthen pots tied to their trunks to catch the ras or sap as it trickled from the tapping cuts.

The morning after our arrival in Dapdapia I woke up to find the shutters raised from without and several pairs of curious eyes looking at us. When I came out, the group of giggling girls scattered in haste but not before one of them had invited me to our cousins' house for breakfast. It was a short walk across the garden, but that was the first time my bare feet sank into soft grass wet with the tender dew of a winter morning. As often happens, it had been misty earlier, and I saw the moisture gleaming in glassy beads on the shrubs and branches. That breakfast was the first time I tasted the pure, undiluted sap of the date-palm, naturally chilled in its earthen pot from exposure to the night air. It is the most natural and uncloying sweetness that I have ever encountered.

As a child I had heard my father talk about drinking this khejur ras straight from the tree. In fact village boys often incur the wrath of farmers who have tied their pots to the trees by climbing up and drinking the ras, quietly replacing the pot and disappearing. Though the date-palm tree looks the same round the year—a shorter, less attractive cousin of the tall coconut—the best sap is generated only during the winter. The first tapping takes place in late autumn and successive tappings go on throughout the short winter. Some parts of Bengal provide better habitats for the date-palm and the coconut tree than others. The districts of Barisal, Faridpur and Khulna are particularly well known and a popular adage in Bangladesh says that the district of Faridpur is noted for its thieves, swindlers and khejur gur! But though the trunk provides such a delightful sweetener, the actual dates from the date-palm tree are nowhere near as tasty as those from desert climates.

The date-palm sap is made into three types of gur: liquid, grainy and the solid chunks of patali. The sap is heated in huge *karais* over wood or coal stoves and it is only an expert who can gauge the different degrees of cooking to achieve the right textures. The arrival of gur in the market is the signal for the professional sweet-makers to start preparing one of their most popular products, sandesh flavoured with the new gur. This nalen gurer sandesh has a browny-pink tinge and is very dear to the plump Bengali's heart. At the beginning of the season, gur is sold in its liquid form, jhola gur. This comes in earthen pots and disappears fast enough. In our home it would be used like maple syrup in America, poured over hot luchis or chapatis and as a sweetener in the milk. It ferments easily and so has to be eaten quickly. In rural areas the fermented gur is made into a kind of cheap liquor which tribals and poor villagers drink. It was this same jhola gur which inspired committed following from exceptional Bengalis like Sukumar Ray, our version of Edward Lear or Lewis Carroll. In one of his delightful poems he spun out an absurdly contradictory list of all the good things of life, and the very best of the best was bread with jhola gur. The solid patali gur can be stored and used for quite a few months after winter is over, and refrigeration gives it even longer life. The most notable application for it is its use in payesh in place of sugar. The pure nutty sweetness of the gur makes this winter payesh a Bengali gourmet's dream.

The house in the village where I had breakfast belonged to

distant relatives, my in-laws, but the shyness between town and country limited our conversation mostly to smiles and nods. As I sat looking at all the activity in the large kitchen, a young girl came in with a bunch of greens and sat down in front of a bonti to chop them. The leaves and stems lost all character and fell in a pile of minute green fragments on the plate placed to catch them. Some of the others noticed my amazement and explained that skill at cutting this koloi shak was one of the factors that went in a girl's favour when the prospective bridegroom's family was appraising her. The greens were fried with chopped garlic and just before serving, some dry red chillies were roasted and crumbled over them. I have never forgotten the taste nor the magic speed of the hands that went into the cutting.

Along with koloi shak there were many items cooked for our lunch that day. But for me the most wonderful experience was seeing the huge rui that was caught from the pond to be made into a jhol. It was a beautiful specimen, weighing at least 5 kg (10 lb), its pinkish scales gleaming in the sun as it lay gasping on the beaten earth of the courtyard. The taste of a fresh and mature fish caught immediately before being cooked was ambrosial.

Evening in the village was mystery and heightened awareness. We walked out to some fields in the late afternoon to admire the vegetables and dals growing there against the infinite distance of a horizon unencumbered by buildings. The green and maroon of the low-lying leafy greens were harmoniously countered by the white of the cauliflowers and the higher plants of the dals, the tomatoes and the brinjals. Soon the darkness came hurtling down on batwings and we hurried back to the house to pick up our shawls, for it was much colder in the village than in the city. Then, with one of my husband's cousins to guide us, we set out along the beaten mud tracks and raised embankments dividing the fields, to eat dinner with a friend of the family at the other end of the village. The darkness was impenetrable, our only visual aid being the lantern carried by our guide. And above was a most unfamiliar sky, cold, moonless and starry with no intervening veil of industrial smog. Halfway down, we came upon a cluster of houses. As we stepped into the courtyard-like space in the centre, doors opened on all sides and people came out with lanterns. Our guide laughed and chatted with them and one by one, the women, impelled by curiosity, came up to me and raised their lanterns to my face in a strange but unconscious parody of a priest holding up his lamp to the face of his divinity.

Another plunge into the darkness of the fields, and a little later we came upon the extended homestead where Kadam Bhai lived with his family. Instead of being taken indoors, we were taken around to the back where our dinner was being cooked in the open. Two pits had been dug in the ground and a wood fire built inside each, a technique which is an old tradition in many villages. Much store is set by the flavour of food cooked over a wood fire and it is generally believed to be good for one's digestion.

Huge handis had been placed over the flames to cook the khichuri and duck meat, a standard combination in Barisal and a common favourite in the winter because that is when the birds are most plump and healthy. In the old days when feudal landlords with huge properties could indulge in all kinds of gustatory refinements, the wretched birds were 'prepared' for eating to produce the extra pleasure similar to that of milk-fed veal. Several ducks, their wings clipped, would be chained to little stakes attached to a large wooden platform, and kept locked up in a pitch-dark outhouse. Once a day a bowlful of rice and yoghurt would be set in front of each bird and every morning the entire platform, together with ducks, would be taken to the pond for bathing and cleaning. But the rest of the time the birds remained cooped up in the dark, unable to move or see. After two or three weeks of such treatment, the birds were considered fit for the plate, their flesh having become exquisitely soft and tender.

Though Kadam Bhai's wife was doing the cooking that evening, he himself was no mean cook. It was from him that I later learnt how to make a duck bhuna which always brings back to me a rush of wintry village atmosphere, the smoke from the wood fire mingling with the savoury smell of meat and spices and the sense of communal enjoyment as a group of relatives and neighbours sat down to their meal. I watched them and remembered a Bengali proverb that my mother is fond of quoting. You kill the duck for the son-in-law so that the whole family can eat its fill.

Both the recipes that follow were made with wild duck. They can, however, be used for cooking chicken too, adjusting the cooking time to the type of chicken so that it does not fall apart by the time it arrives on your plate.

DUCK BHUNA

FOR THREE TO FOUR PEOPLE

INGREDIENTS

A nice plump bird of 1½ kg (3 lb)

120 gm (4 oz) of onion paste

1 tablespoon of ground ginger

2 teaspoons each of ground garlic, chilli, turmeric, cumin and coriander

½ teaspoon of ground black pepper

2 bay leaves

3 pieces of cinnamon, 2.5 cm (1 in) long

120 ml (4 fl oz) of mustard oil

120 ml (4 fl oz) of water

2 small onions
6-7 large cloves of garlic
2 tablespoons of ghee
10-12 whole peppercorns
Salt to taste

METHOD

To make duck bhuna you need a nice plump bird, skinned, cleaned and cut into 12-13 portions—2 drumsticks, 2 thighs, 2 wings, 4 breast pieces and 3-4 assorted pieces from the rest. The stomach can be kept but the liver will be mashed if put in with the rest. In a large thick-bottomed pot combine the duck with onion paste, ground ginger, ground garlic, chilli, turmeric, cumin and coriander, ground black pepper, bay leaves, cinnamon, mustard oil, water and some salt. Mix thoroughly and leave tightly covered on a low heat until the meat is absolutely tender. Stirring is not required but you should shake the covered pot gently from time to time. Remove from the fire and set aside. Chop onions and cloves of garlic as fine as possible. Heat ghee in another pan, add whole peppercorns and the chopped onion and garlic. Fry until golden brown, add the duck, stir for four to five minutes until no moisture is left and the sheen of oil is visible. Check for salt and remove from the stove. Since this is a dry preparation without much gravy, it is best to serve it with khichuri or parotas, together with a tomato, spring onion and chopped coriander salad.

Two years later, Kadam Bhai came to visit us in Dhaka. During his stay he decided to buy a couple of ducks and cook them for me, probably because he remembered my delighted appreciation in the village. This time he used a different method.

DUCK WITH COCONUT MILK

FOR THREE TO FOUR PEOPLE

INGREDIENTS

1 medium-sized duck of 1½ kg (3 lb)
750 ml (1¼ pints) of water
1 teaspoon of whole coriander seeds
A piece of ginger, 2.5 cm (1 in) long
1 whole medium onion
1+2 bay leaves
Milk extracted from 1 medium-sized coconut
175 ml (6 fl oz) of ghee
3 teaspoons of ground ginger
2 teaspoons of ground coriander
1 teaspoon each of chilli and turmeric powder
½ teaspoon of ground black pepper
Salt to taste

METHOD

Kadam Bhai called this simply duck with coconut milk.
The birds were of a medium size and he set aside the fleshy
portions, drumsticks, thighs, breasts. The rest—necks,
wings, lower ribs, back, even heads—he put into a pan
with water to make a stock spiced with whole coriander
seeds, ginger, onion and a bay leaf. This he left, tightly covered,
over a low flame until the meat was completely separated
from the bones. Removing the pan from the stove, he
strained the stock through a cheesecloth, crushing the meat
to extract the last bit of juice before discarding it and the
bones. Next he extracted milk from a coconut the usual
way, grinding the flesh, soaking it for half an hour in 120 ml
(4 fl oz) of hot water and straining it. He was going to use
double the amount of milk with water. Then he put a large
pot on the stove and heated ghee in it. Into this he threw in
bay leaves, ground ginger, ground coriander, chilli and

turmeric powder and ground black pepper and salt. After frying these for two to three minutes he added the pieces of duck. He kept stirring the meat until it became very dark brown, at which point he added the stock to cover the meat together with some salt. Duck takes a long time to cook, and more stock can be added if needed. When the duck was almost done, he added the coconut milk and kept stirring over a high heat. As the gravy thickened, he added the juice of a large lemon, checked for salt and removed the duck from the stove. The rich gamy taste of the bird was successfully complemented by the sweet-and-sour touch of coconut milk and lemon. A polao made with fine white rice was a perfect accompaniment.

It was the wife of a colleague of my husband's who first made me a very well-known Muslim meat dish, the handi kabab. The name comes from the Bengali handi, the peculiar cooking pot, round bottomed and with a pitcher-like narrowing of the neck and a wide rim for easy handling. This dish was something I had heard about from childhood. All kababs are Muslim preparations, but somehow, the handi kabab seemed to have an especially strong flavour of the 'other' community. Strangely, though I lived in Dhaka for almost seven years, and was invited to eat at many homes, this was the only occasion when I was given the handi kabab. That year, the festival of Bakr-id had fallen in the winter and the handi kabab was the ideal way to prepare some of the sacrificial meat. This can be made equally well in a large thick-bottomed pot with raised sides and a fitting lid.

HANDI KABAB

FOR SIX PEOPLE

INGREDIENTS

1 kg (2 lb) of beef or lamb
10–12 onions, finely chopped

180 ml (6 fl oz) of oil

6 cloves

2 sticks of cinnamon

4 cardamoms

2 bay leaves

1 teaspoon each of whole cumin and coriander

2 teaspoons of whole peppercorns

½ teaspoon of crushed nutmeg

A large pinch of mace

3 tablespoons of vinegar

2 teaspoons of garlic paste

2 teaspoons of ginger paste

2 teaspoons of chilli powder

250 ml (8 fl oz) of water

Salt to taste

METHOD

Our hostess's method for making handi kabab seemed fairly simple, but the result was surprisingly good. The meat was thinly sliced instead of being cubed and then pounded on a grinding stone. The finely chopped onions were lightly fried in 120 ml (4 fl oz) of oil, removed and set aside. It is important to press the excess oil out of the onions as you lift them out of the pot. In the same oil she fried cloves, cinnamon, cardamoms, bay leaves, whole cumin and coriander, whole peppercorns, crushed nutmeg and mace. When these were browned, she lifted them out, again pressing the oil against the side of the pot. The spices, together with the onions, were ground on the stone. A pestle and mortar or blender could be used too. Some more oil, about 60 ml (2 fl oz), was added to the pot and the pounded meat, mixed with vinegar, was thrown into the hot oil. To this was added garlic and ginger paste and chilli powder, salt to taste and water. When all the ingredients had been thoroughly stirred once, the pot was left covered on a low flame until the meat was absolutely tender and the water had evaporated. Then she added the ground, fried spices, stirred thoroughly, kept the pot covered for five more minutes, and the meat was ready to serve. This is very good with plain polao or with parotas or luchis.

PLAIN POLAO

FOR EIGHT PEOPLE

INGREDIENTS

500 gm (1 lb) of Basmati rice
120 ml (4 fl oz) of ghee
4 pieces of cinnamon, 2.5 cm (1 in) long
4 cardamoms
4 cloves
2 teaspoons of ginger paste
1.7 l (3½ pints) of hot water
2 tablespoons of keora water
Salt to taste

METHOD

To make plain polao, take the Basmati rice, wash it thoroughly and let it drain in a colander. In a large pot heat the ghee and add the cinnamons, cardamoms and cloves. Mix the ground ginger with a little water and add to the ghee. Stir a couple of times, pour in the hot water and some salt and cover the pot. As soon as the water comes to a boil, add the rice and keep stirring carefully. Let it boil for a minute or so, add the keora water and cover the pot tightly. Reduce the heat to low. Keep the pot covered for about twenty to twenty-two minutes. If the heat cannot be lowered enough to keep the polao from sticking to the pot or burning, you could put a heavy metal tray or a piece of tin between the pot and the stove. Do not uncover or stir the polao. After twenty minutes remove the pot from the stove and leave covered for another twenty to twenty-five minutes before serving. To garnish, you can finely slice some onions and fry them in ghee until light brown. Remove them immediately from the heat and take them out of the pan, pressing the ghee out. Leave them scattered on a plate so that they remain dry and crisp. To serve, dish out the polao on a large oval serving dish and sprinkle the fried onions on top. This garnish is called *bereshta* in Bangladesh. You can also put sliced hard-boiled eggs on top and orange or yellow food colouring to the polao.

Winter, of course, is also the time when the great rivers are at their tamest, without having totally lost their character or potency, as sometimes happens in the hottest of summers. River cruises on steamboats or launches are a frequent pleasure. And the tranquil waters, even at the large junctions of waterways, make the raging torrents of the monsoon an unreal dream. Fishermen have an easy time hauling in their catch, whether it is big fish like rui, katla or hilsa or some of the smaller varieties. But some of the most delectable fruits of the river in winter are several kinds of shrimps and prawns as well as a kind of perch, the koi. Like the hilsa, the prawn has a specially elevated status and its price reflects it. The striped tiger prawn or bagda chingri is cooked with ground coconut or with winter vegetables or made into a paturi like the hilsa, while the big, fat galda chingri, king prawns, are cherished for their wonderful juicy taste and added to a rich cauliflower and potato kalia or made into the classic malaikari. Overfishing with trawlers in estuarine waters and with nets in the rivers has made the galda chingri rare to the point of being an extinct or unaffordable species. But even now, when the favourite son-in-law arrives for a visit, the Bengali parent will scour the markets for these top-heavy, mustachioed monsters, to create a memorable lunch.

The malaikari, which makes every Bengali salivate with pleasure, is a rich red preparation where the sauce, enriched with thick coconut milk, ghee, spices and the oozing juices from the huge heads, serves as a background to the richer red of the shells enclosing the heads. Though considered a Bengali classic, it is doubtful if the malaikari has been in Bengal for more than 150 years. Even Iswarchandra Gupta, the poet of good food and good cooking, who died 131 years ago, did not mention it. There are many theories about the origins of the name malaikari which seems linked to the English word curry. By the nineteenth century it was being used for the various dishes cooked by the people of Ceylon and southern India with coconut milk, as is the malaikari, and flavoured with kari leaves. Another theory argues that the dish should be called Malay curry since the people of the Malay archipelago have been cooking with coconut milk for centuries, a practice which came back to us through the emigrant Indian Tamil settlers there. To my mind, however, there is a big difference between Bengali malaikari and similar recipes in cookbooks on Southeast Asian food. It is the combination of the garom mashla flavour with the coconut milk and the pure ghee.

The very first time my husband came to Calcutta to meet my parents it was March and my mother regretted not being able to find good enough galda chingri. But the next time he came it was Christmas time and she was thrilled to be able to make malaikari for her one and only son-in-law. I watched her with interest, since I had never had the nerve to try making it before.

GALDA CHINGRIR MALAIKARI

FOR FOUR PEOPLE

INGREDIENTS

1 kg (2 lb) of the king prawns

250 ml (8 fl oz) of thick coconut milk

5-6 medium onions

5 cm (2 in) piece of ginger

8 cloves of garlic

3 sticks of cinnamon, 2.5 cm (1 in) long

4 cardamoms

2 cloves

60 ml (2 fl oz) of peanut oil

3 tablespoons of ghee

3-4 teaspoons of sugar

Salt to taste

METHOD

To make the galda chingrir malaikari, 1 kg (2 lb) of the king prawns had been bought. Since their heads make up so much of their weight, you need to buy a lot to serve amply. But the pleasure we get from the juicy heads will not be there unless the cook retains the heads and takes the trouble of cleaning them. In Bengal this is done by inserting a matchstick or something like that and drawing out the green bile sac which tends to make the whole head taste bitter. The coral is left undisturbed. Both the head and the tail with shell are left attached to the body which is peeled and deveined. When cooked, the shell turns red and heightens the rich red of the gravy. The prawns are washed, dusted with salt and turmeric and steamed for three to four minutes (cooking directly in water would mean draining the water together with a good part of the coral which will ooze out).

The steamed prawns were set aside and my mother ground the flesh of a large coconut to extract the milk from it. A small handful of the ground coconut flesh was set aside before thick milk was extracted and diluted by adding water. After this, the onions, ginger and cloves of garlic were ground together on the stone. Then came the garom mashla, sticks of cinnamon, cardamoms and cloves which were made into a paste with a little water. A large karai was put on the stove and peanut oil was heated together with ghee. The onion, ginger and garlic paste was fried until golden-brown. To this was added turmeric powder, chilli powder and half the ground garom mashla. After frying these for a minute, she added the steamed prawns and stirred them carefully until they were nicely coated with the spices. The coconut milk was poured over them and brought to a boil. Salt and sugar were added and the karai kept covered over a low flame until the gravy thickened and the prawns were tender. The final touch was the addition of the coconut paste and the rest of the garom mashla. When everything had been thoroughly blended, the gravy was tasted for the salt and sugar balance. Like all dishes made with coconut milk, the malaikari must have a sweetish taste. If more sugar is needed, you can add it at the end. The sauce should be rich, fragrant and red, and the vivid red shells of the heads and tails of the galda chingri give it an even richer look. Some people use the bagda chingri, tiger prawns, for their malaikari and they also prefer to make it white, in which case turmeric and chilli powder are omitted and green chillies are added for zest.

Tiger prawns are prized in Bengal for their relative fleshiness. The heads are not so big and do not make up the most of the weight of an expensive commodity. They, too, are combined with the coconut but in many different ways. The ultimate in gustatory delight is *dab chingri*, a preparation where the prawns are mixed with a pungent mustard paste, salt, mustard oil and green chillies and stuffed inside a tender green coconut whose top has been removed and the excess water drained out. The coconut is then plastered with mud and slowly baked in a wood fire. Needless to say, this is a typical rural recipe which survived in the great feudal houses in Dhaka and Calcutta with their huge cavernous kitchens and army of servants to build the wood fire and clean up the ashes. In modern Bengali homes where space is a big constraint and there are hardly any live-in servants, such elaborate arrangements are rare. But there is a simpler version which is not subject to any constraints provided the ripe coconut is available.

NARKEL CHINGRI

FOR FOUR PEOPLE

INGREDIENTS

500 gm (1 lb) of tiger prawns
½ a large coconut
2 tablespoons of black mustard seeds
1 teaspoon of turmeric powder
5-6 slit green chillies
60 ml (2 fl oz) + 2 teaspoons of mustard oil
Juice of 1 medium lemon
Salt to taste

METHOD

To make narkel chingri, it is essential to have the black, pungent mustard we use in Bengal, not white or brown mustard. Grind the mustard seeds on a stone or in a blender with a touch of salt and green chilli. The finer the paste, the better. Rinse the prawns carefully in water after shelling and deveining them. You can discard the heads if you want. Squeeze the juice of the lemon over the prawns and leave for ten minutes. Rinse again in cold water. Heat the oil in a karai and throw in the prawns dusted with turmeric. After a minute or so, add the ground coconut, the green chillies, ground mustard and salt to taste. Stir briskly and keep covered over a low flame until the prawns are tender and all the flavours have mingled. Uncover, stir over high heat until any excess moisture has evaporated and remove from the flame. Add 2 teaspoons of fresh mustard oil and keep covered until it is time to serve. This is best with plain boiled rice.

Among the many cherished fishes of winter can be mentioned the koi, the shol and the magur. All of them are always bought live. Since they seem very hard to kill, living for a long time in buckets of water, it is assumed that a dead specimen must be really diseased. Legend tells of a shol fish that was perverse enough to live even after being roasted over a fire. A certain king, unwise enough to incur the wrath of Shani, Saturn, who was persecuted by the malevolent deity until he lost everything and had to become a recluse in the forest, managed to catch a shol one day and roasted it over a fire for his lunch. Just as he was about to eat it, the fish slipped out of his grasp and disappeared into the river.

There are many apocryphal stories about the koi too. Like the hilsa, the koi also becomes fat and oily in winter. But despite its wonderful taste it is an even more dangerous fish than the hilsa. Not being a big fish (the large ones are not more than 20-25 cm [8-10 in] in length), it is served whole and the curved bones of the stomach can be lethal if stuck in the throat. One of my favourite koi dishes is made by my mother with the fish being first lightly fried, coated with chilli and turmeric powder and salt. It is then cooked in the juice of some grated onion and ginger. Green chillies add sharpness and flavour, and the delicate but oily sauce coats the fish lovingly as you eat it with plain rice. Iswarchandra Gupta, when commenting on the Englishman's way of eating fish, sneered at the total absence of spices when the fish is brought to the table and at the compensatory embrace of the fish by table mustard poured over it. In really good Bengali fish preparations too (except the jhol), the sauce embraces the fish with loving tenacity. The koi also features in some of the medieval mangalkabyas, cooked with the juice of ginger or with ground black pepper.

As the first month of winter, Poush, rolls on, the occasional north wind becomes a little too nippy in the mornings, and the dust flies around to settle in a pall over available surfaces. The heavy, still evening air traps the smoke from the factories and open-air charcoal stoves that are still used in some houses and creates a spectral fog. But neither dust nor fog can curb the spirit of fun, for winter is the season for fairs and exhibitions. Shantiniketan in Birbhum district holds an annual Poush Mela which draws crowds from many places. In terms of food, Poush is the specific month for eating two things—one being *mulo*, a species of long white or pinkish white radish, the other being all kinds of rice-wheat-coconut based sweets described by the collective term pitha.

Of the thirteen festivals in twelve months that have become a Bengali proverb, the last day of Poush is probably the only one that is purely based on the pleasures of eating. In the old days when rural and feudal life meant extended families and communal festivities, there was great scope for gifted women to show off their various pithas. Modern urban life is sadly divorced from that, but the art of the pitha lives on. One of the simplest, rasbara, is made from kalai dal paste which is whipped till very frothy, then fried in round balls and finally soaked in syrup. Another very simple pitha, the chitoi pitha, is made from rice flour mixed with water and left in a covered, heated, greased earthen saucer around which some water is sprinkled to keep the pitha from being too dry. Perhaps the most memorable pitha that I have ever tasted, at the home of Professor Abdul Razzaque in Dhaka, was a variation of the chitoi. A small triangular hilsa peti had been baked right into it so that it had absorbed the oil and the characteristic hilsa flavour. I doubt if many other savoury snacks can match the delicacy of that taste. During my winter visit to the village, I had seen another kind of pitha being served with the duck bhuna. Made with home-ground rice flour, this was called ruti pitha or chaler ruti (literally rice bread). Atap rice, soaked for an hour and then dried, is ground on the stone to make the flour. It is then sieved to get rid of the coarser particles, then salted boiling water is added to it to make a sticky dough. It is then left for ten to fifteen minutes on a pan set over a very low flame. This indirect heat cooks the dough. The cooled dough is then kneaded, divided into little balls which are rolled out to form chapatis and toasted on a dry tawa or frying pan. Finally each bread or ruti is held on a wire frame over a direct flame so that it puffs up like a balloon and the inside is properly cooked. Served piping hot, it is the most delicious medium to mop up your portion of meat and gravy.

The bulk of pithas, however, are sweet rather than savoury. In my childhood I looked forward to the puli pitha or puli pithe as we Ghotis used to say. Both my grandmother and my mother regularly made this on the last day of Poush. It is both heavy on the stomach and laborious to make without the extra hands of an extended family, and yet winter could never be complete without it. The vital ingredient is khejur gur which permeates the milk and makes this a treat you long for during the rest of the year. Since khejur gur does not seem to be available outside

Bengal, the only way to make this elsewhere is to substitute white sugar for the portion of khejur gur in the recipe that follows. In the absence of gur a vital flavour of Bengal will be missed, but the pitha itself will provide an essential Bengali delight.

PULI PITHA

FOR THREE TO FOUR PEOPLE

INGREDIENTS

250 gm (8 oz) of cream of wheat
½ coconut, finely ground
120 gm (4 oz) of sugar
900 ml (1½ pints) of whole milk
120 gm (4 oz) of solid khejur gur, crushed coarsely
2-3 cardamoms, finely ground
250 ml (8 fl oz) of water

METHOD

To make puli pitha (or dudh puli), the filling is made first, by cooking the ground coconut with sugar over a low flame until it is sticky and gives off a sheen. This is cooled on a plate. The shell or puli is made by setting the cream of wheat to boil in water. When all the water has been absorbed and the cream of wheat forms a big lump, mash it with a spoon or spatula. You should be able to move it easily in the pan in a little while. Remove from the fire, let cool and divide this dough into little round balls. Take each one, flatten it in your palm, put a little coconut filling in the centre and close the shell to form small rolls tapering at the ends. This is the classic shape of the puli pitha. When all the pulis are ready, set the milk to boil in a pan. When it comes to a boil, reduce the heat and evaporate until it is reduced to about 750 ml (1¼ pints). Add the pulis and leave to cook over a low heat. Meanwhile, take the gur (or more sugar) and add to the milk. Stir once or twice, being careful not to break the pulis and let it cook until the gur and milk are thoroughly blended. Remove and pour into a serving dish. Sprinkle the ground cardamom over it.

For the pious Hindus, the end of Poush means the great concourse of pilgrims for the Ganga Sagar Mela on Sagar, an island in the Bay of Bengal where the Hooghly river joins the sea. On the early morning of the sankranti, hundreds of pilgrims plunge for their ritual bath into the icy waters to ensure salvation in the next world, to wash away the sins of this world. In severe winters many elderly pilgrims die here from exposure to the cold. The holy confluence of the river and the sea has also seen some terrible things in the past. Bengali women who often miscarried or could not get pregnant easily, would often promise their first child to the sea, provided they had two safe births in succession. And hundreds of unfortunate women would be forced (through fear and social pressure) to carry out this grim promise. Sometimes a mother would come all the way with the doomed child but find herself unable to part from it. Anxious family members, determined to avoid the wrath of the gods, would then forcibly take the child away from her and throw it into the water. Tagore has a poem about such a woman who drowns her child, desperately pleads with the sea to give it back to her and finally plunges into the turbulent waters herself.

This is the time when winter (what we have of it) bares its teeth occasionally. The pleasure of sleep, so intense when you have warm quilts and blankets, are denied to those who are too poor to afford them. A humorous Bengali verse describes the three stages of an inadequately covered man through a cold night. He starts out straight as the dhenki board which is used for threshing rice; halfway through the night he has assumed the half-moon shape of a tautly strung bow; and in the early hours of the morning he has curled up in a knot like a dog. In the villages they sometimes light fires outside cottages and warm themselves before going to bed, a luxury not possible in the enclosed town houses. During such short cold waves I have often longed for the small, crackling fires of the countryside.

Though the season is such a cornucopia of new and different vegetables, there are not too many fruits that are particularly available in the winter. The great exception is the orange which grows in the hilly regions of Darjeeling in West Bengal and Sylhet in Bangladesh. The Bengali orange is not the same as the Western fruit of that name. What we call an orange is the tangerine of the West. The transposition of the English name is interesting, for the word orange is derived from the Hindi and Urdu *narangi*. These round, pulpy, juicy, fragrant fruits are much prized and the fruit sellers in the markets set their prices high, knowing they will still manage to sell their quota.

In my family, the orange was mostly eaten as a fruit, the only culinary effort I have seen being the kheer with orange pulp made by my mother. But in Bangladesh I have eaten two wonderful orange dishes that linger vividly on my palate even after so many years. One was, to me, the unthinkable combination of the fruit with the koi fish. Unlike the French duck with orange or Polynesian meat dishes cooked with pineapple, Bengali cuisine rarely combines fruit with fish or meat. The only exceptions I have seen have been in Bangladesh, where once I had a hilsa dish cooked with pineapple and this koi with orange. The latter was made by my friend Nusrat when she invited me for lunch one beautiful winter afternoon. Having heard some of my comments about the comparative richness and heaviness of Muslim cooking versus the lightness of Hindu cooking, she was determined to prove that the Muslims could serve a meal that was both delicious and light. Amazingly, there was no meat, nor polao. Instead she served plain boiled rice with moong dal flavoured with ginger, cumin and green chilli, fried brinjals, koi with orange, brinjal in tamarind sauce and finally a mouthwatering dessert of orange-flavoured sweet rice. The tangerine pulp provided a lovely rich tint from which the dark koi and the green chillies stood out. And the sweet-and-sour taste of the pulp, with the added pungency of mustard oil, heightened the natural flavour of the koi. It was one of the best meals I have had in Bangladesh.

KAMALA KOI

FOR THREE PEOPLE

INGREDIENTS

800 gm (1.6 lb) of koi fish
4 medium onions, finely chopped
3 teaspoons of garlic paste
1½ teaspoons of ground ginger
2½ teaspoons of red chilli powder
7-8 green chillies
120 ml (4 fl oz) of mustard oil
250 ml (8 fl oz) of water
Salt to taste

METHOD

For this dish of kamala koi, the koi fish is eaten whole. The koi is scaled thoroughly and cleaned and gutted with the back part of the head being left attached to the body. The gills are discarded. Like other fish, these kois were also dusted with salt and turmeric, fried lightly in oil and set aside. The painful part of making this dish was dealing with the oranges. Each was peeled, the sections separated, and the pips and translucent cover removed so that only the inner pulp and juice remained. The mustard oil was heated in a karai and the finely chopped onions were browned. All the ground spices were thrown in and stirred until they were dark brown and nearly sticking to the pot. A little water was sprinkled over them and the orange pulp added. This was stirred for three to four minutes, the spatula smashing the bigger portions, and the whole mixture was blended smoothly. Next, the water was poured in and 2 teaspoons of salt added. When the water came to a boil, the fish were placed in the karai with the green chillies and left to cook until the gravy had thickened. Then each fish was turned over and the karai left on a high heat for two to three minutes before being removed from the stove. The salt can be checked at this point, more added if needed, and a few drops of mustard oil have to be added. The fish should then be left covered till serving time. If no other fish or meat is being made then this will suffice only for three people.

The kamala or orange theme suggested by the fish preparation was further developed by a lovely salad made with the inner pulp of the orange sections and thinly sliced green bell peppers, a recently cultivated vegetable in this region. The final denouement was the *kamalar jarda* or orange-flavoured sweet rice served as our dessert. Though West Bengal has plenty of uses for rice, this kind of dessert is not at all common here. Perhaps some Muslim families with a strong tradition of elaborate cooking do make this sometimes, but I have never encountered it this side of the border. From a distance it looks almost like a dish of polao with orange food colouring added to it. But as you get closer, you see the syrup and the fruit juice enveloping the rice as well as the minute shreds of orange pulp. As for the fragrance, the combination of the rich smell of ghee and the fruitiness of the orange is amazing. The garnish of white almonds, green pistachios and brown raisins on top create the impression of a colourful patterned quilt.

ORANGE-FLAVOURED SWEET RICE

FOR SEVEN TO EIGHT PEOPLE

INGREDIENTS

20 medium oranges
500 gm (1 lb) of fine Basmati rice
2.2 l (4 pints) of water (for the rice)
1 kg (2 lb) of sugar
120 ml (4 fl oz) of water (for the sugar syrup)
3 sticks of cinnamon
4 cardamoms
4 cloves
120 ml (4 fl oz) of ghee

METHOD

To make the orange-flavoured sweet rice, the oranges were
first peeled, the sections separated and the pulp and juice
scraped out into a waiting bowl. Enough of the peel was
chopped into tiny slivers to make 120 gm (4 oz). This was
set aside separately. Then she measured out the rice and
rinsed it in a colander under running water. Leaving the
rice in the colander, she put to boil 2.2 litres (4 pints) of
water in a very large pot, adding a touch of orange food
colouring to it. She added the rice to the boiling water and
stirred from time to time until the rice was done. The orange
peel was thrown in just before the rice was ready and kept
there for a couple of minutes. The water was then drained
and the rice left in the colander until it was dry. Then it was
transferred to a large tray and spread out to let all lingering
excess moisture evaporate. Meanwhile, she took another
pot and made a syrup with sugar and water. To this was
added cinnamon, cardamoms and cloves. She stirred the
syrup over a low flame until all the sugar melted. Then she
added the orange pulp, juice and the ghee and cooked the

mixture for three to four minutes before adding the rice. This was stirred and stirred until no moisture was left and the rice gleaming with ghee, but she was careful not to let the rice burn or stick to the pot. At this stage the pot was covered tightly and left on the lowest of low flames for five more minutes. If this is difficult, you can try putting the pot in an oven set at the lowest temperature. When the jarda was finally done, she transferred it to a shallow silver serving dish and left it uncovered until it had cooled. Then she turned it over several times with a fork so that it would not be sticky or lumpy. It is essential for a jarda to be light and fluffy. Before serving she garnished it with almonds, pistachios and raisins.

Towards the end of Magh the cold can be made severe by occasional showers which are usually welcomed as a blessing for the winter crops. They were even more so in the days before extensive irrigation. As Khana the wise woman declared, blessed is the land of the fortunate king where it rains at the end of Magh. Afternoons then become a time of pure bliss, with the worst of the dust washed away and the kindest of suns beaming from blue skies. The Bengali's post-lunch siesta becomes a thing of the past as even the most indolent person enjoys the daylight. I found it particularly pleasant to take a rickshaw and be driven around the quieter streets of Dhaka. On the balconies and porches of houses I would observe the women sitting with their long hair spread over their backs, wet and gleaming from the bath and drying in the sun. Elderly folk, well-wrapped up in shawls would be facing away from the sun, almost bending forward so that the whole stretch of their backs could be warmed by the sun. Silk and woollen clothes would be hanging from clothes lines, being warmed for the umpteenth time to get rid of all lingering mustiness.

This is also the time for developing all kinds of sniffles, colds and coughs and in childhood we often dispensed with conventional medical treatment. For colds my grandmother would dose us with the age-old remedy of tulsi, crushed with honey in a little oval marble mortar reserved for such medicinal purposes. If a dry cough persisted, it was time to brew hot drinks sweetened with crystallized palm sugar or to boil dried sticks of a herb called *jashtimadhu* in water which absorbed the liquorice-like taste and flavour of the herb. In our Vaishnav house the tulsi had a special place since it is a plant favoured by Krishna. Rows of pots stood on the verandas and roof, with the plant growing in them, and every day each person had to eat a few leaves.

By the time winter draws to a close, good eating, increased outdoor activity and brisk weather have put the Bengali in the most contented frame of mind he can ever have. As Magh comes to an end and the occasional southern zephyr sweeps over the land as a prelude to our elusive spring, Bengal clings tenaciously to the last remnants of blissful winter. The shawls, quilts and blankets are used even when not necessary and the last of the koi or the last orange enjoyed with protracted relish.

This contentment and pleasurable, even sensuous, abandonment is the perfect foil for the gentle discipline symbolized by Saraswati, Durga's daughter, chaste white goddess of learning who comes gliding along on her regal white swan on the fifth day of the Magh new moon. She is a dual Muse, for in one hand she carries a book and in the other a veena, a stringed instrument similar to the sitar. Everything about her is white, including her sari, and her tranquil preoccupations make her the antithesis of her sister Lakshmi, red-robed goddess of fortune. It is commonly believed that those favoured by one goddess will be shunned by the other, and there are many amusing stories about how each one tried to establish her superiority over the other.

Perhaps it is an indication of whose favour our family sought that in my grandparents' house Saraswati was worshipped on this day with full ceremony. This was the only big puja I have ever seen at home. A huge image of the goddess would be bought and installed in the dalan or central courtyard and a priest would be hired to do the puja rites. From early morning the house was a bustle of activity as we all got up and took turns to bathe and put on fresh clothes. My grandmother, mother and aunts would sit at several bontis and slice a huge mound of fruits like apples, *shakalus*, *safedas*, which together with bits of sugarcane, bananas, dates and *kul* (a kind of plum) would be offered to the goddess. The bananas offered to Saraswati are a special type, very sweet, but full of large black seeds. The kul cannot be touched before being offered to the goddess. Since it has a very short season, Bengalis eagerly look forward to the goddess's arrival to receive the sanction to eat this sweet-and-sour fruit. This variety of kul is called a *narkel kul*. A sour red species, the *topa kul*, can be made into lovely sweet pickles with gur or salted and dried in the sun.

Once all the fruits were ready, the incense lit and flowers brought in to be offered to the goddess, the priest would lead us through the special prayers. Strangely, the white-clad goddess comes at a time when there are no white flowers. It is the marigold, golden or pale yellow or even rusty red, that is considered her special bloom. For children, one bit of undiluted joy is offering up all schoolbooks to the goddess, since it is forbidden to study on this day. Instead, we would fold our palms and intone the Sanskrit mantra addressing the petal-white, deep-breasted goddess bedecked with snowy pearls and beseech her to grant us comprehensive knowledge. Once the flowers had been placed at her feet, we were free to break our fast before trooping out to see the neighbourhood images.

It is customary for women to wear pale yellow saris on the day of Saraswati puja. The colour is called basanti in Bengali from Basanta, spring, and this is the surest indication that winter will disappear soon. New green leaves and flowers in flaming colours will usher in a changeable, brief season of fluctuating temperatures and festive weddings. But the presence of the goddess provides a natural hiatus between quiet contentment and febrile excitement. In the evening my family would get together to sing, for music is the other way to honour the goddess. Though metaphysical realizations were far from our minds, we children too were conscious of an elevated calm after the day's activities. My youngest aunt, who had a magnificent voice, would sing a Sanskrit hymn beseeching the goddess to bestow the gift of music, the highest form of art, and the slow cadence always struck a responsive chord in our grubby little hearts.

Like all other goddesses, Saraswati also leaves in the evening for the final ceremony of immersion in the river. And departing, the snow-white deity takes some human colour back with her. Sindur glows brightly on her forehead and her beautiful pink lips are stained crimson with the juice of spiced paan crushed against them. As she is moved from home or community pandal to truck to the river, the lavish garlands of marigold round her neck almost obscure her white sari, signalling the blazing sunshine of summer to come. Bengal sighs at the parting, for like a Royal Bengal tiger crouching potent, terrible, yet splendid in the grass, summer too is waiting to pounce, behind the immediacy of spring.

EPILOGUE

recaptured essences

And now, before taking leave of Bengal, we will have a last look at Chhobi's family and see how they have come to terms with the universal human situations of separation, sorrow, forgiveness, reunion and rediscovery in the framework of their domestic life.

From above, as her plane descended, Chhobi could see the February landscape: cultivated plots of land, some harvested to bare brownness, some still green with the remnants of winter crops like mustard, split peas, brown chickpeas; clumps of palm and coconut trees; the odd bodies of water and the thin line of meandering river. Ah river. She smiled as the childhood memories came rushing back. Of Dida telling her stories about the prince who went in search of the princess across the seven seas and thirteen rivers. Of hearing her parents and her uncles talk about the incredible rivers of East Bengal, of their ferocious floods and rolling waters and the daredevil types who lived in those parts. She had seen those rivers herself now. And what rivers they were. Even in winter or the driest of summers they were nothing like the insignificant line of water she could see now. More like shimmering wide ribbons or torpid, engorged pythons.

Well, she had sworn to herself she would see the world and have adventures, like all the princes in Dida's stories and she'd certainly had a few. Like those fabled figures, she too had flown across oceans, though no miraculous winged horse had carried her. Like them, she too had pledged her faith and her affections to a stranger. After all these years Chhobi sometimes wondered at herself, shaking with apprehension but determined to marry a Muslim man who was nothing like the childhood images of Muslims, but disturbingly familiar, just another Bengali like herself. Now, marriage over and done with, saddened but enriched by memories of a life in the 'other' Bengal among those East Bengali Muslims who had seemed such terrifying figures in her schooldays, Chhobi was finally coming home to make peace with her family. The marriage, which had happened during her years as a student in America, had led to a total estrangement from her family and even the subsequent divorce had not changed things immediately. From Bangladesh she had gone to America, to think and recreate a life for herself. But four years later had come this unexpected letter from Bilu, her little cousin now grown up and about to get married himself.

'I refuse to do it without you, Chhobidi,' he had written. 'And this estrangement has gone on long enough. Everybody is miserable. Your parents hardly speak a word, but go around like silent shadows. Our grandmother cries every time I ask her about you and I've even seen our uncles and my father blink away tears. I've told them what I feel about it—that it's stupid to persist in this kind of breach in this day and age. They all agreed with me, but were afraid to write to you for fear of your rejection. Then grandmother asked me to write. Please write back, please say you'll come back for my wedding.'

There had been many more letters, back and forth, from her parents, from her uncles, from Dida and some more from Bilu. Finally here she was, the prodigal coming back home after an absence of twenty years across the seven seas and thirteen rivers. They seemed very easy to cross now that she had been detached from life in that other Bengal.

Irrationally, Chhobi wondered what she would be given for lunch. Or perhaps it was a natural thought: so many family dramas had been enacted around the plate of rice. Why not this one, the most excruciating of them all? Was Keshto still there, thin and dour as ever, and did he still have verbal battles with Dida? And Ma, dear Ma, did she still take as much pleasure in cooking and making those mouthwatering prawns, or banana blossom with potatoes, chickpeas and ground coconut, or those incredible luchis, light and puffy like inflated balloons? Tears pricked in her eyes and she tried to think of something else.

As if to help, memory veered in another direction, to the first meal she had had in Bangladesh in her brother-in-law's house in Dhaka. Despite all assurances, she worried about encountering and initially living with her Muslim husband's eldest brother and his family. As often happens, reality fell far short of her apprehensions. Amazing, how she could still remember every detail of that first day in the ample, beautiful house. Sitting down to lunch with the family, she was taken aback at the different tastes that familiar fish and vegetables seemed to have acquired. The novelty of the gravy coating the fish made her ask how they had been cooked. 'Our new sister wants to know what you've put in the fish, Tofazzal,' her hostess asked of the junior cook. 'She likes it.' The young fellow, very rustic and very young, was obviously flustered and the only reply he could think of was, 'Spices,' accompanied by a self-conscious grin. Chhobi forgot her own shyness and laughed. Spices. But of course. What else could you tell some strange lady from foreign parts? It took her several days to figure out that one of the reasons why everything tasted so different was the ubiquitous onion. Like salt, it was an inevitable ingredient.

In the afternoon, when the whole house was enjoying a post-lunch siesta, Chhobi felt restless. She left her husband sleeping in their room and wandered along the veranda to the garden. As she left the flower beds and came to the kitchen garden she saw that one corner near the house was a hive of activity. Two maids and the junior cook were sitting at their bontis and dismembering several chickens. The back door of the kitchen opened on to this space. As Chhobi walked up to them, the servants smiled shyly.

'What's going on?' she asked.

'There's going to be a big dinner tonight in your honour. Lots of guests are coming.'

Chhobi was horrified at the prospect of being given the
once-over so soon. As she stood there trying to make the best
of it, a plump, bald man came out of the kitchen wearing a vest
and a checked lungi, the skirt-like wraparound that men in
Bangladesh wear at home. He held a *biri*, the native cigarette
made of tobacco leaf instead of paper, in one hand and the long
brass spatula called a khunti in the other. This must be the head
cook, Chhobi thought. The sight of her made him drop the biri
and put on an eager ingratiating smile. She went forward and
followed him into the kitchen, more to divert herself than out
of genuine curiosity. Her nose was immediately assailed by the
strong aroma of meat and spices. There was a huge pot on the
gas stove.

'This is the khashi you see on the fire. I am making a rezala
with it. And once the chicken's ready, I'll cook it with rice and
make a morog polao. The shami kabab, as you can see, is all
done. Just a matter of heating and serving them. Then there
will be a cucumber salad. And for dessert, I've made a pineapple
jarda.'

The man lifted the cover from an oval silver dish on the
kitchen counter and she saw the deep saffron tinted rice of the
jarda decorated with almonds, pistachios, bits of edible silver
foil and dried kheer. Curious, she bent forward to smell this
beautiful creation, and then she could make out the fine shreds
of pineapple.

'You must teach me this sometime,' she said, lifting her
head.

'Of course, Apa. Any time you want. In the winter you can
also make a lovely jarda with oranges. It looks even better
because you can see the bits of grated orange peel in the rice.
I think it smells even better.'

Even after so many years, Chhobi could recall the taste of
every item the old man had made that first night far more

intensely than the people she had met or the conversations she had had. The jarda, in particular, stood out as the most exotic discovery in this parallel culinary universe, its fruity aroma richly modified by the rich caramelly flavour of ghee, its pale yellow tones enhanced by the glint of the edible silver foil garnishing it. No kin this, to that other jarda, the perfumed tobacco she had found so fascinating in her childhood.

But her life in Bangladesh had ended five years ago. And here she was, coming back home to probably the biggest adventure of her life—meeting her family as an adult, ready to accept the difficult gift of forgiveness, dying to love and be accepted again. Look at me, she thought as she trundled her luggage trolley towards the exit door. After all the strange encounters I have had, here I am quaking at the thought of meeting my own family again.

But like so many other difficult things it turned out to be very simple. The minute she came out, Chhobi could make out her mother's face, older, more lined, grey at the temples, but essentially the same dear face that had smiled at her through a film of tears as they said goodbye twenty years ago. And though she had last seen him as a schoolboy, Chhobi had no difficulty picking out the tall handsome young man who must be her cousin Bilu. He was grinning widely as he came rushing forward through the crowd of people.

'You haven't changed much, Chhobidi,' he said hugging her after the respectful gesture of touching her feet.

'But you have,' she said, amazed and secretly proud of his good looks. He had obviously taken after his mother, but seemed to have no touch of her narcissistic coyness.

As Chhobi raised her head after touching her mother's feet, she noticed the familiar little bulge in the right cheek.

'So Ma,' she said, absurdly casual after all these fraught years, 'you haven't stopped taking paan yet.'

'I wanted to look just the way I used to when you went away dear,' said Ma, her voice trembling, her hands stroking her daughter's hair.

'You do,' said Chhobi, and knew she was home. Once again, she would let herself feel the presence of her own kind, the youthful pleasure of submerging herself in a pre-ordained routine, once again be urged to eat more of this or that, once again relinquish responsibility in a hundred minor ways.

Inside the rented car that was to take them back from the airport, the first thing Ma did was to take out a few drooping tulsi leaves from a small box and put them in Chhobi's mouth.

'Your Dida plucked them this morning for you. They should be the first thing you eat, she said.'

I wonder how many of the old tulsi plants she still has on the southern veranda, thought Chhobi, overcome with memories of mornings with Dida.

'Is the kamini still there Ma? And the hasnahana?'

'Yes, dear. Still flowering beautifully.'

Bilu was pointing out the new by-pass road along which they were travelling. Now, he explained, they could get home from the airport in half an hour. 'I bet in the old days it was a nightmare, going through all those narrow lanes of north Calcutta.'

'Oh yes. The journey then took an hour and a half. And if you were unlucky, you could get into a traffic jam that could make you miss the plane.'

Bilu shook his head and started pointing out several new apartment buildings that had come up. Chhobi listened with half an ear. It was hard to rediscover the little boy she had left behind, except in the still quite innocent eyes. How fortuitous his birth, which had healed such a terrible breach in the family. And now, again, he had made it possible for another breach to heal.

'Does your mother still aggravate Dida by forgetting all the rules of ritual purity?' she asked, and saw Ma smiling quietly.

'Oh yes,' said Bilu with an irreverent grin, not averse to discussing either his mother or his grandmother. 'Though things have been very quiet for the last few years. Old age I suppose. But the minute the old lady heard you were coming back, she dropped ten years. And the battle between mother and daughter-in-law is raging all over again. It's really funny, listening to them.'

So, she's excited about seeing me, thought Chhobi, looking out of the window, and hugging the thought close to her heart. It's good to be coming back, good to feel that I matter so much. Like a cool glass of lemonade in the summer. Yet, still, she also felt afraid.

'What about Shejo mamima?' she said, enquiring about her older aunt, 'Does she still invite all the relatives every month and cook khashi for them?'

'Oh no,' said Ma. 'Those days are over. She doesn't have that kind of energy any more.'

'And Baba?' asked Chhobi with a tremor in her voice, looking out of the window, knowing that meeting her father was the hardest thing she had to face. He had reacted far more strongly to her marriage than any other member of her family. Chhobi had, in fact, been thunderstruck at the violence of his rejection of her and her choice. And even forgiveness now could not wipe away the memory of the pain. Her mother must have sensed the qualm behind the question for she quickly said, 'Oh, he wanted to come with us to the airport too. But he's not well you know. We were not sure if your plane would be on time, how long we'd have to wait. But he's most excited about your coming,' Ma concluded, touching her daughter's hand.

'Is he?'

'Oh yes. You should have seen him this morning, conferring

with Keshto about the shopping, since he can't go himself.'

'Keshto! You mean he's still there? He must be a hundred by now.'

'Well, he looks just the same as ever and cooks just as badly. Your father told him to go buy a good rui and some parshe fish, because you always liked them. He didn't want you to have hilsa the very first day. It's so oily, he was afraid it might be too rich for you. Anyway, I cooked both the fish myself. At least your first lunch shouldn't be spoiled by Keshto.'

'This is where I work, Chhobidi,' Bilu was saying, pointing to a tall building.

'How come you are not at work today then?' she asked. 'Did you take the day off in my honour?'

'Shame on you Chhobidi'. Don't you know that today is Id-ul-fitr, the biggest Muslim festival? You, after living in Bangladesh for so many years?'

'I haven't been there for the last five years,' muttered Chhobi uncomfortably. She looked at her mother but her face did not show anything. There, finally it had been brought up, Bangladesh, her life there with the Muslim, among all the Muslims. And why not. The sooner they come to terms with my experiences, the better. Id-ul-fitr. How meaningless it is to all these people, just another holiday, as it was to me when I lived here. No Muslim friends, no Muslim contacts. All we knew was that school was closed and that one did not have to go to work. How far away that first Id in Dhaka seemed now. And yet the details were so clear, like the view of a sky through a telescope. The refreshing iftaar that was brought in during the evenings of Ramadan to break the day's fast. How ceremoniously the first cool drink of lemonade or just plain water was drunk and savoured, to be followed by the little savoury snacks. The end of the month of fasting and the arrival of the great day of Id-ul-fitr. The people out in the streets, visiting each other, dressed in new clothes, the ritual offer of vermicelli cooked in milk or syrup and ghee, the laughter, the greetings, the embraces, the touching of the feet of elders. And at lunchtime, the rich array of festive meats, the effusion of hospitality, chatter and laughter. Another time, another world.

'Well, we are almost there, Chhobidi,' said Bilu looking at her, obviously sensitive to all the complex emotions besieging her. She looked out of the window and there it was, the old well-remembered landmark, the shimul tree covered with scarlet blossoms, and beyond that the well-loved house with its long, entwining verandas. The car stopped, she got out and there they all were: Baba, her uncles and aunts and even Keshto. Dida, she knew from her letters, was too full of aches and pains to come downstairs. With immense effort she walked across the pavement and bent to touch her father's feet.

'Are you well, my dear?' he asked, touching her head in blessing and putting one hand on her shoulder. The tremulousness of his voice told Chhobi of pain, of time passed, of time endured.

'Yes Baba,' she said and realized that here, too, the doors were wide open. A cheerful babble of conversation ensued as everybody came forward with laughter, questions and embraces.

'Keshto doesn't seem to have changed at all,' she said, looking at him and the old servant smiled.

'Dida is waiting for you,' said her father and once again, Chhobi was conscious of that beloved presence which had been so central to her life in this house. No shadow of doubt about Dida's love had clouded her mind during these twenty years of absence, and now she was finally going to see her and be with her. Up the stairs once again to the hexagonal dalan, the suffused daylight coming in through its row of glass windows to illuminate the old rattan furniture, and the final letting go in Dida's arms.

They felt thinner, almost tenuous, but the wise old eyes told her that Dida was all there, more in command of herself than anybody else.

'Come and sit next to me,' she said, patting the sofa, and Chhobi experienced the luxury of doing what she was told.

'Get the girl a glass of water and a *naru*,' Dida commanded Bilu's mother.

'I don't need a naru. I just want a glass of water before lunch.'

'Nonsense. Didn't I always tell you not to have water on an empty stomach? Besides, I made those narus myself, just the way you liked them, with coconut and khejur gur. What do you mean, you don't want them.'

Chhobi laughed. Some things never change. In Dida's house you still had to eat a sweet before you could have a glass of water, no matter what the time of day. This she had tried to explain to her American friends and they had found it baffling, much as they had found her strange habit of cutting vegetables in different shapes. In her fine American kitchen where knives had replaced bontis, Chhobi would insist on cutting the potatoes in different ways for different preparations, just as Dida had, sitting on the floor so many years ago.

As she sat eating her naru, brown and sticky with the khejur gur, the soft resistance of the coconut making a pleasure of chewing, Bilu bombarded her with questions, mostly about her life in America. But it was her second uncle who asked her how she had liked living in Bangladesh. A look at her father's face showed none of the strain she had feared. And Chhobi happily launched into some of her encounters with those Bangals, their strange dialects and their beautiful country.

'What about the rivers of Bangladesh?' asked Bilu.

'They are wonderful. I never thought I could fall in love with rivers, me a scared little Ghoti from West Bengal. But it was an amazing experience, travelling down those rivers in old paddle steamers. I went to Barisal several times, and each time the steamer came to the confluence of the Padma and the Meghna, my heart would stop in wonder. It was like an ocean, that immense stretch of water. And one time, during a trip to Rajshahi, we were caught in a storm in a ferry boat. It made me realize how helpless human beings are, in spite of all our machines, and you know, I could almost see that there might be some truth in old wives' tales. People who live in such surroundings feel more deeply than we do!'

It was Dida who broke up the conversation after a while, telling Chhobi to go and take a bath before lunch. Before going upstairs, Chhobi looked into the old kitchen, still cavernous and gloomy as ever, but no longer full of that dark fascination she had felt as a child. Keshto, however, looked every bit as much the lord of this domain as he used to and showed her all the things that had been already made for lunch. 'Have you become a memsahib, or can you still eat rice and fish with your hands?' he said grinning. 'Just wait and see,' Chhobi grinned back, and lifted the lid of the karai containing the parshe fish in mustard sauce that her mother had made. 'The rui jhol is really good,' said Keshto, uncovering it again. The delicately balanced aroma of cumin-coriander-ginger hit her nose and irresistibly, she bent forward, plucked out a luscious kalai dal bori and put it in her mouth. Nothing had ever tasted so good, it seemed, during the past twenty years! 'I'd better get out of here, before Dida finds me stealing bori,' said Chhobi and left Keshto among his pots. A look into the dining room showed the old dining table still in place, still covered by a sheet of plastic. Upstairs, in her old room, Chhobi sat on the bed for a few minutes, feeling the presence of the old house in her bones. She moved the curtains and once again, the shimul tree nodded at her much as it used to so many years ago. After lunch, she decided

she would go to the southern veranda and look at her other
friend, the kadam.

At lunchtime, the conversation moved back to Bangladesh,
as Chhobi tried to describe the different ways of cooking fish
and meat that she had encountered there.

'Many of the women I got to know there were the most
wonderful cooks and tried to teach me some of their recipes,'
she said.

'Well,' smiled Dida, from her chair, set at a slight distance
from the rest of them around the dining table, 'our Bilu is also
marrying a Bangal. Her family comes from Dhaka, though she
was born here and has never set foot in Bangladesh.'

'I am sure she's a wonderful cook,' said Ma. 'These Bangal
girls are very well trained, unlike our Ghoti girls. I always
regretted not having taught you anything before letting you go
out in the world. But you seemed to have no interest in cooking
and your father did not want me to push you into the kitchen.
So I didn't.'

'I may have had no interest in cooking, but I certainly was
an enthusiastic eater. I must have been your most devoted fan,
in terms of appreciating all the things you made. All these years,
I have remembered the taste and smell of your special dishes,
the mocha, the mustard-hilsa, your wonderful luchis, your
potatoes with tamarind and asafoetida, and so many other things.'

'Have you learned to cook, Chhobidi?' asked Bilu.

'Some things, I suppose. And I am a mixture of many
influences, especially the Muslim cuisine of Bangladesh. Their
variety in cooking meat and poultry dishes is really remarkable.
I never realized how limited our meat cooking was until I went
to live there. The main thing that bothered me was that all
their vegetable dishes tasted the same. Everything was called
a bhaji and everything was cooked with onions and green chillies.
No phorons, no sauces. But then they had, as I have told you

before, the most amazing innovations, like koi fish with oranges!'

'You must tell Brinda about this,' said Bilu smiling. 'She's dying to meet you.'

'Good god, why?'

'Oh, I've been talking to her about my mad, bad cousin who disappeared for twenty years, married a Muslim, got divorced, lived alone for several years and then decided to come back to her tribe. How many people can claim such unusual relatives?'

'Am I such a rebel?' asked Chhobi. 'I think it's there in our blood, this overwhelming urge to have our way in personal matters. Even you are not having an arranged marriage, but have found your own bride.'

Though she was amused at Bilu's determination to openly discuss her life in Bangladesh, Chhobi felt that the first meal of the first day was not the right time to go into intimately personal and painful matters. I don't think I will be leaving soon, she suddenly found herself able to articulate in her head and was amazed at the conviction. For she had made no long-term plans about staying when she had taken the plane out of America. And yet, here she was, sitting in front of her old bell-metal plate eating her rice with parshe fish cooked in a mustard and green chilli sauce, and a cool certainty was filling up the vacuum inside. This is my home and I am going to stay. And slowly we shall bring out all the old sorrows into the open and air them like quilts in the winter sun. In her own head, she knew, she would often go back to that other land across the border, where people spoke the same language with such different inflections, where the same things tasted so different, where the massive rivers rolled on, majestic or destructive. She had not been able to live there forever, but she had been gifted an essential part of it inside herself. What more could she want, after such a felicitous return?

'I told Bilu that I wasn't going to raise any objections about his marrying a Bangal or marrying out of caste,' she heard Chhoto mama, Bilu's father, say. 'After all, we all have done things against the norm at some time or the other. And I don't want my son to be unhappy because of some demand I make of him. That's the least I can do for him. Don't you agree my dear?'

Chhobi nodded and smiled and the conversation turned to the arrangements for the elaborate wedding festival. 'Do you remember, Shejo mamima,' said Chhobi turning to her elder aunt, 'how, as a bride coming to her husband's home for the first time, you had to walk in through the doorway exactly at the moment Keshto had a pan of milk coming to boil in the kitchen? And how, in his excitement he spilled the milk on the stove and all over the floor? And that awful burning smell?'

Everyone laughed at the memory, especially Dida.

'I don't think we'll go that far in observing the popular rituals this time,' she said. 'Times have changed. So many other rules are being broken all the time. We just have to live in a different way.'

'But we are going to send a really traditional *tatto* to the bride's house,' said Chhobi's father with pride. 'I have been discussing it with everyone else, and your mother will do some of her best alpanas on the wooden trays we have had specially made for all the gifts.'

Chhobi remembered the wonderful alpanas Ma used to paint on every festive occasion and how, as a child, she used to love sitting next to her and watching her paint. Those wonderful leaves, flowers, fruits and lamps, even birds and fishes and conch shells, which came to vibrant life on their polished red floor under her mother's exquisite touch. Just staring at that complex pattern of fantastic shapes was enough to transport the little girl to some distant magical land where endless adventures and infinite discoveries awaited her. She looked at her mother and felt a sudden surge of pride and affection. It was also Ma who had decorated the trays on which the ceremonial gifts, the tatto, had been sent out to the brides' homes when each of her uncles had got married. The tatto was sent on the occasion of *gaye halud* which preceded the wedding. This was one of their Ghoti practices in West Bengal, as she used to explain to her friends in Bangladesh. Though all Hindu men took dowry from the bride's family by tradition, the Ghoti groom reciprocated in a very moderate measure by sending this tatto. Apart from expensive saris and jewellery, trays and trays of sweets had to be sent along with several earthen pots of sweet yoghurt. But the most important item of the tatto was an enormous rui fish, symbolizing fertility and prosperity, and decorated with vermilion powder (sindur) and a paste of oil and turmeric (halud). A little bit of the same paste had to be smeared on the face of the groom and some sent in a little container to the bride's house so that she could be anointed with it too. All the gifts served as the accompaniments to this crucial offering of the turmeric paste. In the case of both her uncles, it was Anath, of course, who had supplied the largest rui he could find.

'What news of Anath uncle?' she asked, suddenly reminded of him.

'Oh he passed away about five years ago, poor fellow,' said Mejo mama, Chhobi's second uncle, regretfully. 'We have no friend now to supply us with fish whenever we have a festive occasion or invite guests for dinner. But your father will take charge of all such purchases. He's been resting and conserving his energies for the great occasion.'

'Well, I'd better. This is likely to be the last wedding I am going to see.'

Baba must have regretted his statement immediately, for everyone was avoiding looking at Chhobi. She felt a sudden constriction of guilt inside. I should have let him have that pleasure, I should have stayed here and had a traditional Hindu Bengali wedding where he could have fussed over everyone, arranged every detail in his perfectionist way and beamed proudly at his married daughter and son-in-law afterwards. I was his only child and I denied him that pleasure. He pushed back his chair and started talking about his own wedding, of how terrified he had been about walking around the ceremonial fire with his shawl tied to the anchal of his bride's sari.

'That was my worst nightmare,' he said, smiling at his wife. 'That somehow, the trailing shawl would catch fire and we'd be burnt to death before we could be man and wife.'

'You and your nightmares,' scolded Ma affectionately. 'Don't put such ideas into Bilu's head.'

Keshto had come in and was taking the plates away. One small bell-metal bowl was left in front of each place. Chhobi knew this was for dessert and she also knew that this first time she would not be served any sweets bought from a shop. Ma got up and brought over a large serving dish of payesh, the thickened milk tinted pinky brown, the fine grains of rice forming little bumps on the surface and the whole decorated with raisins and pistachios. Chhobi inhaled at length, trying to recapture the essence of the childhood thrill of tasting the first mouthful of payesh.

'You must have learned to make much better payesh than your old mother,' said Ma as she dished out a large portion into Bilu's bowl and then into Chhobi's.

'Oh come on, Ma. You know you make the best payesh in the world. Can't Dida have some too? This is vegetarian.'

'No didi,' said her grandmother. 'It's too rich for me to have these days. I am an old woman now. Besides, tonight I plan to indulge myself a little. God willing, I will sit with you and have one or two luchis with my didi. But now I just want to see you eat your fill. Your Ma has not had the pleasure of feeding her own child for such a long time. It's time you let her mother you again, even if it means having to eat a little too much.'

'Speaking of feeding,' said Bilu, 'have we decided on a menu for the wedding guests?'

'If you had taken the slightest bit of interest in the preparations,' said his mother acidly, 'you would have known it was all settled several days ago. But all you can think of is disappearing with your girl—as if she's going to run away.'

Chhobi was taken aback at this sudden display of petulance. But why not, she thought; Bilu is her only child, and she's been the only important female in his life till now.

'Things are no longer the same, you know,' said Mejo mama to Chhobi. 'When your uncles got married, we hired cooks and had the cooking done on the roof, but all the serving was done by ourselves and a few intimate family friends like Dilip. Now, there is a whole new group of people called caterers who will take your menu, cook the entire meal somewhere else and turn up with the food before the dinner or lunch starts. They arrange everything to feed your guests. And it's also difficult to have things done the old way. So we too have decided to hire a catering firm, though I regret having to do it. None of the professional cooks we hired in the past are working now. In a way, families have become onlookers at their own festivals as far as meals are concerned. Half the fun of a wedding is gone, without the bustle of shopping and cooking on the premises. The women of course are all for the new ways, they don't have to clean up afterwards like they used to. But that also means that there are no wonderful leftovers from the wedding feast.'

'Oh no,' said Chhobi in dismay, 'You mean there will be no huge pots full of leftover meat and polao, no bowls full of luscious, brown syrupy pantuas smelling of large cardamom and ghee? That was the best part of weddings!'

'Welcome to modern times,' said Bilu. 'What about Bangladesh? Don't they have caterers too?'

'I suppose they do. But I never saw a wedding from inside, none of my in-laws got married while I was there. The older generation were all married, and none of the children were old enough. So the only weddings I attended were those where I was invited as a guest. We went, ate and came back. But the food was very different.'

She smiled to herself, remembering her initial surprise as she went to wedding after wedding and found the same menu repeated with minor variations, and the consistent absence of fish or vegetables on that menu. Dida was amazed when Chhobi told them about this.

'That's incredible, East Bengal is the land of fish—just think of all those wonderful rivers.'

'I know,' said Chhobi, 'that's what I used to think too. But their ideas of ceremonial food are very rigid, and very different from ours. On one of their religious festivals, Shab-e-barat, for instance, they serve many kinds of haluas with thin chapatis made with rice flour. And would you believe, I saw haluas made with yellow split peas, plain flour, eggs, and in one house, even ground meat!'

Though everyone shuddered at the last, they were all quite fascinated and obviously ready to listen forever. How easy it is, thought Chhobi, to slip into the storyteller's role and have them listen to me open-mouthed like children, as long as I talk about food. Avoid the fraught subjects like the man I married, his likes and dislikes, how the marriage was, why we broke up. Just stay on the safe topics of their food and ours. She wondered if, when violent arguments did take place in her family, the overtures of peace still took the form of a painstakingly cooked meal.

Dida was getting up from her chair, slowly, painfully.

'I have to go and lie down a little. And didi, you must do so too. You've been travelling a long time, you need to rest.'

'Not before I've had a sweet-spiced paan,' begged Chhobi like a little girl, looking from her mother to her Shejo mamima. Both laughed, and Shejo mamima said, 'I'll let your Ma have the pleasure of making you your first paan after all this time. Tomorrow you can have one of mine.' Baba too was smiling, knowing disapproval now would be in vain.

As Keshto came in to remove the bowls and glasses, Chhobi decided that this was the time to go to the southern veranda and take a look at the potted plants and the garden below. The mild February sun fell aslant on the hasnahana whose leaves were slightly dusty in the dryness of winter. But the plant itself seemed healthy, as did the kamini and the lilies and the tulsis. Ma was right; despite her age and infirmities, Dida still had not lost her green thumb. And beyond these sheltered pampered creatures, rose the huge kadam in the garden, witness to so many family dramas, repository of so many family secrets. Chhobi was conscious of a happy sense of reconnection and smiled at the tree as at an old friend. She heard footsteps behind her and turned to find her mother coming with the paan, together with Bilu. Though she had been expecting a few cosy moments with her mother while they chewed their paan, Chhobi was touched at the obvious affection that made Bilu follow her around like a devoted puppy.

'This garden is full of all kinds of memories for me, Bilu,' she said. 'By the time you were old enough to go out and play, it was probably too wild and overgrown, wasn't it?'

'Yes. I never liked the idea of going in there. Somehow, I was always afraid there would be snakes in the grass.'

'When our grandfather was alive, the garden was really well-kept. Even towards the end of his life, when I was a little kid, I remember several singing sessions there. They would put up an awning in front of the kadam tree and rugs would be spread on the grass. The images of Radha and Krishna would be taken from your grandmother's puja room and placed on the altar, decorated with garlands and sandalwood paste. And then there were the quiet times, when nobody came to the garden. I would creep downstairs, go to the altar underneath the kadam tree and sit and dream about all the different adventures I was going to have some day.'

'Tell him about the day when you played with the tree,' said Ma with an indulgent smile.

'Oh God, yes. I'd nearly forgotten about that. It was the festival of Doljatra or Holi. Some of my schoolfriends were supposed to come over and we were all going out to throw those coloured powders at people in the traditional way. Baba had bought me all these different coloured powders the night before. But on the morning, I waited and waited and nobody turned up. We did not have a phone then, so I couldn't call anybody. Nor could I go out all by myself. I cried at first in my rage and frustration. But then I decided I was going to have as much of a good time as they were. I took my powdered colours, and my liquid colours, and a little plastic bucket and sprayed colours on all the shrubs, bushes and finally, the kadam tree. The funny thing was, that though I was pretty miserable when I started, in a short time I was quite enjoying myself. The kadam, by long association, was like an old friend, and so were the other shrubs and bushes.'

'After the wedding, I'll have the garden cleared and taken care of,' said Bilu, touched by his experienced cousin's vulnerability. 'Maybe we can revive the old custom, maybe we can have musical sessions out there in the summer and invite our friends and relatives to come. It doesn't have to be devotional music, does it?'

The mild warmth of the sun slanting across the veranda was

making Chhobi sleepy and Ma was quick to see it.

'Go on upstairs, dear. I think you should have a short nap. I am going to sit with your Dida and give her a massage. But you need some rest today. There will be plenty of time later to talk about all kinds of things.'

'Are the dates all set for the wedding, Bilu?' Chhobi asked her cousin as he followed her upstairs.

'Yes. Ten days from now.'

'And which room will you have after you are married?'

'The two rooms on the southeast corner. My parents have moved down to the first floor. So, once the second floor is painted, those two rooms will be set up with the new furniture she's bringing as part of her dowry and with my things. We'll be up there together, your parents, you, me and Brinda. It should be fun. The other room on the southwest corner will be left empty. Who knows, we might need extra storage space for all the wedding gifts we can't use immediately. Brinda, I think, will prefer to have them stowed away somewhere, rather than cluttering up our daily life.'

'You seem to know her pretty well,' said Chhobi.

'I have had some time with her, you know. More than you did when you married your husband. What was he really like?' he added in a rush, unable to control his curiosity.

'One day I'll tell you. As Ma said, there will be plenty of time later. I need some time to fit into things here. But we'll talk, don't you worry.'

She parted from her cousin in front of her room and went inside, glad to be alone again, to sit and think. So many years lived, so much to remember, so much to forget. The day of Bilu's annaprasan came back to her. That day too, she had come into this room after lunch and sat on the bed sorting out impressions and colours in her head. That day too the sun had been mild, but it had become overshadowed by rain clouds later. Then, as now, she had pulled out the worn, velvet-soft cotton quilt from under the pillow and thrown it over herself as she stretched out on the bed. That day too, she had parted the curtains near her head and looked out at the shimul clothed in scarlet flowers. And she had lain there and imagined all the adventures she was going to have like the prince in Dida's stories. Now she was here, many adventures later, and the shimul still stood guard over the old house and looked enquiringly at her. Many adventures, yes. But the greatest adventure of them all, letting herself be known by her own kind and getting to know them again, of recapturing essence and form, still lay ahead of her. Her grandfather's resonant voice singing the rich notes of the late evening raga, Darbari, sounded in her head. Those days with their particular joyousness were gone forever. But a new time of joy was about to begin, she felt. She would never lose her moorings again, nor be fragmented in her being. The basic continuity of life in the old house would provide her with the anchor she had always needed and missed. And all the small family dramas would still be enacted around the dining table, family dramas that would bond them together, even in their divisiveness. Fluffy white rice would be served every day in the centre of the golden bell-metal plates and all around, like the motifs in a patterned quilt, would be the green, brown, yellow, ochre tones of the food Ma or Dida or her aunts made.

GLOSSARY OF BENGALI TERMS

Akhni
: A kind of perfumed water made by boiling several spices in a bundle until the original volume of water is reduced to a third. This perfumed water is used to cook the rice for a polao.

Alu
: Potato.

Alur chop
: A kind of fried potato cake made by dipping balls of spiced mashed potatoes in batter and deep-frying in oil.

Annaprasan
: A ceremony that formally marks a child's transition in diet from milk to solid foods, including rice, *anna*.

Ata
: A kind of fruit with a green and black knobbly surface and creamy white flesh inside with large black seeds. Available only during autumn. Atar payesh is the flesh of this fruit cooked in milk as a dessert.

Atap
: Literally, untouched by heat. The term denotes husked rice which has not been parboiled.

Balam
: A variety of long-grained rice from the Bangladesh district of Barisal, much prized for its taste.

Bangal
: A person from East Bengal, now Bangladesh.

Bara/bora
: Round balls of fish or vegetables, usually deep-fried.

Barsha
: The rainy season, the monsoon.

Basanta
: Spring. Also smallpox.

Bhabra   A savoury snack made with spiced ground
              fermented chickpea flour fried in oil. These
              used to be fairly common in parts of rural West
              Bengal.

Bhakti   Literally, devotion. The medieval Bhakti
              movement in Bengal was started by Sri Chaitanya
              (also known as Nimai) who declared that god
              could be reached only through the deepest and
              purest of loves, not through knowledge or
              ritual.

Bhashan   Literally, setting afloat in water. All images of
              gods and goddesses are put into the nearest
              river after the end of their particular festival.

Bhat   Plain boiled rice.

Bhog   An offering of food given to the gods.

Bichar-achar A complex set of rules governing the purity of
              the kitchen and the home. Most of the rules
              centre around the pot of cooked rice and
              vegetarian and non-vegetarian food.

Biraha   Separation. One of the great themes of
              medieval poetry is the painful separation
              between Radha and Krishna after the latter
              leaves his native Brindaban and assumes the
              kingship of Mathura.

Bonti   A curved, raised blade attached to a long, flat
              piece of wood or a metal frame, and used for
              cutting vegetables, fish and meat. Knives are
              a relatively recent import in the Bengali
              kitchen. The bonti used for fish and meat is
              kept separate from the one used for chopping
              vegetables and is called an ansh-bonti. The word
              ansh literally means the scales of fish.

Bori   Small pellets of ground, spiced dal, dried in

	the sun and stored throughout the year, to be used in stews and vegetable preparations. More common among the Bengali Hindus.
Chaitanya	Also called Sri Chaitanya, the founder of the Bhakti movement in medieval Bengal. His followers were from the Vaishnav sect.
Chal	Uncooked husked rice. The word also means roof.
Charak	A summer festival in the honour of the god Shiva.
Chhana	The solid part of milk curdled by the addition of acid. Chhana is used to make a host of Bengali sweets.
Chholar dal	Yellow split peas.
Chingri	A generic term denoting all kinds of shrimps and prawns. Striped tiger prawns are called bagda chingri, while the top-heavy king prawns are called galda chingri. Very small shrimps are called kuncho chingri.
Chira	Flattened rice.
Chitol	A large fish, prized especially by the people of East Bengal, with a very soft oily stomach or frontal portion, and a very bony back portion.
Choruibhati	Literally, rice for the sparrows. The term means a picnic meal cooked outdoors, usually by children in villages.
Dab	The green coconut.
Daga	The back portion of the fish, longitudinally separated from the front portion, peti. This portion is usually more bony.
Dal	A generic term denoting any kind of pulses.
Dalan	A central space in a house, or a house built around such a space.

Danta	Any kind of succulent stalk which is eaten with or without its leaves as a vegetable.
Dhan	Unhusked rice paddy.
Dhenki	Instrument for manual rice threshing, now almost obsolete. In Bengali adage, a symbol of unrewarding hard work.
Dhenki shak	A fern-like leafy green, much prized as a vegetable among the people of East Bengal.
Dhonka	Literally, a hoax. In culinary terms dhonkas are made out of ground, pressed dal to form squares which are then cooked in a rich sauce and served in place of meat.
Doi	Yoghurt.
Doljatra	The great spring festival of the Hindus, where people pelt each other with coloured powders (or even spray coloured water), commemorating the game of colours played by Krishna with Radha and her friends.
Durga puja	The most important Hindu festival in Bengal, the three-day worship of Durga, wife of Shiva, goddess of deliverance.
Enthho	Literally, contaminated by mouth or touch. A whole complex set of rules governs the subject of enthho and the orthodox Hindu kitchen is run along those strictures. Associated with bichar-achar. Enthho para means to clean or wipe the place where food has been eaten.
Garom mashla	Literally, hot spice. Usually it means the combination of cinnamon, cardamom and cloves, with black peppercorns being optional. The spices are often used whole to flavour meat dishes, and ground or made into a paste to add the final touch to some vegetable and meat preparations.

Gaye halud	Literally, turmeric on the body, the word halud meaning both the spice and the colour yellow. This is an important ceremony preceding a Hindu wedding. A paste of oil and ground turmeric is smeared on the foreheads of both bride and groom as a symbol of auspiciousness. The ceremonial gift of a whole fish sent by the West Bengali groom to his bride is also smeared with the same paste. Fresh turmeric is also considered an aid to beauty and traditionally Bengali girls used to anoint their whole bodies with turmeric paste before their bath so that the skin would retain a golden glow.
Ghee	Clarified butter.
Ghoti	A person from West Bengal.
Gobindabhog	A particular kind of fragrant, small-grained atap rice.
Golapshoru	A similar kind of atap rice.
Gondhi	Literally, with smell. Used to describe a large variety of very fragrant lemon.
Gotashedhdho	Literally, boiled whole. Specifically, this term means several winter vegetables boiled whole and seasoned with salt, oil and green chillies which are eaten by the Bengali Hindus on the day after the winter festival of Saraswati puja.
Grishma	Summer.
Gur	Indigenous sugar. Aakher gur means unrefined cane sugar. Khejur gur means the brown sugar obtained by processing the sap from the trunks of khejur or date-palm tree during the winter.
Habishanno	Rice and vegetables boiled together in an earthen pot, prescribed for mourners after the

death of a family member.

Halua   A sweet dish made by cooking cream of wheat,
                 eggs, flour and other things in ghee and sugar.
                 Like the Middle Eastern halva.

Handi   A cooking pot with a rounded bottom, slightly
                 narrowed at the neck with a wide rim to
                 facilitate holding. Rice is traditionally cooked
                 in a handi.

Haram   Among Muslims, a term denoting something
                 absolutely forbidden.

Hemanta   Late autumn, usually when the main rice crop
                 is harvested.

Id-ul-fitr   The biggest Muslim festival, it comes after the
                 month-long fasting of Ramadan or Ramzan.

Id-uz-zoha   The second biggest Muslim festival, also called
                 Bakr-Id in Bangladesh. This commemorates the
                 prophet Abraham's willingness to sacrifice his
                 son to Allah. The son was changed to a lamb,
                 bakri, which was sacrificed. Animals are still
                 sacrificed on this occasion and their meat is
                 called korbani, sacrificial meat.

Iftaar   The breaking of the daily fast during the month
                 of Ramadan among the Muslims. This is usually
                 a light evening meal of cool drinks and snacks,
                 preceding dinner.

Ilish   The Bengali name for hilsa.

Ilshe guri   A very fine misty rain during the monsoon,
                 the season for hilsa.

Jalkhabar   Usually a light afternoon snack, the equivalent
                 of the English tea.

Jamaishashthi   The sixth day after the new moon during the
                 second calendar month, Jaishtha. This is a day
                 when the jamai, son-in-law, is ceremoniously

invited by his parents-in-law and fed an elaborate meal and given gifts.

Janmashtomi	The birthday of the lord Krishna, during the monsoon.
Jarda	Perfumed tobacco, taken with betel leaves. In Bangladesh, the term also means a kind of dessert made with rice, cooked in ghee and syrup, often with shredded fruit like pineapples or oranges.
Jhola gur	Liquid gur, made by boiling the sap from the date-palm tree to a thick liquid consistency, like that of maple syrup.
Kachchi biryani	A Muslim preparation where uncooked rice and meat are cooked together over a very low flame.
Kachu	Any of several kinds of colocasia.
Kachu shak	The stems, not leaves of colocasia, eaten as a vegetable.
Kachuri	A stuffed fried bread.
Kagaji	A variety of lemon with a delicate fragrance, preferred in making lemonade.
Kalai dal	A kind of pulse very popular among the people of West Bengal, especially in the summer as it is supposed to keep the body cool.
Kalbaisakhi	A short, violent northwestern storm, usually in the early part of summer.
Kali puja	The worship of the goddess Kali during the autumn new moon.
Kalojam	A small berry, black on the outside and purple on the inside, available during the monsoon. The word is also applied to a sweet, a kind of pantua fried very dark on the outside to resemble this berry.

Kalo jeera   Literally, black cumin. A small black seed (nigella) with a delicate flavour, used in the cooking of fish and vegetables. Sometimes called onion seeds in English.

Kamala   The orange.

Kamini atap   A small-grained variety of atap rice.

Kancha   Raw or uncooked. Kancha moong dal means unroasted moong dal.

Karai   A cooking pot, shaped like a Chinese wok, but much deeper, used for deep frying, stir-frying as well as for preparations with sauces and gravy. The Bengali karai can be made of iron or aluminium, and usually has two loop-shaped handles.

Karamcha   A pinkish-white, very sour berry available during the monsoon. Used in making sour fish dishes or chutneys and pickles.

Karola   The larger variety of bitter gourd.

Kasundi   A sour mustard pickle, usually made in the summer, eaten with rice and fried vegetables.

Katla   One of the several kinds of freshwater carp.

Keora water   Water perfumed with extract of screwpine (keora) flowers, used in Muslim meat and rice dishes.

Khashi   The castrated goat.

Kheer   Evaporated milk.

Khichuri   Rice and dal cooked together with a variety of spices. Usually associated with the rainy season.

Khoi   Popped rice.

Khunti   A kind of spatula, usually of brass or iron, with a long thin handle.

Kirtan   Religious songs, mostly about the love between Radha and Krishna.

Koi	A kind of fish, served whole, sometimes called a climbing perch. Mostly available in the winter.
Kojagori	The night of the autumn full moon, when the goddess Lakshmi is worshipped. The term literally means 'who is awake' and devotees are not supposed to sleep that night.
Korbani	Sacrifice, sacrificial meat.
Krishna	An incarnation of Vishnu, the second of the Hindu trinity. The Vaishnav sect in Bengal are devotees of Krishna. The word literally means black or dark, and Krishna is supposed to have been dark.
Kul	A plum-like fruit available in the winter. The sweet variety is called narkel kul and is used as an offering to the goddess Saraswati, while the sour topa kul is used to make pickles and chutneys.
Kumor	The potter.
Kumro	The pumpkin. Chal kumro, literally pumpkin on the roof, is a native Bengali gourd. The pumpkin was a late import and was originally called biliti or foreign kumro.
Lakshmi puja	The worship of the goddess Lakshmi, goddess of wealth and prosperity, on the autumn full moon.
Langcha	A kind of sweet, like a pantua, but shaped like a bolster.
Langra	A variety of mango, much prized all over India.
Lau	The favourite Bengali gourd, pale green on the outside and white inside. Believed to have cooling properties, and to be a preventive against cholera.

Luchi	A circular fried bread, either puffy like a balloon or flaky.
Maan kachu	A kind of very large white colocasia, prized for its delicacy of taste and its supposed beneficial qualities. The word maan also means repute.
Machh	Fish.
Machher jhol	Fish stew.
Magur	A kind of fish of the catfish variety.
Malaikari	A preparation of prawns made with coconut milk.
Malomash	Literally, inauspicious month. Hindu weddings are forbidden during certain specified inauspicious calendar months.
Malpo	A home-made sweet.
Malsha	An earthen pot in which rice, dal or vegetables are cooked, especially for ritual purposes.
Masoor dal	The lentil.
Matar dal	Dal made from green peas.
Matarshuti	Green peas. Matarshutir kachuri has ground green peas as the filling inside the bread.
Mela	A fair.
Mirgel	A smaller variety of carp.
Mishti	Sweet (adjective) or sweets (as a collective noun).
Mishti doi	Sweet yoghurt.
Moa	Round balls of puffed rice or popped rice, sweetened with date-palm sugar or white sugar and sometimes flavoured with kheer and cardamom seeds.
Mocha	Banana blossom.
Moira	The professional sweet-maker.
Moong dal	A kind of small-grained yellow pulse, also called mung beans in English. They are cooked

	plain or after being roasted in a metal pan.
Muithya	A term used by the people of East Bengal to denote fish balls made by shaping them in the fist or muthi.
Mulo	The native radish, available during the winter.
Muri	Puffed rice.
Muror dal	A preparation combining roasted moong dal with a muro or fish head and spices.
Nabanno	Literally, new rice. A rural festival, especially among the Hindus, to celebrate the harvesting of the main rice crop during the autumn.
Nalen gur	The new gur.
Narkel	The ripe coconut. Narkel chingri is a dish of prawns cooked with ground coconut.
Nechi	Small balls of dough which are patted between the palms before being rolled out.
Neem, Neem begun	The margosa tree, whose small, bitter leaves are considered beneficial to the health during the spring and the summer. The leaves are fried crisp and combined with tiny pieces of aubergine to make neem begun, a first item served with rice.
Nora	The stone pestle rubbed horizontally against a flat stone to grind spices.
Paan	Betel leaves. These are spiced with betel nuts, cardamoms, fennel seeds, lime solution and sometimes tobacco, and chewed after a meal as a chaser. Real addicts will have paan with tobacco many times a day, like smokers.
Panch phoron	Literally, five flavours. Usually a combination of five whole spices, cumin, kalo jeera, mustard, fennel and fenugreek. Mostly used to flavour dal, vegetables and fish preparations. A great

favourite with Hindu Bengalis.

Pandal   An area covered with an awning over bamboo frames in which the image of a god or goddess is placed for community worship. Pandals are also made for weddings and other festivals, mostly to feed people.

Panta bhat   Leftover fermented rice, eaten by the poor out of necessity, but also considered cooling and beneficial in the summer.

Papor   The Bengali word for papadam, thin sheets of spiced ground dal, dried in the sun or in an oven, and fried just before serving.

Parota   The Bengali word for paratha. Fried bread, circular or triangular in shape, often with two or three layers, but sometimes more. The famous Dhakai parota is flaky as the best pastry and can have fifty layers.

Patali gur   The solidified sap of the date-palm tree, made by repeated boilings. This usually keeps for a few months after it has been made.

Patishapta   A home-made sweet, like crêpes, usually stuffed with ground coconut and khejur gur.

Patol   A small, green gourd-shaped vegetable mostly available during the summer and monsoon and considered a great favourite.

Paturi   Anything cooked wrapped in a leaf (pata) and left over a slow flame or stuck in the embers of a coal stove.

Payesh   Anything, usually rice, cooked in milk.

Peti   The front or stomach portion of a big fish.

Phalahar   Literally, a meal of fruit. Usually this means fruit combined with popped rice or flattened rice and yoghurt or milk. Often served during the summer because it is believed to keep the

	system cool.
Phan	The gruel drained out after cooking rice.
Phoron	A flavouring agent. All dals are first boiled in water, then flavoured with a specific combination of spices fried in oil or ghee.
Phul bori	A particularly light bori, made with ground kalai dal.
Pinda	Literally, a lump. Usually this means an offering of cooked rice and fish, made into little balls and set out to appease the ancestors and the dead person during the Hindu funeral. A dead person's soul cannot be set free from earthly longings without this offering.
Pitha	Sweet or savoury items made from rice flour or cream of wheat, usually during the winter when the newly harvested atap rice is ground to make the flour.
Pithaparban	The winter festival of making pithas.
Polao	The Bengali word for pilaf.
Posto	Poppy seeds.
Pui shak	A succulent leafy green with a slightly astringent taste, available during the monsoon. Considered non-vegetarian, and therefore forbidden to Hindu widows who have to be strict vegetarians.
Puja	Among Hindus, the act of worship. Religious festivals for particular gods are also called pujas. In Bengal, however, the word by itself also denotes the biggest festival of the year, Durga puja.
Puli pitha	A kind of stuffed pitha in a sweetened milky syrup.
Pronam	The respectful gesture of touching the feet of

	elders. Divinities also receive pronam, but the gesture is usually folding the palms together and touching them to the forehead, accompanied with a prayer.
Radha	The milkmaid in Brindaban who was Krishna's beloved, though she was not his wife. To Vaishnavs in Bengal, Radha is the ultimate symbol of selfless love.
Raita	Among Bengali Muslims, a salad of yoghurt and cucumbers.
Rajbhog	A large spherical sweet made with chhana, floating in syrup. Similar to the rasogolla.
Ramadan/ Ramzan	The holy month of fasting in the Islamic calendar, preceding the festival of Id-ul-fitr.
Ras	Literally, juice. Specifically it also means the first tapping of syrup from the trunk of the date-palm tree. Instead of being made into gur, this thin liquid is often drunk as a refreshing morning drink.
Rasogollas	Perhaps the most famous Bengali sweet along with sandesh. These are balls made with chhana and boiled in a plain syrup.
Rasomalai	A kind of sweet with rasogollas floating in sweetened evaporated milk.
Rathajatra	The chariot festival, the major event for the Hindus during the monsoon month of Asharh.
Rui	The most prized variety of freshwater carp.
Sandesh	Like the rasogolla, a famous Bengali sweet made with chhana. But it is sweetened with sugar or gur in the cooking, instead of being boiled in syrup.
Sankranti	The last day of any month.
Saraswati puja	The worship of the goddess Saraswati, goddess

	of learning, during the spring.
Shab-e-barat	Literally, the night of destiny. An important Muslim festival.
Shadh	Literally, wish or desire. It is also the term used for a special elaborate meal served to a pregnant woman towards the end of her pregnancy in the belief that if all her cravings are satisfied she will bear a healthy child.
Shak	Any kind of leafy green, eaten as a vegetable.
Shakto	A Hindu sect, followers of Shakti, the mother goddess.
Shapla	The water lily, whose stems are eaten as a vegetable.
Sharat	Early autumn.
Shashthi	The sixth day of the moon.
Sheet	Winter.
Sheetal	Cool.
Shidhdha	Boiled. Parboiled rice is called shidhdha chal.
Shil	The flat, pitted stone on which spices are ground with a nora.
Shim	A kind of buttery-textured flat bean, available in the winter.
Shingara	Triangular flour shells stuffed with vegetables or meat and deep-fried in oil. A favourite with afternoon tea. These are better known outside Bengal as samosas.
Shojne/Shajina	A kind of long, stick-like pod, available during the spring and early summer, much prized as a delicacy and used in fish stews or mixed vegetable dishes.
Shol	A kind of fish, mostly available in the winter and never eaten unless bought live.
Shorshe	Mustard. Hilsa cooked in a mustard sauce is

called shorshe ilish.

Shradhdha	The Hindu funeral ceremony.
Shukto	A bitter vegetable dish, served as a first course with rice, especially during the summer. Shukto is never served at dinner, only at lunch.
Sindur	A vermilion powder worn by Hindu married women on their partings. Also an auspicious element, used to decorate the foreheads of goddesses.
Supuri	Betel nuts. These are chopped fine and put inside paan leaves to be chewed slowly. Sometimes, chopped betel nuts are also chewed by themselves.
Taal	The fruit of the palm tree. Taaler bara means the small balls made by combining the pulp of the ripe fruit with coconut, flour and sugar and deep-frying them. A monsoon delight.
Tatto	The ceremonial array of gifts sent by the groom to his bride before the wedding. A West Bengali Hindu practice.
Tele bhaja	Literally, fried in oil. A collective term denoting any of several vegetables dipped in batter and fried in oil as a savoury snack or to be served with rice.
Thakur ghar	The room in a Hindu home where the images of the gods are kept.
Tulsi	The wild basil which Bengali Vaishnavs consider holy since Krishna is supposed to have loved it.
Uchche	The smaller variety of bitter gourd.
Vaishnav	Followers of Vishnu, one of whose incarnations was Krishna.

COMMON BENGALI PREPARATIONS

Ambal
A sour dish made either with several vegetables or with fish, the sourness being produced by the addition of tamarind pulp or sour berries like karamcha or fruits like tomatoes or green mangoes. Ambals are meant to be eaten at the end of a meal, before dessert and are more common in summer.

Bhaja
Anything fried, either by itself or in batter.

Bharta or Bhate
Any vegetable, such as potatoes, beans, brinjals, pumpkins or even dal, first boiled whole, then mashed and seasoned with mustard oil and spices. Sometimes ghee is used instead of mustard oil. This is usually eaten as a first item with rice.

Bhuna
A Muslim term, meaning fried for a long time with ground and whole spices over high heat. Usually applied to meat.

Chachchari
Usually a vegetable dish of one or more varieties of vegetables cut into longish strips sometimes with the stalk of leafy greens added, all lightly seasoned with ground spices like mustard or poppy seeds and flavoured with a phoron. Small fish can be made into a chachchari, as can the skin and bones of large

fish like bhetki or chitol. The latter is also called kanta chachchari, kanta meaning bone.

Chhanchra	A combination dish made with different vegetables, portions of fish head and fish oil.

Chhenchki   Tiny pieces of one or more vegetables—or sometimes even the peel (of potatoes, white gourd, pumpkin, cucumber or patol, for example)—usually flavoured with panch phoron or whole mustard seeds or kalo jeera. Chopped onion and garlic can also be used, but hardly any ground spices.

Dalna   Mixed vegetables or eggs, with a medium-thick gravy seasoned with ground spices, especially garom mashla and a touch of ghee.

Dam   Vegetables, especially potatoes, or meat cooked in a covered pot slowly over a low heat.

Ghanto   A great standby dish, especially when guests come. Different complementary vegetables (e.g., cabbage, green peas, potatoes or banana blossom, ground coconut, potatoes, chickpeas) are chopped or grated fine and cooked with both a phoron and with complex ground spices. Dried pellets of dal (boris) are often added to a ghanto. Ghee is commonly added at the end. In nineteenth-century East Bengal the ghanto was often called beshwari, probably from the medieval beshoar meaning dried and powdered. Non-vegetarian ghantos are also made, with fish or fish heads added to vegetables. The famous murighanto is made with fish heads cooked with a fine variety of rice. But fish ghanto is more common among the Hindus of East Bengal than in West Bengal. Some ghantos are very dry, others thick and juicy.

Jhal   Literally, hot. A great favourite in West Bengali households, this is made with fish or shrimp or crab, first lightly fried and then cooked in a light sauce of ground red chilli or ground mustard and a flavouring of panch phoron or kalo jeera. Being dryish, it is often eaten with a little bit of dal poured over the rice. In Bangladesh the term jhal gosht means a very hot and spicy preparation of beef or khashi meat, but it can also have a gravy.

Jhol   A light fish or vegetable stew seasoned with ground spices like ginger, cumin, coriander, chilli, turmeric, with pieces of fish and longitudinal slices of vegetables floating in it. The gravy is thin yet extremely flavourful, and is meant to be eaten with a lot of rice. Whole green chillies are usually added at the end and green coriander is used in season for extra taste.

Kalia   A very rich preparation of fish or meat or vegetables using a lot of oil and ghee with a sauce usually based on ground ginger and onion paste and garom mashla. Served at weddings and other festive occasions.

Korma   A Muslim term, meaning meat or chicken

cooked in a mild yoghurt-based sauce with ghee instead of oil. Some people use thick evaporated milk instead of yoghurt.

Pora   Literally, burnt. Though we do not have a closed oven for baking, many vegetables are wrapped in leaves and roasted over a wood or charcoal fire. Some, like brinjals, are put directly over the flames. Before eating, the roasted vegetable is mixed with oil and spices like a bharta.

Tarkari   A general term often used in Bengal the way 'curry' is used in English. Originally from Persian, the word first meant uncooked garden vegetables. From this it was a natural extension to mean cooked vegetables or even fish preparations.

SUGGESTED MENUS

Boiled rice
Fried brinjal slices (p. 54)
Kancha moong dal (p. 9)
Lau-ghanto (p. 18)
Machher jhol (p. 14)
Sweet yoghurt

Boiled rice
Shukto (p. 6)
Masoor dal (p. 10)
Lau-chingri (p. 17)
Chitol kopta (p. 43)
Doi machh (p. 42)
Posto chutney (p. 35)

Boiled rice
Alu posto (p. 37)
Doi-patol (p. 20)
Narkel chingri (p. 167)
Lamb with posto (p. 40)
Cucumber in yoghurt salad

Plain polao (p. 162)
Roasted moong dal (p. 8)
Galda chingrir malaikari (p. 164)
Khashir rezala (p. 29)
Cucumber and tomato salad
    with chopped coriander leaves

Boiled rice
Masoor dal (p. 10)

Boiled rice
Lemon dal (p. 11)
Spring onions with shrimps and
    coconut (p. 64)
Pumpkin with coconut (p. 66)
Hilsa with coconut milk (p. 75)

Boiled rice
Kalo jeera bharta (p. 86)
Kancha moong dal (p. 9)
Carp roe boras (p. 78)
Crab jhal (p. 79)

Luchi (p. 96)
Alur dam (p. 136)
Bandhakopir ghanto (p. 143)
Chholar dal (p. 100)
Chicken with posto (p. 38)
Payesh (p. 112)

Plain polao (p. 162)
Cauliflower bhaji (p. 138)
Begun pora (p. 123)
Roasted moong dal (p. 8)
Meat without onions and garlic
    (p. 103)
Sweet yoghurt and sweets

Boiled rice
Gotasheddho (p. 142)
Potatoes cooked with green peas

Mochar ghanto (p. 68)
Fried hilsa pieces with hilsa oil (p. 72)
Shorshe ilish (p. 72)

Khichuri (p. 51)
Fried brinjal slices (p. 54)
Fried pumpkin slices (p. 66)
Fried hilsa pieces with hilsa oil (p. 72)
Pineapple chutney (p. 84)

and tomatoes (p. 137)
Masoor dal (p. 10)
Handi kabab (p. 160)

Luchi (p. 96)
Dhonkar dalna (p. 127)
Duck bhuna or (p. 157)
    Duck with coconut milk (p. 159)
Beguner tak (p. 145)
Orange-flavoured sweet rice (p. 176)

SELECT BIBLIOGRAPHY

Bhaura, Prof. Kartik (ed.). *Bharatchandrer Annadamangal.* Calcutta: S. Banerjee & Co., July 1985 (4th edn).

Bhattacharya, Bijanbihari. *Bangobhasha O Bangosanskriti.* Calcutta: Ananda Publishers, August 1985.

Das, Dr Khudiram (ed.). *Kabikankan Chandi*, Part I. Calcutta: Calcutta University, B. Chand & Sons, 1987.

Gupta, Bijoy. *Padmapuran / Manasamangal.* Collected by Basantakumar Bhattacharya. Calcutta: Bani Niketan, 1930.

Gupta, R.P. *Machh Ar Bangali.* Calcutta: Ananda Publishers, January 1989.

Ray, Pranab. *Banglar Khabar.* Calcutta: Sahityalok, July 1987.

Sen, Dr Dinesh Chandra. *Brihat Banga.* Calcutta: Calcutta University edition, 1949.

Sen, Sukumar (ed.). *Sharatsahitya Samagra.* Calcutta: Ananda Publishers, 1986.

Tagore, Rabindranath. *Galpoguchchha.* Shantiniketan: Vishwabharati, 1964.

INDEX